High Tech

How to Find and Profit from Today's New Super Stocks

Albert Toney and Thomas Tilling

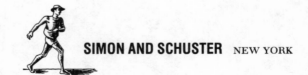

SIMON AND SCHUSTER   NEW YORK

SIMON AND SCHUSTER and colophon are registered
trademarks of Simon & Schuster, Inc.
Designed by Irving Perkins Associates
Manufactured in the United States of America
1 2 3 4 5 6 7 8 9 10

Library of Congress Cataloging in Publication Data

Toney, Albert
High tech: how to find and profit from today's new super stocks.
1. Investments—Handbooks, manuals, etc.   2. Stocks—
Handbooks, manuals, etc.   I. Tilling, Thomas.
II. Title.   III. Title: Super stocks.
HG4527.T66   1983   332.6′722   83-4767
ISBN 0-671-46235-0

The information and statistical data contained herein have been obtained from sources the authors believe to be reliable but in no way are warranted by the authors as to accuracy or completeness. The authors do not undertake to advise you as to any change in figures or in their views. This is not a solicitation of any order to buy or sell securities. The authors and their families may or may not have a position in or with respect to the securities mentioned or related securities. The authors may from time to time have a consulting client relationship with a company mentioned.

Acknowledgments

We would like first to thank Neill Wolf for his inspired and timely effort in producing the personal computer financial analysis programs of Appendix B in truly real time, interactive fashion—in the best tradition of high technology business.

Much appreciation also to Sophia Ahlas and Helen Blanchard of Hambrecht & Quist Equity Management for their cheerful and resourceful support, while overworked in the startup of a new business. Equal thanks to Michael Jackson, Al Toney's partner, who filled in many times when deadlines could not be denied. And to Mary Jane Moran, who faithfully packed and shipped the voluminous research material for this project. We also wish to thank Lynn Archer, who patiently typed and retyped the manuscript many times.

And of course, thanks are due to Leslie, Eleanor, Alexa and Christopher Toney for doing without, putting up with and encouraging surly authors over the course of a very long year.

To Leslie with love for the best years of my life

Contents

9

What to Look for in a High-Tech Investment

High Tech: A Phoenix Rises from the Rust Bowl

When she was sixteen, Theresa Aubut left school in her home town of Lowell, Massachusetts, to go to work in the mills. She entered the cavernous, sprawling red-brick complex, as her father and her grandfather before her had done, in the expectation of holding a lifelong job there. But like so many other mills in Lowell, one of America's first great industrial centers, Theresa's outdated plant shut down, a victim of the competition from inexpensive foreign labor and the innovations of industrial progress.

The end of the story is neither welfare nor unemployment, however, for Theresa and the thousands of other workers in the area idled from their traditional jobs. Lowell's eleven big mills closed down slowly, over a period of decades. Eventually, the proximity of the old mill town to MIT and Harvard University fostered its redevelopment as a high-tech haven. Only recently was the last of the old brick mills converted into a production facility for emerging companies.

Theresa Aubut herself works as a printed-circuit-board assembler for Wang Laboratories, an office-automation computer company. Wang, with 5,500 employees, has more people on its payroll than any of the old textile mills ever did. Not only that, but Theresa, though still a manual worker, now has such fringe benefits as membership in the Wang Country Club, medical and dental care, and, perhaps most significantly, a profit-sharing stock-purchase plan. Wang stock, having gone from 1¼ per share to over 40 per share during the decade of the 1970s, is highly representative of the powerful wealth-gathering investment engine of the high-tech industry —to which you must learn to couple your savings if you want them to outpace the growth of the economy as a whole.

It's fitting enough that the particular high-tech company

that revitalized Lowell was a computer company. For the industry that built the city in the first place made its technological leap forward through data processing. We don't normally think of weaving as conveying information, except perhaps, to a very minor degree, in the case of artistic hangings and their imagery. Nonetheless, the intricate patterns developed on the loom by the crossings of the woof and warp may be thought of as products of coding information, and the impetus behind New England's great textile mills was the Jacquard loom, originated in 1801. Modification followed modification in the rapidly developing technology of the Jacquard weave, but the basic draw engine, which permitted all the motions of the weaving to be controlled from one spot on the loom, combined with a series of punch cards to heddle the warp automatically, laying down the cloth's design, remained the same as conceived by J. M. Jacquard himself. The punch cards, furthermore, albeit in greatly modified form, eventually became the familiar "Do not fold, mutilate, or spindle" that shaped the computer industry through the fifties, sixties, and even into the seventies.

So what, you may well be asking by now, has all this to do with high-tech investing in the eighties? Surprisingly, a great deal.

Knowledge is critical if you intend to invest in high-technology stocks. It is critical, for that matter, if you intend to invest in anything at all. But while the knowledge involved in purchasing bonds may involve interest-rate expectations, and that involving stocks as a whole may involve the economy in general, high-tech investing requires that you know something not only about a particular product, but about the great web of technology of which that product is a part. This doesn't mean that if you're bent on investing in optical fibers, you need a laboratory in your basement. You do need, however, to research the optical/electronics industry and its broadly related product markets, and you need to consider the results of that research in the light of the past in order to profit from the future.

On a broad scale, economists and investors alike today recognize that the traditional technological industries—aviation, automotive, chemical, and steel—which produced the great economic boom of the fifties and sixties are at best on a post-peak plateau. More likely they are on a continuing decline into what Midwestern wags call "the rust bowl," their once mightily expanding markets being reduced to the status of the replacement trade. Right now, what is keeping many of these industry segments afloat is the innovations of younger industries—the current high-tech companies. Only computer control, computer design, data processing, robotics, and their kin are preventing unchecked labor costs and outdated management from allowing the floodgates of imports to open even wider than they already have done.

With such a mass of high-tech products already in place, then, it's surprising to think that these new technologies are as yet in their most nascent stage. Almost everyone will agree that solar energy and biogenetics are in their infancy. But they will certainly not agree that data processing and computers are in the same cradle. Teenagers today are as familiar with video games as with skateboards. Surely a technology that pervasive could not still be in its early stages of development, hence with its most difficult—and potentially most profitable—investment period still to come. Yet that is precisely the viewpoint put forth by MIT's System Dynamics Group, a top-flight economic research team.

The MIT group reaches its conclusions in part by measuring an industry's output as a percentage of the total GNP and calculating the spread of the industry's impact on our lives as a whole. For instance, airplanes were a growth industry during the barnstorming twenties much as computers are in the eighties. But even by the 1930s, aviation-related products accounted for only 0.07 percent of the GNP. It wasn't until major innovations—the radial air-cooled engine, variable-pitch propellers, wing flaps, and new structural materials—put the classic DC-3 on the technology hit parade in 1935 that aviation became a genuine, practical, comfortable economic alternative to the railroads.

Today computers, representing 1 percent of the GNP, are in a position analogous to that of the airplanes of the thirties. As all-pervasive as computers seem to be, until the realization of such foreseeable advances as automated computer programming—which will enable the user simply to go and do his thing without the inconvenience of having to know how to program—the true growth in computer-related industries will remain in the future.

Interestingly enough, the great leap forward that takes a

technology from merely being there to massive application and growth usually occurs during a period of overall stagnation, or even depression. It is just such a milieu that many economists seem to predict for the remainder of the eighties.

Consider the economic history of the automobile. Detroit is groaning under the weight of outdated and excess capacity in a saturated market as if this were an entirely new phenomenon for the industry. Yet go back to the Great Depression, and you find that by the end of 1929 the automobile industry had expanded its capacity into the eight-million-vehicle range— double what had been produced in any given previous year, and sufficient for sales not to be actually realized until 1950.

Meanwhile, as the automotive and other smokestack industries such as steel were expanding their capacity based on historic demand trends, the developing technology of aviation was where all the innovation was going. In a sense, the auto industry's overexpansion and capital depletion helped to spawn its own future competition.

There is a critical mass at which a new technological industry begins to achieve economies of scale which lower product costs and thus stimulate demand. That stage has quickly been attained in many of today's high-tech industries. The computer concept might seem to have exhausted this force, but even it has a long way to go. The period of economic stagnation evident in the early eighties, however, is almost certain to bring nascent fields into their own. Slack consumer buying is a great incentive to lower costs, since the easy price increases of inflationary times are not possible in a buyer's market.

If history has any bearing on the present, the current sluggish economy will probably turn out to be a crucial key to high-tech investing. According to Professor Gerhard Mensch of Case Western Reserve, the commercialization of the largest number of major basic technological innovations occurs during periods of economic disaster. It was in the course of the economic havoc of the 1820s and 1830s that the railroads came to the fore, changing the economic map of the nation and pulling in forty years of prosperity. The depression of the 1870s and 1880s saw the developmental application of the incandescent bulb and the telephone, the dynamic duo that launched an economic expansion all the way into the roaring twenties. The story of chasm-bridging technological leaps forward continues on up to the aforementioned automobile and airplane revolutions.

According to Mensch, these bursts of technological development occur during depressions because investors are more willing to pump large quantities of their capital into high-risk ventures once traditional investment vehicles lose their profitability. Think about it for a minute. Do you feel you'd be more likely to make a fortune today investing in the right automobile company, the right airline, or the right biogenetics company?

The answer is obvious, but the word "right" is crucial. Let's explore what you should know in order to make sure your decision is right, not merely a hopeful, fingers-crossed stab in the dark.

We can't promise you a technological rose garden. What we can provide you with is the means to be sure that you have done everything possible short of rigging the market to make certain the odds are as much in favor of your investment as they can be. For, above all, you have to learn to master the world of high-tech investing by yourself.

No broker or adviser cares as much as you do about making money for you. No broker or adviser can lead you through the constantly changing maze of high-tech development. For that matter, no book, including this one, can do the job for you. What this book can do is to show you how you can educate yourself in a variety of highly profitable high-tech fields.

High-tech industries differ from standard investments in a number of ways, of which newness is not really one. Given enough capital, you can start a new automobile company or a new hamburger chain or any new company. But high-tech companies are not only searching for new solutions. Rather, quite often, they are looking for a problem itself—to which they already have a technological solution.

Home computers, as they were once known, are an excellent example of this inversion. While the exact origin of the appellation "home computer" would be difficult for a dedicated linguist to trace scientifically—even using a computer —it probably owes a lot to a ragtag group of electronic whiz kids in Silicon Valley. Banding together in a modern-day version of the artistic coffeehouse crowd, they discussed, instead of sonnets and sculpture, syllogisms and circuits. Instead of exchanging the latest literary magazines, they swapped software and computer components—often of unknown and unquestioned origin.

The first meeting of the Homebrew Computer Club, held in a Menlo Park, California, garage on March 5, 1975, largely concerned itself with an article in *Popular Electronics* describing the Altair, the original kit computer. Suddenly, for a few hundred dollars, anyone could build his own computer. And hobbyists by the thousands did just that.

Then, driven by a combination of idealism—computers could solve almost all of man's problems, and if everyone had a computer, the world couldn't help but be a better place—and the good old American entrepreneurial spirit, these homebrewers bubbled over into manufacturing for the masses. Name almost any personal computer company around today, be it Apple, Commodore, or Osborne, and you will find that if not the founders, then at least the engineers behind the machines at one time or another shared this amalgam of curiosity and the desire to possess one's very own computer.

IBM, DEC, and the rest of the big computer companies laughed at these computer freaks and their "Computer Faires," and their laughter was not unwarranted. For, it turned out, no one besides the hobbyists really wanted a home computer. What, after all, could one accomplish with such a device? To that question the hobbyists could provide no ready answer.

So the fledgling firms in the forefront of the home-computer revolution, companies such as IMSAI, Polymorphic Systems, and Processor Technology, vanished with a great product that didn't really do much of anything. Games were not enough. Other homely, heralded-in-the-press tasks such as filing recipes or turning on the coffeepot in the morning were more simply accomplished by means of the conventional file box, the scrapbook, or a timer.

But a few companies, among them Apple and Cromemco, began, by some marketing inspiration, to woo the businessman and the scientist as their natural targets. The word "home" vanished, to be replaced by "personal." To the question "What can I do with it?" was shot back the answer "Just about everything you can do with the big one at the office."

Selling microcomputers to people already familiar with the large-scale version was simplicity itself. Computer-savvy individuals were delighted to find that for a few thousand dollars they could have a machine of their own capable of doing scientific calculations, business projections, stock-market analysis, cost estimating, and a host of other time-consuming tasks.

Then software innovations began to enrich the marketplace. Companies such as VisiCorp tackled problems like the necessity of interminably rewriting calculations to determine cost and profit projections and developed solutions to them. The electronic spreadsheet VisiCalc, for instance, did all the refiguring for the classic "What if" question automatically. The operator could change one number of a financial projection, and the computer would change all the others at the press of a button. The sales figures for personal computers began to skyrocket, going from a few thousand per annum to tens of thousands to hundreds of thousands in the space of four years.

Exact sales figures for the market escalator ride of microcomputers are hard to come by, since many of the hottest companies, such as Osborne and Cromemco, are privately owned electronic gold mines. But a consensus estimate puts sales of personal computers for 1982 at around two million units—which exemplifies one of the basic differences between high-tech investing and the more mundane moneymaking ventures. Once a product niche has been established, the rate of change in both sales volume and development is much more rapid than in the standard industries.

Not only that, but the rate of change accelerates at a breathtaking speed as product acceptance expands geometrically. Video games, which are much more limited in their application than the all-purpose personal computer, produced around $1.7 billion in revenues during 1982, and this astounding sum will easily explode to over $3 billion by 1984. All in all, it will have taken video games less than ten years to reach this sales figure. Hollywood has been at it for over seventy years, and sales of movie tickets are only now reaching the $3 billion level.

Rapid change is a fact of life in high-tech industries, and not only in sales figures. The entire industry is in constant turmoil, with companies regularly gobbling each other up,

Pac-Man fashion, and key management members splitting off from parent companies like electronic amoebas to start their own operations. People in the high-tech industries are extremely mobile, going from job to job like the tinkering gypsies of yore. Even at the production level, skills are short and demand is high. No wonder many high-tech firms supply their employees with company swimming pools, three-day weekends, paid ski holidays, and other perks that would seem ludicrous in basic industry.

The lure of the perquisites notwithstanding, the chance to do one's own thing—and possibly to make a million in the process—often becomes irresistible. Josiah River and Herman Ward both work for the three-year-old Pick-It-Now Computer Company, an established producer of inventory control software. They've written half the programs themselves and are linchpins in the organization. However, even with great salaries and perks, River and Ward aren't happy, because the head honchos are always on their backs. Besides, they could do a better job of running the company themselves, they both agree over Friday-night beers. By Saturday they're serious. Sunday they've worked out a business plan. On Monday they hire an attorney, mortgage their houses, sublease some office space, and Pick-It-Sooner Computer Company is on its way to becoming a star—or a falling star.

Contrast River and Ward with good old Arthur G. Higginbottom IV. You can ask Aunt Irma about Higginbottom. She'll tell you how she once went to a shareholders' meeting of American Tire and Tunnel back in '38, clutching her thirty shares, and how she heard Higginbottom himself describe the great strides being made by AT&T in bringing Americans together through transportation. Today Higginbottom's name still graces the annual report, and what with a dividend repurchase plan and several splits, Aunt Irma has 260 shares. The fact that their value in true purchasing power is hardly more than that of the original shares is another story. From an investor's viewpoint, the difference is a matter of stability.

While management is more mobile in high-tech industries than in traditional enterprises, that mobility is at the same time also more important, allowing the creative temperament of a gypsy to come to the fore. The fields of endeavor are new, the guideposts few. The entrepreneurial management of a high-tech company is often, out of necessity, of the fly-by-the-seat-of-your-pants variety. Good gut feelings on the part of a product-aware manager are likely to be worth more than a clutch of M.B.A.s from Harvard. The Harvard graduates may know business, but if they don't love a product as a member of the family, if they haven't nurtured it from that first eureka flash in the bathtub through the first early prototype, they're not involved to the point where creative drive overcomes the pessimism of reason.

Look at Frederick Smith. While completing his graduate studies at business school, he wrote a thesis on the need for a guaranteed overnight small-package express system in this country. His advisers told him the concept was totally impractical. His advisers are unknown to the public, but everyone has heard of Federal Express, the company Smith founded because he knew he was right.

Such a key consideration as company loyalty on the part of management is often considered an archaic stumbling block in the competition for personal fortune, tough in almost any business but positively cutthroat in the high-tech segment. Not only is the rivalry ruthless, but it is becoming more so. The Japanese dragon can be seen standing behind the door as each new venture opens up a profitable market. Even the "little dragons," as *Electronic Business* magazine calls Hong Kong, Singapore, South Korea, and Taiwan, are sidling up to the threshold, ready to bring $2-an-hour labor and $800-a-month engineers into the fray for any technology market that grows beyond the developmental stage.

As an investor, you may remember National Video, that mighty maker of television picture tubes that was the darling of speculators during the sixties. But have you heard of Samsung Electronics Company? Probably not. All the same, National Video vanished into the halls of the bankruptcy courts within a decade, while the little South Korean dragon Samsung is now the world's largest producer of black-and-white television sets. Hong Kong supports a business pace so hot it has the highest per capita telex-machine population in the world. And so it goes. Every government sees the same opportunities to hype the slowing economy of its country. The sharpest players are all attracted by the highest potential profits.

This vying for new markets, with every country and state trying to get a piece of the high-tech action, means that start-up companies are continuously stepping forth bearing slightly better "me too" products. All that emulation and rivalry leads to an extremely volatile equity situation. If the old buy-and-hold investment strategy is not yet dead for the stock market as a whole, it certainly is for high-tech stocks. The chances of anyone's buying a share of a new IBM and passing it on to one's children multiplied by tens, its value increased by thousands, is simply not realistic.

High-tech stocks these days mean high price-to-earnings ratio, or P/E, stocks. And if you own high-flying stock such as Datapoint with a P/E of 100, which means that it's selling for a hundred times what it is currently earning in a year, you're a little more nervous than you would be with steady old Arizona Public Service with a P/E of 6. So are all the other market players, who, in trying to win, have driven the company's share price up to the point where it would take the company a hundred years at this year's earnings rate to match the value investors have put on the stock.

Disappointing company performances are inevitable. You need to be able to spot them before they arrive, or you'll end up holding something like Datapoint as it makes its breathtaking, wallet-busting dive from a price in, say, the fifties to one in the low teens because of a single poor earnings report. When the bad news hits, everyone heads for the exit at once. They even use the windows!

Another circumstance setting high-tech investments apart from other stock holdings is the fact that there is so little available in the way of conventional statistics and research on them. The fields are simply too new. Most investors don't have access to the sources of information about more than a few of the better-known high-tech companies, much less to the information itself. But you're different. You have the sources and background you need for that research in your hand right now, assembled in a single volume for the first time anywhere.

Fortunes are being made—and lost—as the world is swept by the most profound economic change since the dawn of the Industrial Revolution. Which direction your personal money supply takes in the uncertain future will depend almost solely on whether or not you seize the opportunities offered by this industrial upheaval. The possibilities for financial growth are staggering, abounding as never before. But they are also briefer and more difficult to discern, sometimes appearing unexpectedly, like mushrooms, almost overnight. How to recognize and profit from these sudden opportunities is what this book is all about.

II

Picking Apples Instead of Lemons

The constant splitting off of entrepreneurial splinter groups in established high-tech industries is the obvious cause of the proliferation of new companies. But merely the desire, drive, and knowledge are not enough to plant the seed of a new company—it all comes down to the nourishment of a few cupfuls of capital.

Remarkably enough, the total thirst of a start-up company may be relatively small. Successful multimillion-dollar software companies have been established with an initial capitalization of only a few thousand dollars. Electronics as a whole is not capital-intensive compared to traditional ventures, and with a potential super-return on investment, venture capital is easier to come by.

Other entry barriers are low as well. There are few social or political obstacles. An overall cultural endorsement prevails. Change is perceived as good, and risk takers are the heroes of our time.

Add to these enticements the lower tax rate on capital gains, which allows early investors in a company to create genuine wealth through their stock purchases, and you have an almost irresistible spawning ground for an ever-increasing number of high-tech companies in the eighties. As with fish spawning, of course, not many of those that hatch will make it to pubescence, much less to maturity.

To pick the real winners, as opposed to the mere survivors, will take some adroit maneuvering on your part. And you won't succeed all the time. But after reading this book, your investments should be right more often than they are wrong. And that's what counts in the long run.

For the short run, there are ten key questions to ask, and to reflect upon, when you are checking out the factors affecting the success of any high-tech company. Ask these questions whenever you are investigating a company in any field of high technology with the thought of making an investment.

1. What does the company do?

Note that we do not ask, more specifically, what it makes. That's because there are service companies such as software houses besides manufacturing companies in the high-tech field, and assuredly they are not to be overlooked. In order to be successful, either a company must satisfy an existing need better than do its current competitors or it must create a demand for new products or services which it can then help to meet.

Is the company's product truly new or better? Innovation and improvement are what the high-tech investment game is all about, but don't be fooled into thinking that *different* is the same as *better*. Fads are different; innovations create benefits for users.

2. When is the product or service available?

Now is the only answer. Soon doesn't make money. In 1977, a fantastic laser-based computer memory was soon to burst on the market. It's still fizzling. A great deal of high-tech industry uses premature product announcements for market testing or for the attempted raising of capital.

3. How much does the product or service cost?

Giving the customer more benefits for the same price is good. So is giving the same benefits for less money. But true customer happiness consists in getting more for less. Another successful variation, which depends on customer control— meaning the customer can't drop your product—is to give more benefits for more money. The leading practitioner of this policy has been IBM, but it has many high-tech emulators. The trick is to give a greater gain in product performance than in product price.

4. What is the trend of unit sales?

Unit sales are what growth is all about. If units don't grow, the only way in which revenues can increase is by way of price, and in that direction lies displacement or extinction. A

young company in a new market can sell small quantities, but
a larger company must have unit sales which increase at
either a constant high or a rising percentage rate.

5. How large is the company?

If a company is too large, even a spectacular new product
with explosive sales may not affect the bottom line sufficiently
to be reflected in the share price, at least significantly so.
Usually what you want is a company with a market capitalization of under $100 million, although there are exceptions.
Some companies are growing so rapidly, and in such large
markets, that it is better to look at their age in years. They
should be under ten years old. MCI Communications is a
good example of a fast-growing company over the $100 mil-
lion mark, in a multibillion-dollar market, yet a company
young in years.

Market capitalization is simply the number of shares of common stock outstanding times the price per share. Let's look at
Biological Gear Works, Inc. Listed on the Imaginary Exchange at $22 a share, the company has 1.5 million shares
outstanding. Multiplying 22 × 1.5 million gives you a figure
of $33 million as the firm's market capitalization, a sum well
within the boundaries of your search.

Companies with over $100 million in market capitalization
have effectively "emerged." That is to say, usually they have
been discovered by a broad base of investors and analysts
alike, and their share prices have been driven up to such
levels that their most volatile growth has already been dis-
counted. A recent study by Professor Rolf W. Banz of Northwestern University shows that over a fifty-four-year period the
total rate of return of companies listed on the New York Stock
Exchange with a market capitalization of $50 million or less
was 11.6 percent annually. For companies with a larger market capitalization, annual returns were only 8.8 percent.

Like all general rules, this one will have its exceptions,
Comsat being, at this writing, a case in point. Comsat has
eleven million shares outstanding, currently priced at roughly
$70 a share, giving Comsat a market capitalization of $770
million. Still, Comsat is one of those exceptions that prove the
rules. Its hold on the communications-satellite market has
been so strong that it virtually has a monopoly. This market

strength combined with a phenomenal growth in the demand for its product assures it of a special niche in the high-tech investment world, at least for a few more orbits.

An interesting corollary, broadly relevant to the economy as a whole, may be drawn from the employment figures for small versus large firms. The little companies are where the new jobs come from. According to data released by J. Peter Grace, president of the W.R. Grace Company, in the period between 1969 and 1976, companies with over five hundred employees were responsible for 13.3 percent of all new jobs. In the same period, companies with fewer than twenty employees created 66.0 percent of the new jobs; and small businesses as a whole, the companies with fewer than a hundred employees, accounted for 81.5 percent of all the new jobs.

So not only does the investor stand to profit handsomely from a well-chosen selection of emerging companies' stock, but the job market stands to benefit from these new enterprises as well. The increase in individual earnings thus generated propels the economy as a whole upward. If the 1980s are to realize boom times, it is the emerging companies that will lead the way, in so doing firing up the economy, which can then, in turn, support and increase these companies' growth. This is the way economic spirals begin.

6. *What is the company's annual revenue per employee?*

Since high-tech companies are knowledge-intensive rather than capital-intensive, the revenue-per-employee figure should be much higher than it is for basic industries. If it is not, something is usually wrong. High-tech-company revenues should be in the $50,000-per-full-time-employee-per-year range.

To determine a company's revenue per employee, simply divide its annual revenues by the average number of full-time employees for the year. The figure is easy to come by using the revenue and employee statistics to be found in a company's annual report or drawn from the Standard and Poor's sheets. It should be used with caution, however, and it must be weighed with care against the figures for other companies in the industry. You'll also have to be wary of spectacularly high revenue-per-employee statistics. They can be caused by such factors as the company's distribution methods. For instance, if company A uses an outside sales force and company B its own, company A's sales-per-employee figure will obviously be inflated relative to that of company B.

7. *How hungry is the market?*

If you want to get fat, you sit down to a big meal. The companies you investigate as potential investments can be small initially. But the overall market for their products in the industry as a whole should have the potential to expand to beyond $1 billion in annual sales within a decade. Remember that $1 billion isn't what it used to be. The massive growth in world population, as destructive as it may prove to be in the long run, has easily extended the market for almost any "necessary" device into the $1-billion-volume range.

8. *If the volume's there, where are the profits?*

Dollar volume alone is meaningless. International Harvester has a multibillion-dollar sales volume—in a decibillion-dollar market—as of this writing. But whether the company will still exist by the time you read these words is in doubt, because the company is losing money. Simply making decent money isn't good enough. What you're looking for is earnings potentials with a *real* growth rate of 15 percent per year—that's 15 percent *after taking inflation into account*.

Quantitative factors such as these, so crucial in evaluating the high-tech companies, are elusive, but not impossible to measure. They do require some detective work, and for that task this book is your investigator's manual. With it you'll be able to unearth company details you may never before have realized were available, information even your broker doesn't have but would love to lay his hands on.

Using this book, you'll also be able to assemble a picture of the nonquantitative factors that can spell the difference between investment failure and success.

9. *Does the company's management have a successful background related to the technical field of endeavor?*

General management techniques may be fine for directing discount stores, steel mills, and railroads. For the high-tech industry, they're simply not enough. In this business, the building of dynamic, growing companies requires a new breed of management, management that knows the technologies and the markets involved well enough to break old rules with innovation—leading markets rather than reacting to them.

American industry in the last decades has increasingly turned to executives with financial or legal backgrounds to fill top management slots. Their jobs, by standard management rules, have been perceived as those of skilled strategists with a knowledge of resource allocation and a knack for quick and decisive judgment in taking over new businesses while divesting themselves of losers. And so a whole generation of top executives have honed their skills as gunslingers, three-card-monte players, and portfolio managers rather than focusing on product and production innovation.

The need to concern oneself with the more painstaking tasks (and longer-term rewards) of inventing, building, and developing future businesses has often been relegated to the scrap heap along with related obligations to workers, customers, suppliers, and even fellow managers. The sterility of this morally bankrupt attitude has been amply highlighted by the success of Japan in competing with many companies run in such a fashion. In technology, look for marketing and engineering people. The worst thing you can discover when you are investigating the management of a company is a collection of lawyers.

10. Is management managing a company or a stock?

Managing a company is quite different from managing a stock's price. Many investors value the comfortable certainty of regularly increasing quarterly company revenues and profits. Even if those regular penny increases in earnings per share translate to only a fraction of a percent in actual return on the investment, the arrangement somehow presents a feeling of orderly progress and predictability. But these regular increases may be purchased at the expense of needed spending on future company growth. The truth of the matter is that short-term performance and long-term growth frequently conflict.

The operations of good companies often undergo disappointing flat, or down, quarters for perfectly good reasons relating to long-term growth objectives. An attempt to show immediate gains at such a juncture may keep the price of shares up for the short term, but it almost always does so at the expense of future growth. A good case could be made for not focusing on quarterly results at all, were it not for the fact that professional investors (the real odd-lotters of today's market) tend to do so, and stock prices will react to them. From an investor's viewpoint, using the same time horizon as that employed by company management, namely, one to three years, makes a lot of sense. You'll also sleep better! Furthermore, long-term capital gains are taxed at a maximum 20 percent, while the tax on short-term gains can be as high as 50 percent, not counting any state and local taxes. Even Uncle Sam tries to point you toward the longer term.

But why, you may well ask, should any well-managed company have disappointing earnings quarters—unless the whole economy is crumbling? And if occasional earnings disappointments are inevitable, how can an investor tell a "bad" bad quarter from a "good" bad quarter? These are excellent questions, both of them, and while they are tough to answer unconditionally, the general rule is as follows: If the company *warns* you about the disappointing earnings *beforehand,* it's probably okay; if not, then the company—and your investment—is likely to have problems.

You don't have to be privy to secrets or inside information in order to follow this rule. For example, suppose the management of a company announces that it's building up its sales force and reducing its dependency on outside reps. You as an investor should be aware of the implications of such a changeover. Hiring and expanding over a short period, however beneficial it might be for future earnings, can't help but put a crimp in profits for a quarter or so. Until the sales force's orders actively enter the earnings stream, the salary demands will cut into profits. If management says that it has hired ten new top-flight members for its research and development team, and that their salaries and bonuses will affect earnings negatively for two quarters, that's probably okay too.

When everything is coming up roses and management announces that another blockbusting quarter can be expected— as soon as eight of the company's new and improved ambidextrous robot arms are tested and shipped—and the announcement is followed by a quarter of disappointing earnings, then a potential problem, perhaps a serious one, is lurking some-where. There could be a valid reason why shipment did not proceed on schedule. The buyer might have asked for a delay. The shipping delay would constitute a temporary setback, al-though it could also be indicative of a recession or slowdown in the industry that particular company is supplying. More seriously, the ambidextrous robot arms could have failed a customer's acceptance test. At best this could mean a delay and a subsequent slowdown in the company's growth. At worst it could indicate production or design problems which should have been recognized much earlier. Such problems, if they involve a company's main product, can cause a severe setback in or even a major loss of competitive position.

If all of this is beginning to smack of a bit of work to come, we must say that while there is indeed work to be done, once you know how and where to look for the crucial company information that is the driving force behind high-tech stock prices, the time required to keep your personal investments on the profitable top of the financial world should be no more than, on the average, two to four hours a week. Assuming you work a forty-hour week for your money, that 5 or 10 percent of your working time spent on making your money work hard for you is not a lot—particularly when you consider that each capital-gains dollar you make is worth so much more than your workaday, ordinary-income dollar.

III

Why Patents Don't Count, and Other Marketing Paradoxes

For years, telephone operators' headsets were heavy, klutzy affairs larger than a B-52 pilot's earmuffs. It didn't make much difference to the telephone companies. After all, an operator just sat there all day pulling and pushing jacks. Mobility was not an important factor and, from an engineering point of view, neither was the telephone operator.

Then Plantronics designed the Star Set. A featherweight, almost invisible headset connected to the console by a gossamer umbilical cord, it allowed almost unlimited movement and flexibility. Plantronics opened up a whole new market. No longer was the headset the domain of telephone operators chained to their switchboards. Stockbrokers, freight forwarders, billers, estimators—just about anyone whose day-to-day business involved constant telephoning—found the Star Set to be a handy timesaver. No longer was it necessary to hold the telephone receiver in one hand or crooked in the shoulder. Both hands were free, movement was convenient, and production shot up. So did Plantronics stock—by 1,000 percent.

Most people think of high-tech companies as representing some great new breakthrough. But a company need not invent something as basic as television in order to show phenomenal growth. In fact, a breakthrough invention often leads to failure. Witness Du Mont. Allen B. Du Mont invented the consumer television, and Du Mont went broke.

Execution is usually 90 percent of the battle in winning the high-tech race, the idea itself being only 10 percent. Knowing a company's strategy, then, is fully as important as understanding its product.

One important and quite basic part of many a high-tech company's strategy is *not* taking out patents. To the uninitiated investor, this may seem a plan of dubious merit. But the truth of the matter is that patents aren't what they used to be. In fact, they often turn out to be no more than a license to litigate.

Ideally, patents are like a fence. They're supposed to keep people out of a company's territory. But if the company isn't careful, it may well find itself held prisoner in its own backyard instead. In our litigious society, the culprit is most often money.

Defending a patent from infringers takes a lot of money. It takes a lot of money even to find out who is infringing on your patents. No less a cash machine than Apple Computer was slow to launch its investigation into Far Eastern knockoffs of its Apple II, simply because of the expense and difficulty of locating the offenders. When Apple finally decided the problem was going to grow, not simply go away, the company was unable to eliminate it. At best, patents help large companies. Large companies have money; little companies do not.

Patents are of use to large companies in another way besides that of protecting their own. There are staffs who do nothing but sift through patents pending or issued to other companies. If they find something potentially profitable, the companies then put their research staffs to work designing around the patent. Modifying patented devices so as to circumvent their protection may be cheap-shot research, but it works for the big companies—to the detriment of the smaller ones.

If a small company introduces a very successful product, the necessity for a larger, more established firm to figure out a way of finessing its way through the patent barrier may not even arise. All it need do is wait for the newcomer to develop an excessive backlog. As the little company falls farther and farther behind in filling the flood of orders, the other company can jump right in and infringe to its pocketbook's delight, knowing that the originator of the device has already stretched its financial and managerial resources to the limit and is in no position to litigate. Without the benefit of the patent filing, the large company might not know how the product had been devised.

Some patents are easier to get around than others, of course. As a rule of thumb, device patents are stronger than process patents. If you invent a new friction-reducing bearing, a patent that pretty well covers all the contingencies and ripoff possibilities can be written for it. A process patent, on the other hand, because most processes are composed of so many complex steps, is relatively easy to get around, simply by modifying some of the steps. Suppose your patented process goes from A to H by way of B C D E F G, and someone else's process goes from A to H by way of B E D F G. While the end results may be the same, the processes are not, and the patent has been skirted quite legally.

Patent problems are particularly onerous in the electronics field. Software patent law is barely out of diapers, and weak to boot. Most legal rulings to date have left software subject to the less complete copyright protection rather than granting patent rights, on the basis that software is an intangible process and therefore not patentable.

In the electronics field as a whole, electronic design and fabrication processes underlying the technology have patent support almost as weak as that of the software by means of which design applications are executed. That's why many companies rely instead on trade secrets, keeping knowledge hidden not only from the competition but, by implication, from investors as well.

For the would-be investor, then, investigative emphasis must be on analyzing a product's market potential and sales possibilities rather than on seeking to understand all the technological developments underlying its design. In a way, this circumstance makes the investor's task easier. Market analysis, after all, doesn't require quite the technical expertise involved in truly comprehending what is going on in the amazing world of microelectronics.

One exception to the patent problem is to be found in the fields of pharmaceuticals and genetic engineering. Although these specialties employ process patents primarily, the product development times involved are tremendous. The slight differences that can be introduced in electronic processing to bypass patent protection can usually be interjected into the sequences of genetic engineering as well. But in electronics, once a company has found a way to slip around a patent barrier, commercial production can usually be up and running in a matter of months, whereas in the case of genetic engineering the start-up time for the me-too product is measured in almost the same number of years as it would have taken the company to come up with a product entirely on its own. The reason is that there are no shortcuts in the testing of new drug products for safety and efficacy. Even a modification in fabrication sequence leading to the finished product means that the company goes back to square one in the long approval process. It does so, furthermore, for each country in which it plans to market the product. Here, then, a patent is a definite ace up a company's sleeve.

Patent or no, certain basic marketing principles are essential to any high-tech company. First of all, it must heed the "window" principle. For every right product, there is a right time to bring it out, to push it through the opened window in the normally impenetrable brick wall of tradition. The best of products can miss its opportunity and die waiting if it is brought out before the market is ready. The best of products can be undermined by an inferior imitation if its release is delayed.

Sometimes an executive will succeed in one high-tech field and then carry his success to another company. Al Shugart founded Shugart Associates and led it to the top of the floppy-disk-drive stack before selling out to Xerox and going fishing —literally. After a while, the lure of high technology beckoned once more, and he started Seagate Technology, the hard-disk-drive company everyone expects to become a dominant force in the industry. But notice that he did not start another floppy-disk firm. He adjusted his strategy for the next start-up.

The market may be different the second time around. It may be slower to develop. The team may not click the same way. Then too, the folks working under Mr. Wonderful may have actually been responsible for the first company's success. The worst danger confronting an executive founding another company is that he might try to repeat a successful formula without allowing for the inevitable changes wrought by time among his competitors and his markets.

Then there's the matter of growing markets. The world is full of them. However, for far too many, companies and investors alike, the promised growth is a mirage. Quadraphonic sound, plated-wire memories, and fluidic logic systems were all exciting, real technologies gazing toward expanding horizons only a decade or so ago. But the future, for various reasons, never came for them. In the case of quadraphonic sound, consumers simply weren't willing to go the extra dollar, so stereo remained king. Fluidic logic systems had a broadly based control and logic market, which it was slowly stealing from transistor producers. But along came integrated logic circuits to clobber them both.

A deeper problem underlay the development of these ideas, namely, lack of sponsorship. The stock of a company may be selling for a P/E of one, and the company may have a fantastic growth record, but if you and your aunt are the only people buying shares, the stock price is not going up very high. When investment companies and big stockholders suddenly decide they want to own part of the company, and buy in, the share price begins to reflect this sponsorship and shoot up.

Not many manufacturers pushed quadraphonic sound, plated-wire memories, and fluidic logic devices. The majority of them were more interested in making component stereos, disk memories, and integrated circuits. With strong sponsorship, these innovations grew into robust technologies. Remember that, when you are considering investing in a company which has developed the perfect rattrap. If all the rest of the rodent-repelling industry is working on poisons, you may end up being caught.

But if everyone and his brother are working on a product, how do you, as an investor, pick the winner from among them all? Well, for one thing, you determine how focused the various companies are. The entrepreneurs who start high-tech companies are very good at bulling their ideas through to production. However, someone also has to determine which applications factors and features should dominate in order to assure a developing product's eventual success, how long a given product can stay on top, and in which technologies to invest. Sometimes a discerning innovator can cover all these bases, but only sometimes.

During the early seventies, Bob Noyce and Gordon Moore of Intel saw that a certain type of semiconductor technology had an immense number of potential applications in a broad range of products, making possible as it did components which were faster, cooler, and better at working with standard power-supply voltages. So they pushed Intel to the red line in developing this technology. While Intel was thus conceptually focused, its competitors were diffusing their research efforts among several competing semiconductor technologies. Intel quickly dominated the new semiconductor-dependent microprocessor marketplace.

Had this kind of dramatic grab for the lion's share of a market occurred in the steel industry, there would have been no competition left. But the semiconductor industry is so dynamic and expansive that all Intel really did was to hobble the competition for a while. Timely new products make for new markets and new heroes.

A winning strategy has a focused approach, consistent and coherent in all its elements: image, price, distribution channels, and performance all reinforcing each other rather than operating in conflict. A company can carve out a very profitable niche for itself by, say, selling ultracheap personal computers through mail order, the way Sinclair has done with its under-$100 models. Sell the same computer through specialty retail stores and you'll have too expensive a distribution system for the product revenues to support.

The Boston Consulting Group, a favorite adviser on corporate strategy, has devised a chart (see Figure 1) which pretty well sums up the considerations of price versus performance in the market appeal of a product for various buyer categories. The adjectival descriptions in each box of the money matrix convey the product image, and chances are that any given high-tech company that is going to be a winner will have a product line which tends toward the neutral axis. A successful company may have products in several boxes, but only if it's an industry leader, whose image can support such a soup-to-nuts resource allocation.

A company's ability to focus its products and target a market soon becomes obvious on the bottom line. Your success as an investor depends on spotting the development early. Telling indicators of an emerging high-tech winner include:

1. Rapid revenue growth.
2. High profit margins relative to the competition.
3. An above-industry average return on equity (ROE). (Return on equity is measured by taking company earnings as a per-

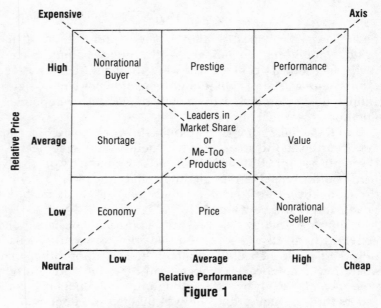

Figure 1

**BOSTON CONSULTING GROUP PRICE
VERSUS PERFORMANCE CHART**

centage of company net worth. For instance, a company with $100 million net worth earning $10 million has an ROE of 10 percent.)

4. A good balance sheet not too highly leveraged. (Technology companies should have less than average financial leverage because they have a good deal of business operating leverage. For manufacturing companies in general, the rule of thumb is that they should have no more than one part debt to two parts equity. Technology companies should have less debt. The faster they are growing, the less debt is allowable.)

5. A dominant position in an emerging industry or a significant and growing market share of a fragmented industry.

6. Few institutional stockholders.

7. Research and development outlays representing 6 to 16 percent of annual revenues.

In order to qualify for your investment consideration, a company should have at least five out of these seven winning characteristics.

If a company you are considering meets these positive criteria, you should go on to check for the *absence* of certain factors before you invest. Even in a potentially prosperous high-technology field, there are forces at work that could severely limit the growth of, or even kill, a company.

First of all, there is the matter of regulation. Government regulation is the great leveler, equalizing strong and weak, good and bad companies. Most important, from an investor's point of view, regulation narrows the difference between profitable companies and those less so. For the well-managed company, it evens profits down, not up.

Consider the late history of trucking. Having grown fat and rich and noncompetitive over the years, the industry almost collapsed when it was deregulated recently. A few years after the turmoil dies down, however, those companies that survive will be spinning off more profits than ever.

Regulation is a particularly leveling burden in established industries such as utilities. By contrast, certain of the newer high-tech enterprises may temporarily prosper under regulation. For instance, the cellular-mobile-radio regulations in effect give the operating telephone companies semi-monopolistic control over designated broadcasting areas by ensuring that every licensed market has only one telephone competitor, which is certainly a benefit initially. But the benefit is bought at the cost of oversight control. The companies' earnings will reflect the costs of pioneering before the real costs of the business are well understood. Cellular-mobile-radio broadcasters may have some early hot times in the stock market, but for the long haul, shares in the companies producing the concomitant hardware will probably do better. Although the service side of the industry is regulated, the equipment manufacturers are not.

Beware of the company that relies heavily on one major customer, someone like Sears, say, or one agency of the United States government. Being on the Sears approved list can do wonders for a company's product volume, but if Sears is the principal buyer, sleepless nights may well ensue. A principal buyer has marketplace leverage in reverse, calling the tune on prices, delivery dates, and even product design. Eventually, of course, the principal buyer also calls the tune on profits—what's left of them. Watch out whenever one customer accounts for over 10 percent of a company's revenues.

You must also be alert to no-growth growth. During inflationary periods, a company can sell its products for higher and higher prices, simply because of steady demand and the ease with which higher costs can be passed on. Overall sales revenues and earnings increase even when there is no growth in unit sales.

But if there is no real growth in demand, no growth in the market for *more* of the product, then when deflation comes along, as it always does, the company doesn't stand a chance. Earnings don't merely fall, they plunge when senior-citizen growth companies are exposed to a declining economy or other pressures on their pricing. So make sure that the growth you perceive in any company you are investigating as a possible investment candidate comes from rising demand, not merely from inflated prices.

Consider the big mainframe computer companies, for instance. They are certainly high-tech. But are they winning high-tech? The actual number of new installations in the industry is growing by only 6 to 8 percent a year. The profit growth is 13 to 15 percent, because the companies can sell more and more performance to the same old customers for higher and higher prices. But the extra 7 to 9 percent in growth is an illusion. The microcomputer and minicomputer invasion is going to put large mainframe computer prices under severe pressure. The true low growth of the mainframe computer companies will be revealed—much to the regret of unwary high-tech investors. You, however, will know enough not to be caught in the trap. So let's go on to explore some of the other pitfalls and potentials, both individual and industrial, that the high-tech investor of the eighties may encounter.

IV

My Word Processor Has a Human Operator, and Other Problems

Direction can be a real problem in investing. In fact, it's becoming a real problem everywhere, on the industrial as well as on the individual level. No one knows where we're all heading, because the current growth of knowledge is simply too great for it all to be channeled effectively. Despite the immense accumulation of information over the last two hundred years, and the last two decades in particular, we have, as mutual-fund director John Templeton puts it, "only a fleeting glimpse of the future. We are not at the tag end of the creative progress but at a new beginning. . . . we are perched on the frontiers of future knowledge."

The fact is, should the information explosion continue at the present rate, which it's likely to do for at least a number of decades to come, a child born today would graduate from college in a world accommodating four times the knowledge it held on his birthdate. By the time he was fifty years old, the amount of knowledge would be thirty-two times as great. To put it another way, 97 percent of everything known to man would have been accumulated since the time the child was born. So it seems there's a lot of picking and choosing ahead for your financial future. Even as a specialist in any one given technological area, you will have to take a lot of educated guesses based on as much information as you can absorb and sort out. When the total amount of information available reaches the staggering quantity it already has, an ability to "feel" the future with some accuracy becomes a necessary substitute for knowing it all.

Part of your research will be devoted to developing a feel for the *rate* of change in the industries you choose to follow

41

as well as for the changes themselves, because the expansion of product markets is usually directly related to the velocity of the industries' overall development. According to John Young, president of Hewlett-Packard, by the year 2000 electronics can be expected to be the second-largest industry in the country, a runner-up only to energy. That's less than two decades distant. Computer power is presently doubling every two and a half years, or, to view it from a pricing standpoint, every two and a half years the cost of computing power is cut in half. Had a Rolls-Royce undergone the same price and power changes over the last couple of decades, the automobile would now cost less than $5 and get several thousand miles to the gallon. Dream on.

These are rather staggering changes, and the Rolls analogy simply attempts to put them in perspective. Perspective on economic worth is usually developed through quantitative measures. Such measures are very hard to come by for the elusive "quality" that makes or breaks a high-tech company. Nevertheless, we have found a few, as mentioned in the beginning of this book.

Without an adequate market, the best company in the world cannot grow. Since growth is central to profitable high-tech investing, let's break down market size in greater detail than we accorded it in our earlier brief introduction to this factor.

First of all, the market size of a high-tech company headed for success must be at least $1 billion, or, if it is not, it must have the potential to become so in relatively short order. To determine market size for the company you are investigating requires only a minimum of research. Most industry specialty magazines and analysts publish such estimates on a continually updated basis. Current market projections are in this book, chapter by chapter, industry by industry. A company with sales of $75 million now—which is a good size for investment purposes—growing at 30 percent a year—which is a nice revenue-growth rate—will have sales of over $1 billion within ten years. Go ahead, try it on your calculator.

Another factor to be considered is your target company's share of the market (SOM), also available from trade publications and analysts. Its share of the market can be less than 5 percent when a firm is starting out, but the company must have a decent chance of growing until it has a major share (over 20 percent). The SOM number needed will depend on how concentrated or fragmented the relevant market is. What counts is being number one or two in SOM rank—however large or small the percent number works out to be. Number one tends to set prices for the industry, and number two can usually live with them. The rest eat less well. In maturing markets (and even our fast-moving subjects will get there eventually), the leader may have a majority (over 51 percent) share. Once it reaches this stage, its growth will depend more on the continued expansion of the market than on grabbing a further market share. The fact is, once a company's share of the market reaches 60 or 70 percent, increasing its market share becomes exceedingly difficult, both legally and from a selling point of view.

Yet another quantitative measure of a high-tech company's current performance and future potential is its sales per employee. Appropriate ranges for high-tech companies engaged in the various fields covered in this volume are:

applications software packages	$75,000–150,000
cellular mobile radio	$40,000–100,000 *
computer graphics	$50,000–100,000
consumer products	$80,000–125,000
custom circuits	$30,000–85,000
data base services	$75,000–150,000
fiber optics, lasers, and microwaves	$30,000–85,000
genetic engineering	$50,000–125,000 *
medical technology	$30,000–85,000
military technology	$40,000–65,000
office automation	$50,000–150,000
personal computers	$50,000–150,000
robotics	$30,000–75,000 *
video and advertising technology	$30,000–55,000

* These are speculative figures, since no public companies currently have revenues or profits from these sources that constitute a sufficient percentage of their total income to be representative.

The best companies in their respective industries should usually have a per-employee sales figure toward the higher end of the scale. Abnormally high sales per employee, however, might not be a good sign. Often such a disproportion indicates that the growth of the sales force has not kept up with the growth of the company. Worse yet, it could indicate that the company is coasting on past efforts, with inadequate numbers of service and support or research people to sustain sales in the future.

Profits are what the investment game is all about, of course, and whereas the average American industrial company earns 4 percent on revenues after taxes, good high-tech situations should result in pretax profit margins of 12 to 28 percent or after-tax profit margins of 7 to 14 percent. That's assuming earnings are fully taxed. If a company pays the IRS less than the average 40 to 50 percent of its pretax earnings, you should do a little calculating, as follows.

Take the company's revenues and pretax profits, both listed in its quarterly and annual reports, and subject them to the formula below.

$$\frac{\text{pretax profits} \times 100}{\text{revenues}} = \text{return before taxes, stated in percent}$$

Applying the formula to a company with, say, $30 million in quarterly revenues and $5 million in quarterly profits before taxes, one turns up the result below:

$$\frac{5 \times 100}{30} = 16.7 \text{ percent}$$

The 16.7 percent figure is within the acceptable profit-margin range, so the hypothetical company is definitely worth investigating further. Higher margins, incidentally, not only would be nice, but are quite possible. However, they are usually due to a company so dominating a market that 15, 16, or even 20 percent revenues after taxes become practicable. Unfortunately, that sort of dream situation is an open invitation to competitors, who rarely stay away for long under such circumstances. So watch your company as its stock skyrockets—someone may be gaining on it quickly.

As a check on a company's profit standing, use its return-on-assets figure, derived in a fashion very similar to the calculation of its pretax profit margin. Simply substitute the company's total assets (the bottom figure on either side of the balance sheet which you will find in the annual report) for the revenue figure. If you use quarterly revenues, don't forget to make them annual by multiplying by 4.

The return on assets for a well-managed, successful company in an unregulated industry is normally within the range of 7 to 21 percent after taxes. In other words, annual profits should be 7 to 21 percent of the company's assets. This measure combined with quantified profit margins should help you to rank companies in order of desirability, since the return on assets is relatively constant across industry lines.

Company growth rates, on the other hand, are far from constant across industry lines. To be considered a good investment, a well-run high-tech company must grow at 20 to 50 percent per year (including inflation) while small, and at 15 to 30 percent as it matures in size. It's hard to maintain, say, a 40 percent rate for very long. A company doing so would grow to twenty-nine times its original size in only ten years. To put it another way, a company with an initial market capitalization of $350 million would grow to a $15 billion company in the same ten-year period. That's why you want to do your hunting among companies with a market capitalization of $10 million to $100 million. Such companies have the potential of a few years' explosive growth ahead of them before sheer size impedes their momentum.

As a company reaches the behemoth stage, however, another investment opportunity—or another problem, depending on your vantage point—sometimes makes itself available. The entrepreneur who started, say, Electro-Hydro Sump ends up not liking the confinement of a large company. He feels a loss of control and personal involvement. So he cashes in his chips and goes fishing. He can afford it—usually within one to three years after the company has gone public and there's a strong market into which to sell his shares.

The second echelon, the founder's early partners, Goldfinger and Midas, also have some chips, although not as many of them. Instead of going fishing, they go across the street and set up Son of Electro-Hydro Sump, deciding to do things *their* way this time around—in competition with the original company, of course. You won't hear much about this clone company at first, for it won't be public initially, so Wall Street will pay it no heed. Eventually, if Son of Electro-Hydro Sump does go public, you may have a second investment opportunity in the field. But meanwhile, the original Electro-Hydro Sump may not be doing as well as it had in the past, for reasons not discernible—except to you. Having followed the industry as a whole, including perusing its trade journals, you will have seen Son of's superior product advertised, and more important, you will have noted the departure of Messrs. Goldfinger and Midas in the trade-press coverage of the debut of Son of Electro-Hydro Sump.

Precisely therein lies the difference between high-tech investing and throwing your money away. There is no automatic way to pick high-tech winners, no surefire "system." Some tasks in your investment search can be automated. For instance, Appendix B at the back of this book contains an Apple II–based set of programs and linking steps that will allow anyone with access to an Apple II personal computer and the appropriate software to calculate the various parameters of roughly twenty-eight stocks at a time, facilitating investment decisions. The programs also allow you to graph these parameters for visual presentation, to help give that crucial "feel" for how the stocks are capable of performing.

Using a computer to help select high-tech stocks seems somehow fitting. But if you don't have a personal computer, you can still use all the material in this volume. It will merely take you a little longer to process the information manually.

A computer, properly tuned, can help to speed up the decision-making process once it has the information we have chosen as pertinent. However, the computer is not going to make the decisions. At least it shouldn't. There are computer programs designed to flash buy and sell signals while tracking the market, but they simply don't pick stocks as profitably as the human mind can do.

The best approach to high-tech investing is to choose investment areas that pique your curiosity, either because of your work interests or hobbies, or because they seem interesting and might, in turn, evolve into new and perhaps even gainful hobbies. An investment specialty that broadens the horizons of your regular field of work can be a surprisingly profitable career move. Once you've read Part Two of this book and found the industries that really interest you, use the following worksheet to make a preliminary evaluation of the high-tech investment areas best for you.

HIGH-TECH INDUSTRY SELECTION WORKSHEET

DATE ______________________

INDUSTRY ____

Market Factors

1. Size
   To determine the relevant industry market size, use the projected figure for the ending year of your projected investment period, not the start.

   EXAMPLE: If you are buying a stock in 1983, with a planned three-year holding period, use the projected 1986 market size (see the "Projected Market Growth" bar graphs in each of the chapters dealing with the specialized industries).

   Score 2 for a market over $500 million. Score 1 for an industry market between $200 million and $500 million, 0 for a market under $200 million. ____

2. Growth Rate
   Make sure you measure the industry market growth rate over the time horizon you expect your investment to cover.

   EXAMPLE: For a three-year investment in robotics, check the 1983 and 1986 market size figures (see Chapter VII). They are $220 million and $450 million respectively, indicating a 2.04× increase, equivalent to a compound annual growth rate (CAGR) of 27 percent per year.

   Using an inexpensive business calculator makes it a snap to determine the compound annual growth rate (CAGR). The formula for hand calculation of the CAGR is given in Appendix B on page 362. Although presented as part of the computer program described in that appendix, the formula can be used with a calculator—or, for that matter, a pencil. There are also special CAGR tables published. A local real estate agent would probably have one. Similar to mortgage interest tables, they are equally easy to use. Score 2 for a CAGR of 25 percent or better, 1 for a CAGR of 15 to 25 percent, 0 for growth below 15 percent.   ____

Subtotal ____

Structural Factors

Score 1 point for each yes, 0 for each no.

1. It's easy to start a small company in this industry, since capital and personnel needs are low.   ____

2. The technical expertise required to start such a company is considerable.   ____

3. The industry is on the leading edge of a technology. Or the industry is a simple extension of another successful industry and thus does not need the integration of several different technologies.   ____

4. Products or services in the industry have international as well as national sales potential.   ____

Subtotal ____

Regulatory Factors

Score 2 points for each yes, 0 for each no.

1. The products or services have no known harmful effects or difficult waste-disposal problems.   ____

2. The industry is not currently under any form of government regulation.   ____

Subtotal ____

Customer Factors

Score 2 points for each yes, 0 for each no.

1. Product selling prices are $1,000 or less, and there are at least 750,000 potential customers. Or product

selling prices are between $1,000 and $50,000, and there are 50,000 to 500,000 potential customers. Or product selling prices are $100,000 or more, and there are at least 5,000 to 10,000 potential customers.   _____

2. Potential customers may spend money without voter intervention. (Voters may be university trustees or people in similar control positions, not necessarily political voters.)   _____

Subtotal _____

Personal Factors

Score 2 points for each yes, 0 for each no.

1. I have expertise in the industry or in a closely related one. (Expertise may be academic experience, on-the-job training, or knowledge gained from being a supplier to the industry. No points are allowed if it has been more than five years since your contact with the industry.) Or I have a friend who is one of the above—and I really respect his or her opinions. (Be honest. Your friend will never know, and it's your money.)   _____

2. I find the industry intrinsically interesting, and after looking at some of the trade journals, I've decided I'd rather read them than cereal boxes with my breakfast.   _____

Subtotal _____

Total _____

Your overall score for the industry should be at least 12 before you consider involving yourself in the research necessary to pick the investment winners. If you have categories with a subtotal score of zero, you should explore the industry further before making any decisions on it. Subcategory totals of zero represent unevaluated risks. Unevaluated risks are to be avoided. They will zap you every time.

Update this sheet annually. Industries change dramatically —and so, sometimes, do your interests.

V

The Right Information Makes the Crucial Difference

We live in the information age. We may well drown in the information age. The relentless stream of data flows through our lives in the form of television, radio, newspapers, magazines, cassettes, government forms by the cabinetful, licenses, applications, permits—there's simply too much of it. Yet the right information is crucial to financial success. The secret is how to find and use it.

A great deal of information is presented in Part Two of this book. After reading it, your next step will be to put a lot of it aside temporarily, for you will need to focus your investment deliberations on one or two specialized areas, areas you find interesting, areas that have aroused your curiosity. The High-Tech Industry Selection Worksheet in Chapter IV will help you to establish the particular industries on which you wish to spend further research time. Your next step will be to map out your own way of obtaining detailed coverage of your chosen field or fields. Now how do you go about doing that?

A good way to start is by attending one of the professional-association, trade, or industry shows listed in the industry chapters that follow in Part Two. This is baptism by fire. You'll be thrust into everything at once.

You'll also have a tax-deductible vacation, since expenses related to investment research are tax-deductible, and not even the IRS would consider attending an electronics trade show a vacation, unless you fail to spend most of your daytime hours at exhibits and sessions. Keep a diary of your day as it relates to your investment investigations. Going to a hospitality suite for drinks and canapés is a perfectly legitimate way to gather information at these affairs. Evenings, furthermore, are your own. Inasmuch as most of the conventions are purposely held in places like Las Vegas, Montreal, San Francisco,

Boston, and Monaco, show-going can be a very interesting way to work.

There is the expense to be weighed, of course, and such trips are not exactly necessary. On the other hand, consider a $10,000 portfolio. Were you to put that amount into a commission-charging mutual fund, the commission and management fees would probably come close to equaling a week's worth of investment research in New York or Los Angeles, plane fare included. So why not pursue your own investigations?

Assuming you do decide to attend one of these industry gatherings, what can you expect to gain besides sore feet (and they're a sure thing)? First of all, you'll have the opportunity to see all the latest products, and see them demonstrated. You'll have a chance to collect literature on them for your research files and to question company salesmen (watch out —they're always optimistic about their products) as well as, quite often, company executives. They're all there to sell their firms as much as their wares.

You'll also be able to pick up free copies of all the latest trade publications. These will contain the subscription cards you need to order the periodicals on a regular basis. Besides signing up for the magazines you decide might be helpful, you can put your name on the mailing lists for product announcements and financial news such as the quarterly and annual reports of publicly held companies. You'll discover publicly held companies of which you weren't aware before, in fact, plus a lot of private companies that bear watching against the day they might go public.

Then there are the tutorial sessions, providing a chance to rest your feet while learning about new industry developments and trends. Among these tutorials are usually a surprising number of investment-relevant ones. Most high-tech company engineers and scientists need help on financial matters. Expertise in the ways of managing their companies' growth is not their forte. Thus there are a lot of presentations on marketing, sales trends, and potential market niches that can be very useful to an investor.

Security analysts are also frequently to be found at these conventions. They are often good sources of investment information, voicing their opinions informally at trade exhibits, hospitality suites, and after-the-show bars, in a manner quite unlike their office demeanor. Overheard snatches of discussions and gossip fall into that amorphous category of information known as getting a feel for the industry and the companies involved. Into the same category go noticing how crowded the booths are and whether people are just looking or really ordering. It may all sound a bit like playing detective, and in a sense it is. It's also an excellent way to pick up leads, however.

But, you object, you're not quite ready to spring for a $1,000-plus research vacation, even if it's tax-deductible. Where do you start in that case?

First of all, orient yourself with the help of some general high-technology publications. Besides the specialty periodicals listed in the chapters on specific industries, there are sources giving more of a broad overview of high-tech developments. What you as an investor will be particularly interested in will be the survey, prediction, or update issues periodically put out by the various technical publications below. Copies of at least some of these issues should be available for perusal at your local library if it's a large one. If you live near a major city, chances are there's a business or university library containing most of them.

The periodicals listed provide useful background information for more than one high-tech industry, although, of course, no single publication covers every high-tech field. The references are listed in order of probable usefulness to the investor plus cost-effectiveness. Look them over, see which ones you can read comfortably, then select at least three for regular background study.

Electronic News

Fairchild Publications
7 East 12th Street
New York, NY 10003
Telephone: (201) 899-5566 for subscriptions
Subscription: $25 per year for weekly newspaper

Coverage of computers, electronics, and telecommunications is provided by this publication. It is not a good resource for cable television, entertainment, genetics, medical technology, robotics, or software. Roughly every other issue is devoted to an industry subsegment update. These overviews are basically condensations of consultant studies, contributed by various consulting firms in the hope that readers will order the full (and expensive) study, supplemented by interviews with industry participants. They don't offer much in the way of basic industry understanding, but they are all right as updates.

Electronic Business

Cahners Publishing Company Division of
   Reed Holdings, Inc.
221 Columbus Avenue
Boston, MA 02116
Telephone: (303) 388-4511 for subscriptions
   Subscription: $35 per year for monthly periodical
               (address inquiries to 270 St. Paul Street,
               Denver, CO 80206)

Electronics-industry analyses, forecasts, reviews of new issues, notes on management changes, and a calendar of events are offered by this monthly periodical, which also has at least one business-segment update and projection in each issue. The magazine generally furnishes more details to aid you than do most other comparable publications.

The Rosen Electronics Letter

Rosen Research, Inc.
200 Park Avenue
New York, NY 10166
Telephone: (212) 586-3530
   Subscription: $395 per year for irregular (roughly
               biweekly) publication

The Rosen letter supplies topical coverage of all phases of microelectronics and personal computers. It's the leading electronics-industry gossip sheet.

Venture

Venture Magazine, Inc.
35 West 45th Street
New York, NY 10036
Telephone: (212) 840-5580, (800) 247-5470 for
   subscriptions
   Subscription: $18 per year for monthly periodical

Small-company-oriented articles to help the entrepreneur are the emphasis of this publication. It has a significant high-tech slant.

Inc.

Inc. Magazine
P.O. Box 2538
Boulder, CO 80322
Telephone: (800) 525-0643 for subscriptions
    Subscription: $18 per year for monthly periodical
Similar to *Venture* in its approach, *Inc.* also compiles an annual list of the hundred fastest-growing public companies plus a similar list of the fastest-growing private firms.

High Technology

Technology Publishing Company
P.O. Box 2810
Boulder, CO 80322
Telephone: (303) 447-9330
    Subscription: $15 per year for monthly periodical
High Technology gives broad coverage to high-tech developments and trends and tries to explain the technology. It contains a short investment section.

Spectrum

The Institute of Electrical and Electronic Engineers, Inc.
345 East 47th Street
New York, NY 10017
Telephone: (212) 644-7555, (201) 981-0060 for
    subscriptions
    Subscription: $6 per year to institute members for
                  monthly periodical, the subscription cost
                  included in the membership dues of $30
                  per year (address inquiries to the IEEE
                  Service Center, 445 Hoes Lane,
                  Piscataway, NJ 08854)
Technically oriented articles on developments in many fields are written for readers on the Bachelor of Science level. This publication does a terrific job of explaining the technology underlying your potential investments.

Wall Street Transcript

Wall Street Transcript Corporation
120 Wall Street
New York, NY 10005
Telephone: (212) 747-9500
   Subscription: $780 for weekly newspaper
The *Wall Street Transcript* is a bit overwhelming to take in, as it simply contains too much information. However, the publisher does sell reprints of industry analyst round tables for $25 a copy. These discussions run twenty-five pages or so in length and feature four to six participants representing leading brokerage and investment firms. In the course of their deliberations, the analysts as a group tend to give you some understanding of the particular industry under debate—and you'll never access them as cheaply as this. In fact, the analysts' firms often distribute free reprints of the conference proceedings to professional investors. In recent months, there have been round tables on advertising, aerospace, broadcasting, computer services, consumer electronic products, hospital management and supply, office equipment, publishing, semiconductors, and telecommunications.

Survey of Wall Street Research

Nelson Publications
11 Elm Place
Rye, NY 10580
Telephone: (914) 967-9100
   Subscription: $95 per year for bimonthly periodical
Expensive for an individual, the survey may be available through your broker or library. It tells you who follows what, listing as well the addresses and telephone numbers of 3,000 companies and hundreds of analysts. It also lists company contacts. In addition to the bimonthly survey, the publisher compiles a yearly *Directory of Securities Research*, available for $123.

OTC Review

Review Publishing Corporation
110 Pennsylvania Avenue
Oreland, PA 19075
         or

Mailing address:
Box 110
Jenkintown, PA 19046
Telephone: (215) 887-9000
   Subscription: $36 per year for monthly periodical
As the name suggests, this publication covers over-the-counter stocks (and most high-tech stocks are OTC) and is aimed at brokers and investors who need information on these often neglected companies. The editorial style is refreshingly direct and pungent, unlike so much flack-produced material. A good buy at the price, the magazine also provides a reader service card for literature requests from companies featured in each issue.

Research: Ideas for Investors
Research Services
P.O. Box 9040
Van Nuys, CA 91409
Telephone: (213) 997-7441
   Subscription: This bimonthly periodical is free to
                      stockbrokers
Research presents company information in a format designed to make it easily understood by brokers and their customers. Companies review the material before publication. Brokers may obtain free reprints and videotapes of the material, certainly helpful as starting points—but don't stop with company-cleared information.

In addition to these industry sources, if you are a *Business Week* reader, be sure you receive the Industrial Edition. (The legend "Industrial Edition" appears in the upper-left-hand corner of the contents page. The price is the same for the regular edition.) The industrial version of the magazine contains additional editorial pages on high-technology industry developments in roughly every other issue.
   At the opposite end of the periodicals scale from the widely read *Business Week* are the controlled-circulation specialty magazines such as *Broadcasting* and *International Fiber Optics and Communications.* Controlled-circulation magazines restrict their audience to very special groups, say, electronics-company executives or chemical engineers employed in the

plastics industry. Because they reach a very well-defined audience, these magazines can charge higher advertising rates than their small circulation would otherwise justify. In turn, these periodicals don't want general-purpose readers like us among their defined subscribers, because we distort their circulation figures. If you send in one of those large "Subscribe free" data cards bound into controlled-circulation magazines, chances are you'll never hear anything further from the publisher, unless you indulge in a little creative maneuvering. Far be it from us to suggest that you stretch the truth, but a lot of people faced with questions on subscription cards such as "What best describes the principal end product or service of your work?" and "Do you influence the purchase of equipment and/or services?" answer with an ambiguous "Research" and a definitive "Yes." After all, they say, they are in fact one-person research and development firms dedicated to industrial economic analysis.

There is, however, a more legitimate way around the wall of silence. Money talks, and publishers listen. Nearly all of these exclusive outfits will allow you to subscribe if you pay for the privilege. You'll find the price (usually in the range of $25 to $50 per year) and other subscription details in the fine print on the masthead page somewhere not far from the place where the words *controlled circulation* appear.

Whichever approach you decide to take, the hardest part of your quest may well be obtaining a sample copy of the specialty magazine you think might interest you in the first place. Business schools, libraries, and corporate reception rooms are sometimes great places to look over these magazines and pull out subscription cards. A quicker solution is to write or call the periodicals pertinent to your field of interest listed in this book and request that they each send you a sample copy and a subscription form. After you've perused all the magazines in a given field, chances are you'll settle for the three or four among them that are both readable and adequate sources of the information you need.

Reading alone won't supply all the information you should have at hand in order to maximize your investment profits, of course. People can tell you a lot, and the right people can tell you the right lot. *Right* is the crucial word here, for there are far more misinformed and poorly informed people in high technology than there are those who can be truly helpful. That's why, once you find the people with the right information, you need to treat them well. Don't keep constantly nagging for more information. Use their time with discretion—and use yours to seek more sources.

Cross-checks are vital in the ever-changing field of high-tech investing. Three opinions are worth a great deal more than one opinion expressed three times, for everyone's opinion is biased. In the case of multiple sources, the biases tend to cancel each other out, leaving you with a more objective viewpoint.

But who are all these people whose opinions we urge you to seek, and where are they to be found? Here's a rundown of the ideal board of consultants for your investment portfolio. You probably won't be able to contact them all. On the other hand, you'll be surprised how many sources you can reach once you start pursuing them.

Security analysts at brokerage houses, banks, insurance companies, and mutual funds have the same financial objective as you have in your information gathering, namely, to determine how to buy low and sell high. Analysts are some of the best sources of interpretation of market conditions, as they affect the stock of reasonably sized publicly held companies. The catch is that these analysts are usually difficult to approach. Why should they talk to a small investor?

The answer is that they may do so if you have your broker's recommendation. If you are a good customer, and if your broker has stature in his firm, he can probably get you a few minutes on the phone with his firm's analysts.

Another option is to deal with a brokerage firm, mutual fund, or bank which has a member analyst expert in your chosen field (refer to the industry chapters of this book for listings of such specialty analysts), with the understanding that you will be buying stocks in this industry segment and would appreciate occasional access to his opinions. Just don't overdo your contact. This admonition is not that difficult to follow, however, since on the whole you will be buying shares for the long haul rather than trading on a day-to-day basis or a week-to-week basis. A brief conference once or twice a year should be adequate to keep you up-to-date on major trends.

However you decide to contact your analyst sources, do

your homework first. Try to obtain copies of their recent presentations on the industries they follow and the companies they recommend. Any good full-service broker, as opposed to a discount broker, should be able to provide reports by his firm's analysts for you. Also many companies are willing to send you copies of analysts' reports written about their firms or the industry of which they are a part. Such reports will give you more sources of potentially valuable information and provide more cross-checks. But remember that a company is not likely to send you a copy of a very negative report, particularly if it reflects poorly on that company's management.

Once you have the reports, go over them carefully. See what worthwhile questions remain to be asked, points not covered in or raised by the written material. Which stock you should buy or sell is *not* a worthwhile question to ask an analyst. Unlike your broker, who should know your financial circumstances and investment objectives, an analyst simply isn't equipped to evaluate your personal concerns. Security analysts study companies and industries, not investors. Ask what's the best stock for you, and chances are the analyst will simply decline to answer.

Ask for an opinion on the two most important things an investor should be aware of in a given industry, on the other hand, and chances are the analyst will start talking. The question is open-ended and different enough from those usually asked that it will elicit some thought, as opposed to a standard spiel used at the most recent brokers' review meeting.

One caveat should be stated: Most analysts will tend to be kind to companies that are investment banking clients of their firms. You can tell whether a client relationship is involved by checking the most recent company prospectus. It will list the firms which are its principal underwriters right on the cover.

There are often other worthwhile opinions about a company to be gleaned from such peripherally related sources as attorneys, accountants, customer-company executives, supplier-company personnel, commercial bankers, and so forth. People who have some professional involvement with your target company or industry may all be helpful. Each of them will have limitations and biases associated with his own standpoint, however. In determining the views of such contributors, whatever you do, don't try to obtain confidential information. You will quickly lose a contact—as well as any profits should you be judged to be trading on the basis of inside information.

Industry executives, not surprisingly, are one of your best personal sources of investment information. Chances are, like most people, you don't hobnob with many industry executives. However, that doesn't mean you'll never have a chance to talk to them. It simply means you must create your own opportunities to do so.

First of all, let's return for a moment to those conventions. Almost any scheduled flight from any major city to a convention city arriving the day the show opens or the day before will be chockablock full of conventioneers. Among them will be a number of company executives. (Note, however, for your return flight, that most of the bigwigs leave the day before the last day of the show.) Talk to the people next to you on the plane. In an airplane, you have a captive audience. And most people like to talk about themselves and their business. If you have the right questions to ask when such an opportunity strikes, chances are you'll find worthwhile answers to them.

Professional-society and industry-association meetings are also excellent places for informal yet informative contacts. But don't leave matters altogether to chance. Go straight to the sources. Set up an interview with a knowledgeable officer of any company in which you are planning to invest.

High-tech companies are different from established blue-chip firms, which is why we often list as contacts for the various firms in this book such executives as chief financial officers and vice-presidents. Young high-tech companies don't yet have expensive investor-relations staffs; those will come later. Meanwhile the corporate officers don't want would-be investors talking to junior staff members, who may not know which information is for public release. As likely as not, at the up-and-coming Peewee Corporation the president himself frequently handles investors' queries.

When a company hasn't been public all that long, the investment world is new and fun to its corporate executives. They don't have a lot of analysts beating on their doors yet, so investor attention is flattering. They enjoy talking about their company. More than flattery is at stake, however. They need a good market for their company's stock. Without active trading, a company's share price languishes, and developing a pool of interested investors helps to spark trading.

Having explained why high-tech company executives are by and large so much more accessible than those of larger, more established firms, however, we should hasten to add that before you set up an appointment to talk to them, you need to do your homework. Call the company and request:

1. The latest annual report and Securities and Exchange Commission (SEC) Form 10-K, which discusses the company's financial condition in more detail than does the annual report.
2. The most recent quarterly report to shareholders and SEC Form 10-Q, the quarterly counterpart of the 10-K.
3. The proxy statement for the latest annual shareholders' meeting.
4. The prospectus from the company's most recent stock offering, if available.
5. Any recent reports on the company by security analysts.

Read and study these records in detail. In particular, you want to determine the company's major products and the relative importance of each to overall sales and profits. You want to ascertain the company's strengths, especially in relation to those of its competitors. For that you need to know the company's marketing strategy and how its products are positioned in price/performance (review the early pages of Chapter II). Pay close attention to current orders for the company's products and to its revenues and operating (before interest and taxes) profits.

Another variable to study is what keeps the company actually operating—the facilities, people, and cost structures involved. Are they adequate in relation to the company's projected growth and that of its product market?

Compare the firm's standing on these counts with that of the competition. If the company's position differs greatly from that of its competitors on any of these fronts, what is the reason for the discrepancy? If the company compares less than favorably with the competition, why does it do so? There may be a very good reason, in fact. For instance, what might seem an excessive number of employees could well be due to a sizable recent increase in research and development staff, engaged to develop a potentially profitable product.

Try to garner as good an overview of the company as possible. What is its history? Occasionally you'll discover an old firm given a new name to help hide the fact that it has just emerged from bankruptcy. How much of the company do the executives and directors own? What relevant experience do they have to offer the company? In some cases, directors are merely old friends of the founder who enjoy the prestige of being listed as board members but have little to contribute to the firm's future success.

To help sort out and evaluate all the various bits of information you glean on a company, fill out the following High-Tech Company Selection Worksheet, adding missing information as you track it down. A score of 20 or better indicates definite investment potential.

HIGH-TECH COMPANY
SELECTION WORKSHEET

DATE _____

COMPANY _____

INDUSTRY _____

Company Data

1. Market Capitalization
   Score 2 for market capitalization of from $20 million
   to $75 million. Score 1 for a capitalization between
   $75 million and $150 million, 0 for capitalization
   over $150 million. _____

2. Price-to-Earnings Ratio (on estimated following
   year's earnings per share)
   Score 2 for a price-to-earnings ratio of 10 or below, 1
   for a ratio of 11 to 20, 0 for a ratio of 21 or above. _____

3. Return on Assets
   Score 2 for a return on assets of 17 percent or above,
   1 for a return between 8 percent and 17 percent, 0
   for a return of 7 percent or below. _____

4. Annual Earnings-per-Share Growth Rate
   Score 2 for a yearly growth rate in earnings per share
   of 30 percent or above, 1 for a rate of 20 to 29 percent, 0 for a rate of 19 percent or below. _____

5. Revenue per Employee
   Score 1 for yes, 0 for no.
   The revenue-per-employee figure for the company
   falls within the ideal range given earlier in the book
   (see Part Two) for firms in that particular industry. _____

Financial Factors

1. Score 2 for a company with no debt, except for its
   trade credit on the balance sheet. Score 1 for debt
   less than 25 percent of total company assets. Score 0
   for total debt more than 25 percent of total assets. _____

2. Score 2 for a tax rate of 40 percent or higher. Score 1 for a 30 percent to 40 percent tax rate. Score 0 for a rate lower than 30 percent. _____

3. Score 2 for a cash flow (net earnings after taxes plus depreciation) greater than capital spending (additions to property, plant, equipment). Score 0 for a cash-flow figure less than that for capital spending. _____

4. Score 2 for a research and development (R&D) budget over 15 percent of annual revenues. Score 1 for R&D between 6 and 15 percent. Score 0 for R&D less than 6 percent. _____

5. Score 1 for a "clean" auditor's opinion letter in the annual report (*clean* here means the absence of any phrase like "subject to the outcome of the matter in paragraph x"). For anything other than a clean letter, *subtract* 2 points. _____

Management Factors

1. Score 2 for indications in a recent prospectus, trade publication, or personal contact that key managers of the company have had successful previous experience in the same industry. Score 1 for a successful record in a different industry. Score 0 if no information is available. For key managers with financial or legal expertise but with no experience in the industry, *subtract* 2 points. _____

2. Score 2 for a company on which no brokerage firms have estimated earnings available. Score 1 for a company endorsed by leading analysts at brokerage firms which are not investment bankers for the company. Score 0 for a company endorsed by analysts of the company's investment banker. _____

3. Score 2 for a company less than 10 percent of whose stock is held by institutions. Score 1 for institutional stock ownership of between 10 percent and 25 percent. Score 0 for institutional holdings of more than 25 percent. (Information on institutional ownership is available from a variety of stock-reporting ser-

The Right Information   65

vices. If Standard and Poor's has a write-up on its loose-leaf sheets, you can find the figures there, although they tend to be six months old. Even so, they will provide an indication of buying trends and the attitude of institutional buyers toward a given company.)   _____

Competitive Factors

Competition ranks as perhaps the single factor most underestimated, most frequently changeable, and most difficult to quantify in company evaluation. Don't talk yourself into points.

1. Score 2 for a company that ranks first in the industry. Score 1 for a company ranking second or third but having greater than 10 percent market share. Score 0 for a company in second or third place but with less than 10 percent market share. For a company below third place in the industry, *subtract* 1 point.   _____

2. Score 2 for a company having no competitors. Score 1 for a company with no Japanese competitors.   _____

Conceptual Factors

Score 2 if you can express in one sentence, in a way which clearly indicates the company's competitive edge, what products or services the company provides. Score 0 if the description requires two or more sentences (sentences with more than two clauses are disqualified).   _____

The overall score for a company should probably be close to 20 (out of a possible 30) before you consider purchasing its stock. A score above 25 in conjunction with a rising market makes for a very compelling investment idea. A score lower than 10 probably indicates a company that only an investor who can sell short and still sleep at night should look at twice.

If, after going through all the information you can unearth on a company, you find there are still some unanswered questions about it in your mind or on your questionnaire, then it's time to contact a company representative directly. Here you have two choices. You can call or you can pay a visit in person. Of the two alternatives, the personal visit is by far the best selection, and quite often it's neither too difficult nor too expensive to call upon at least some companies if you live in a high-tech metropolitan area such as Atlanta, Boston, Chicago, Dallas, Los Angeles, Minneapolis, New York, or San Francisco. A personal visit offers not only the advantage of a first-hand look at the environs of your potential investment, but the ease of conversation which a face-to-face meeting affords, permitting confidences not often proffered to a strange voice on the telephone (which, among other things, could be that of a competitor trying to pull a fast one).

The prelude to either a call or a visit is the setting up of an appointment. Explain that you are a potentially substantial investor, considering taking an investment position in the company because your research indicates that it shows promise, but that you have a few as yet unanswered questions in need of reply before you make your decision. Make a definite appointment for a specific date and time, and don't forget to leave your telephone number so you can be reached in case unexpected problems necessitate a rescheduling of your appointment.

The day before your visit or call, review the company data you have collected once more. You will be taking up important time for the company executive, and common courtesy dictates that you be well prepared. More significantly to you, the well-informed investor is the one who elicits results.

You can put those results on paper. You can take notes. But don't ask to record the conversation. People don't open up with a microphone around.

One thing you will find, by the time you've reached the stage in your investigations where you need to call on company executives, is that, having saturated yourself with industry information, your confidence about the field has increased tremendously. You're ready to talk to professional analysts and company presidents alike because you are familiar with not only the jargon of the field, but the latest industry developments as well. You can say, "That new multipurpose spreadsheet/word processor software of Sequitur's I saw at COMDEX looks like a really cost-effective product"—and back your statement up with reasons.

Suddenly you may have information or ideas to trade. Analysts, executives, accountants, attorneys, and other professionals are all more likely to talk meaningfully to investors who appear to be in the know, even if those investors' information is not new, but merely confirms their own opinions. By becoming knowledgeable in a field, you circumvent Catch-22. You become useful—part of the answer to someone else's question—and so, in turn, your own questions are answered. In the investment game, having your questions answered means a great deal of progress toward making money.

In the chapters to come, each of the industries chosen as currently the most appropriate for inclusion in this volume is given a broad overview and an expected growth projection. As a unit, these chapters provide you with the equivalent of an old-boy, new-tech network, a group of contacts and information sources familiar with what's happening in these diverse industries on an up-to-date and specific basis.

The high-tech industries themselves are ranked by growth and risk dimensions, with genetic engineering first as the riskiest and, at the same time, the fastest-growing industry. Military technology, the last industry covered, has the slowest foreseeable growth and the least risk—at least as far as economics is concerned. War has always been with us as a growth industry and can be expected to remain so, although war of the Space Invaders video variety currently has a faster-growing product market considered on a percentage basis.

Within each high-tech industry, the companies are listed alphabetically so as not to imply any ranking in terms of investment value. Such a ranking could in any case change considerably within a year or two. Of necessity, it will be up to you to update the matching of companies with your investment personality and future developments, using principles and ideas presented in the other sections of this book.

Some companies participate in more than one technological industry. In such an event, you will find them listed once, in their area of greatest importance. The classifications are inevitably somewhat arbitrary, since there is considerable interrelation and overlap among the technological industries covered. By way of illustration, a slowing in the gains in semiconductor custom circuits could affect many of the other industries' ability to deliver lower costs and greater performance, thus in turn slowing their growth rates.

Large companies are not listed unless they represent a relatively dominant force in a given industry. Many well-known, high-quality companies are omitted for this reason. No criticism is intended. It's merely the result of focusing on small, potentially super-fast-growing high-tech companies.

On the flip side of that coin, the inclusion of a smaller company should not be interpreted as an endorsement of either its quality or its advisability as an investment. Some industries have fewer players, and so their lists may be of lower overall quality as well as quantity.

There are many interesting companies not included simply because they didn't fall within the boundaries of the high-tech industries covered. Again the omission is not a criticism. There's a whole universe of stocks to explore, using the criteria in this volume as a means of investment selection. The companies listed represent one large world of selections, enough to keep you busy for quite a while, but nonrestrictive. New companies are coming down the line every day. Don't ignore them.

Companies may merge, be acquired, go bankrupt (let's hope that's never the fate of one you've picked). Analysts may, and frequently do, change their firm affiliations. But with the guidelines of this book, you'll be able to navigate your high-tech investment portfolio successfully through the shoals of change. And you'll be part of the high-tech network yourself, as profitably up to date as can be.

Part Two

Where to Find the Right High-Tech Investment

VI

Genetic Engineering: Alterations to Suit

Genetic engineering is the ne plus ultra in high tech for the popular media. Robots mowing lawns and serving croissants and café au lait along with the Sunday paper are exciting enough and fun to write about. But stories of little men in white coats running around secret cliffside laboratories creating two-uddered cows, self-harvesting watermelon-sized strawberries, and cells cloned from elephant testicles to cure lymphatic cancer are simply irresistible to feature editors. Fortunately or unfortunately, depending on your viewpoint, the media-hyped realm of sci-fi is not where the genetic engineering action really is—or where it is likely to be for many a decade, if ever.

Overtones of alchemy and supertechtronics aside, genetic engineering is a fairly prosaic industry. An offshoot of biotechnology, which is largely responsible for the hybrid corn, rice, and livestock developed over the last fifty years to feed much of the world's current population, genetic engineering dates more or less from the period of the sixties and seventies when the genetic code was being broken and the electrochemical balances within living things were beginning to fall into an understandable pattern—understandable at least to the scientists and technicians working on the research frontiers.

From an investor's viewpoint, genetic engineering can be roughly divided into three fields. First there's the altered-microbe industry, in which existing microbes are "improved" through stress, isolation, and purification in order to develop mutants capable of performing certain desired tasks. Strictly speaking, the methods employed are not those of true genetic engineering. The cultures are modified by natural processes.

A second, more accurately categorized field of genetic engineering is gene splicing. Here's where the press zeroes in.

71

And genetic modification is a genuinely incredible achievement. However, incredible profits in this area of inquiry, while quite possible, are also quite probably incredibly far off.

The third of the categories includes the pick-and-shovel companies. Not so exciting, not so speculative, these companies are nevertheless the most likely financial winners in the brilliantly researched field of genetic engineering, at least over the near term.

Looking more closely at the first category, one can readily determine that the main thrust of altered-microbe research is to find bacteria to devour various specific substances. Bacteria can outeat Pac-Man any day, although they're fussy eaters—which is both their value and their drawback. Their fussiness means the scientist must find just the right bacteria to do the job at hand. Once found and isolated, however, those bacteria can usually be counted on to perform very specific functions without adding unexpected or uncontrolled factors to the process. As John F. Spisak, chief metallurgist at Anschutz Mining Corporation, has put it, "There is a living system that can duplicate virtually every industrial system in the world today."

If by now, putting two and two together, you are beginning to wonder whether metal-eating microbes live out there, you're right on target. Anschutz's goal is to develop a bacteria-based method of mining.

If you can do it with metal ores, then why not with oil? There's no reason at all why you can't. Hence small new companies such as Advanced Mineral Technologies, Inc., and Salk Institute Biotechnology/Industrial Associates have joined mainstream corporations like General Electric, INCO, and Tosco in researching microbial-enhanced oil recovery.

The oil angle developed from studies conducted by Ananda M. Chakrabarty. Now with Petrogen, Inc., he carried out while at General Electric his original investigation into the possibility of developing a strain of microbes that would devour crude oil. The particular microbes involved were subjected to a landmark 1980 Supreme Court decision when the robed mighty of the high court decreed that altered life forms were patentable.

Although Chakrabarty's original microbes eventually failed

their field test, their patentability resulted in a real research boom—whose most promising results to date have been in the mundane world of waste disposal. Microbes have been used in waste treatment for centuries, of course. In the outhouse and the municipal sewage plant alike, bacteria are what do the work. See what we mean about bioengineering's being rather prosaic at times?

The difference between your run-of-the-mill sewage microbes and your high-tech microbes, the laboratory-designed mutants developed for waste disposal, is a matter of diet—and dollars. To give an example, Allied Corporation is spending $500,000 on a chemical-waste-treatment facility for phenol, cyanide, and ammonia. Therein bacteria will devour the toxic wastes at a third to half the cost of using solvents or burn-off technology. O. H. Materials Company, in another instance, saved a total of nearly $350,000 by cleaning industrial-solvent-soaked soil with bacteria instead of digging up the soil and burying it in landfill. The bacterial method, of course, offers the additional ecological and cost benefits of actually destroying the contaminants—as opposed to simply hiding them until the day they begin to leach out into aquifers, à la Love Canal.

Finding out what eats what and then developing a pure strain of mutants to do the desired consuming is what altered-microbe technology is all about. All things considered, it is less capital-intensive and in some ways more readily realizable than gene splicing, the great second category of investment in genetic engineering.

The biotechnology of gene splicing, or DNA recombination, is spawning what some scientists call the golden age of biology. And the breeding grounds are the Gene Gulch right next to Silicon Valley. A sprawling biotechnology web has now evolved around the Bay Area of San Francisco, with a clone outside of Boston to match that city's computer-lined Route 128. Cetus and Genentech are the big biotech names on the western shore, but there are amazing tales to be told about small, little-known companies such as DNAX of Palo Alto. Capitalized at $6 million one year and gobbled up by Schering-Plough for $19 million the next, DNAX represents the kind of explosive growth of which high-tech dreams are made.

Whatever the company, the basic approaches to genetic modification remain, for the moment, the same. Take, for instance, recombinant DNA, as that technique was conceived by Herbert Boyer and Stanley Cohen over a sandwich break during a science conference in Hawaii. (The formulation of the principle led to an almost inevitable joke: "What do you get when you combine two biochemists and a corned-beef sandwich?" "Designer genes.") Dr. Boyer is now with Genentech and Dr. Cohen is now an adviser to Cetus; both of them are designing genes, under separate labels.

In their recombinant DNA process, a small circular molecule called a plasmid is actually opened, a gene from another species of bacteria is inserted, and what issues is a recombined DNA in a rebuilt plasmid. The characteristics of this new gene will now modify the original bacteria in the desired way.

What counts for the investor is that the designer genes can be tailored to fit industrial processes with more precision than pants fit Brooke Shields. The range of possible end products efficiently and inexpensively produced by recombinant DNA is staggering—fructose, citric acid, insulin, human growth hormones, interferon, alkene, venereal-disease-testing media, and pig scour vaccines, to give you an inkling of the possible scope of applications. No wonder Genentech's stock record includes jumps from $35 a share to $89 in a single day.

But where is the profit in all this? The technological and commercial achievements in the field to date have both been considerable, with revenues for gene splicing exceeding $25 million in 1981. But the failure of investors to distinguish between the possible and the actual has led to the beginnings of a shakeout in this two-year-old industry that already boasts over a hundred entrants, who among themselves have soaked up some $500 million in initial funding. Instant intrigue there is, but the emperor's bottom line is practically naked. Cetus and Genentech each have a market capitalization of well over $200 million at this writing. Yet neither can boast revenues as high as 15 percent of that figure, their earnings per share are insignificant, and in fact those earnings primarily reflect the interest paid on cash still around from the companies' stock offerings.

The problems facing this industry segment are several. For one, there is the question of patentability, a key foundation stone of many genetic engineering companies. The Supreme Court ordained that Dr. Chakrabarty could patent an altered life form. The patent office granted Drs. Boyer and Cohen a patent on the basic gene-splicing process. Yet the two researchers were denied a later patent for a modified process. So to the traditional patent problems of too much disclosure and too much expensive litigation the biotechnology industry must add, it seems, the predicament of having some of its most basic claims to proprietary rights unsustained.

Of course, the biotech companies can, and probably will, take the microelectronics route to circumventing this particular problem—developing restricted know-how, trade secrets, and a technological edge. But that will make it more difficult for investors to pick the biotechnology winners.

A second crucial problem facing the genetic-engineering industry lies with fermentation technology, another of the major underpinnings of this field. An old technology present in civilization since man first discovered that more can be made out of grapes than raisins, fermentation is at one and the same time undependable and mature in its development.

In the late 1950s, Bzura Chemical set out to conquer Pfizer's dominance of the citric acid market by means of a fermentation venture. Bzura's process produced extremely inexpensive citric acid in the laboratory. Bzura's process produced extremely inexpensive citric acid in the pilot plant. Bzura's process produced extremely quick bankruptcy in the full-sized plant. The process simply didn't work on a mass-production scale, because the bacteria involved were not stable.

Bacteria mutate quickly. John W. Sibert, a technologist with Atlantic Richfield Company, recently remarked, in describing microbial-enhanced oil recovery, "You may put a genetically engineered bug down an oil well one week, and three weeks later you may have a completely different organism." Traditional oil-recovery-enhancement techniques try scrupulously to keep bacteria out of underground reservoirs for fear that they will plug up the porous rock and impede the oil flow.

Yet another obstacle genetic engineering companies face is production costs. Getting souped-up bacteria to deliver might cursorily seem akin to pharmaceutics, wherein materials typically account for 5 to 10 percent of product cost, and where small-batch runs are highly profitable. In actuality, genetic engineering is more related to the specialty-chemicals industry, where material costs are high and large-scale production is necessary to yield profits. But specialty chemicals can be sold as bulk commodities, making the concomitant large-scale production worthwhile, whereas even all the Iowa pork producers put together probably wouldn't need pig scour vaccines in quantities considered bulk.

Genetic engineering's high production costs can be traced to several factors. One expensive circumstance is that the chemicals used in the processes have such short life spans that the research teams must work around the clock in order to use them before they degrade. Then, too, since the teams are composed mainly of holders of doctorates and master's degrees, salary costs are staggering. Where do you think the microcomputer industry would be today if it were necessary to staff the production lines for computer chips with electrical engineers instead of minimum-wage Far Eastern labor?

On top of these hurdles, there's a severe labor shortage. There simply aren't many molecular biologists looking for a job.

The solution is obviously to automate at least some of the steps in genetic engineering. This is where the pick-and-shovel companies come in. Back in the gold-rush days, a few prospectors made their fortunes, most lost their shirts, and the guys who really cleaned up were the ones who sold the picks and shovels and bread to the rest of them.

The biotechnological picks and shovels are the newly developed "gene machines." Automating the DNA implantation sequences to even a minor degree will produce quantum production jumps, and the primitive first-generation gene machines now making their way to market are expected to reduce production costs to a fraction of what they are today. Just as important, the gene machines will free desperately needed manpower for further research.

No wonder, then, that the number of start-up operations in the gene-machine line is almost equal to the aggregate of genetic-engineering companies themselves. As many as fifty of these companies may have joined such firms as Bio Logicals, Genetic Systems, and Vega Biochemicals in the manufacture of gene machines by the time you read this book. And the producers of these wonder machines are probably the best investment bets in biotechnology for the short run. They seem likely to make money much sooner than the industry they supply, if perhaps not so much money in the long run.

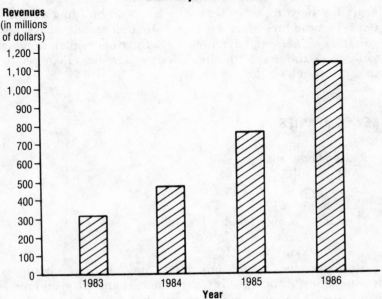

**Projected Market Growth of
Genetic-Engineering Companies
Currently Public**

Expected compound annual growth rate: 50 percent

Note: To date there have been no reliable figures available for the genetic-engineering market. Previously published estimates of market growth have assumed the entire market available to older competing products to be open to genetically engineered products as well—a questionable assumption at best.

INDUSTRY INVESTMENT DIRECTIONS

Regulatory approval for any given new product in the field of genetic engineering takes about five years: Three years of safety testing and two years of efficacy testing are required to determine if the product actually does any good. So don't become overly excited about a new development in genetic engineering until you know how far down the pipeline it is.

Usually it doesn't pay to invest in a company because of a specific product unless it is three to four years into the testing cycle.

"Look but don't touch" is probably the best investment approach to genetic-engineering companies for the next couple of years. Suppliers to the field, on the other hand, tend to be reasonably priced and profitably situated in a growing market. If genetic engineering is your field of interest, these support firms are the companies with which to start building a portfolio. When the furor dies down and you don't read much about genetic engineering anymore, that's the time to pick up what looks to be the best of the lot. There will be fewer companies to sort through by then.

KEY COMPANIES

Amicon Corporation
25 Hartwell Avenue
Lexington, MA 02173
Telephone: (617) 861-9600
Contact: Norman Jacobs, President
          Market: OTC
          Symbol: AMIC
Strong in membrane separation and polymer chemistry technologies, Amicon sells to laboratories, industry, and medical users. It has an irregular record, but exciting technology. At this writing, W. R. Grace has agreed to acquire Amicon.

Bio Logicals, Inc.
20 Victoria Street
Toronto, Ontario M5C 2N8
Canada
Telephone: (416) 364-2371
Contact: R. Bender, Chief Executive Officer
          Market: OTC
          Symbol: BIOLF
A company in the developmental stage, Bio Logicals makes high-speed DNA synthesis instrumentation and related products.

Bio-Response
550 Ridgefield Road
Wilton, CT 06897
Telephone: (203) 762-0331
Contact: S. D. Liebler, Chief Executive Officer
     Market: OTC
     Symbol: BIOR
The Heart Research Institute, San Francisco, is the site of
this company's research on selected antibodies. Bio-Response
is working on lymph-based fluid tissue culture media, with
deficit operations.

Centocor, Inc.
244 Great Valley Parkway, Great Valley Corporate Center
Malvern, PA 19355
Telephone: (215) 296-4488
Contact: Hubert Schoemaker, Executive Vice-President
     Market: OTC
     Symbol: CNTO
A development-stage company only beginning to sell its
products, Centocor concentrates on monoclonal antibodies
and immune factors. The company's first market lines are detection test kits for hepatitis and gastrointestinal cancer.

Cetus Corporation
600 Bancroft Way
Berkeley, CA 94710
Telephone: (415) 549-3300
Contact: Ronald Edinger, Chief Executive Officer
     Market: OTC
     Symbol: CTUS
Cetus employs a multidisciplinary approach to new-mi-
croorganism development for commercial products and pro-
cesses. It has deficit operations.

Charles River Breeding Laboratories, Inc.
251 Ballardvale Street
Wilmington, MA 01887
Telephone: (617) 658-6000
Contact: W. H. Keough, Treasurer
     Market: OTC
     Symbol: CRIV

The Charles River research unit is the largest supplier of laboratory test animals, aseptically delivered by Caesarian section, in the world. The company has a very consistent record. One-third of its profits are from overseas.

Collaborative Research
128 Spring Street
Lexington, MA 02173
Telephone: (617) 861-9700
Contact: Orrie Friedman, Chief Executive Officer
     Market: OTC
     Symbol: CRIC

Collaborative Research, which has ties with the Green Cross Corporation of Japan, is working on interferon production as well as on other recombinant DNA growth factors for all tissues. Operations are deficit.

Collagen Corporation
2455 Faber Place
Palo Alto, CA 94303
Telephone: (415) 856-0200
Contact: Howard Palefsky, Chief Executive Officer
     Market: OTC
     Symbol: CGEN

Zyderm collagen implant (ZCI), used in tissue-contour improvement, is the major product of this company. The intradermal implant has "device" approval from the Food and Drug Administration (FDA), a classification more advantageous than that of "drug."

Dynatech Corporation
3 New England Executive Park
Burlington, MA 01803
Telephone: (617) 272-3304
Contact: Elizabeth Harbison
     Market: OTC
     Symbol: DYTC

Dynatech's products and services are about 40 percent medical-and-biochemical-related, and the company has a good record. It is a profitable but peripheral player in the field.

Enzo Biochem, Inc.

325 Hudson Street
New York, NY 10013
Telephone: (212) 741-3838
Contact: S. K. Rabbain
Market: OTC
Symbol: ENZO

Like most companies in the field, Enzo has no profits and
few revenues supporting its DNA and other research. Johnson
& Johnson bought roughly 15 percent of the company in June
1982.

Flow General, Inc.

7655 Old Springhouse Road
McLean, VA 22102
Telephone: (703) 893-5915
Contact: M. A. Wall
Market: NYSE
Symbol: FGN

Flow General used to be General Research Corporation,
and it used to be a Street darling, but not since 1981. Biomedical products contributed two-thirds of its profits in fiscal year
1981, and the play was superbead microcarriers for interferon
production.

Genentech, Inc.

460 Point San Bruno Boulevard
South San Francisco, CA 94080
Telephone: (415) 952-1000
Contact: R. A. Swanson, Chief Executive Officer
Market: OTC
Symbol: GENE

Started in 1976, Genentech is by now an old-timer in the
gene-splicing business. Operating at a deficit, it is currently
channeling efforts into the production of human insulin and
human growth hormones. Contract research is still the company's mainstay.

Genetic Engineering, Inc.

136th Avenue and North Washington Street
Denver, CO 80233

Telephone: (303) 457-1311
Contact: E. L. Adair, President
Market: OTC
Symbol: GEEN

This company, with deficit operations, is in the developmental stages of producing animal embryo modification and sperm separation for artificial insemination.

Genetic Systems Corporation

3005 First Avenue
Seattle, WA 98121
Telephone: (206) 624-4300
Contact: Robert Nowinski
Market: OTC
Symbol: GENS

Monoclonal antibodies, produced by means of hybridoma-immunological techniques and used in the diagnosis and treatment of disease, are the subject of this company's research. Linked with Cutter Laboratories, it has deficit operations.

Hybritech, Inc.

11085 Torreyana Road
San Diego, CA 92121
Telephone: (714) 455-6700
Contact: Ted Greene, Chief Executive Officer
Market: OTC
Symbol: HYBR

Started in 1978, Hybritech is another monoclonal-antibody developer for hospitals and clinical laboratories, operating at a deficit. Its main products are tandem assay kits, cell-differentiation assays, and histochemical tests for cancer diagnosis.

Interferon Sciences, Inc.

748 Jersey Avenue
New Brunswick, NJ 08901
Telephone: (201) 249-3232
Contact: S. H. Ronel, President
Market: OTC
Symbol: IFSC

Working on research for the production of human interferon, this company is 75 percent owned by National Development Corporation.

InterPharm Laboratories, Ltd.
Science-Based Industrial Park
Kiryat Weizmann
Nes Ziona
Israel
Telephone: (054) 75785
Contact: I. Mokov, President
          Market: OTC
          Symbol: IPLLF
Ares Applied Research Systems of Geneva, Switzerland, has majority control of InterPharm, which is working on human growth hormones.

Monoclonal Antibodies, Inc.
2319 Charleston Road
Mountain View, CA 94043
Telephone: (415) 960-1320
Contact: Gregory Sessler
          Market: OTC
          Symbol: MABS
MABS develops products incorporating monoclonal antibodies derived from hybridoma cell lines. Most of its efforts to date have been in diagnostic test kits, and it has FDA clearance for a pregnancy detection kit.

New Brunswick Scientific Company
P.O. Box 986, 44 Talmadge Road
Edison, NJ 08817
Telephone: (201) 287-1200
Contact: D. Freedman, President
          Market: OTC
          Symbol: NBSC
Biological shakers and fermentation equipment provide another peripheral investment possibility in a profitable company.

Novo Industri

Novo Alle, DK-2880
Bagsvaerd
Denmark
Contact: T. Ryan, Robert Morton and Associates,
 485 Madison Avenue, New York, NY 10022,
 telephone (212) 371-2200.
 Market; NYSE
 Symbol: NVO

A major world producer of enzymes for industrial use, Novo
is also the leader in insulin products. It had a big stock-market
following in the United States in 1982.

TechAmerica Group, Inc.

Elka Estates Industrial Park
Elwood, KA 66024
Telephone: (913) 365-9076
Contact: D. Burket, telephone (816) 474-9407
 Market: ASE
 Symbol: TCH

A veterinary player in the genetics field, TechAmerica
slipped into the red in the second quarter of 1982—and has
been sued by investors over its 1981 offering.

LEADING ANALYSTS

Kathy Behrens
Sutro and Company, Inc.
201 California Street
San Francisco, CA 94111
Telephone: (415) 445-8500

Richard Emmitt and Scott King
F. Eberstadt and Company
61 Broadway
New York, NY 10006
Telephone: (212) 480-0887 and (212) 480-0835

Gene Gargiulo
Goldman, Sachs and Company
55 Broad Street

New York, NY 10004
Telephone: (212) 676-7190

Sarah Kendall
Oppenheimer and Company, Inc.
One New York Plaza
New York, NY 10004
Telephone: (212) 825-3723

David MacCallum and Nina Siegler
Paine Webber Mitchell Hutchins, Inc.
140 Broadway
New York, NY 10005
Telephone: (212) 437-7332 and (212) 437-2620

Annette Campbell White
Hambrecht and Quist, Inc.
235 Montgomery Street
San Francisco, CA 94104
Telephone: (415) 986-5500

PERTINENT PUBLICATIONS

Agricultural Genetics Report
Mary Ann Liebert, Inc.
500 East 85th Street
New York, NY 10028
Telephone: (212) 289-2300
   Subscription: $115 per year for bimonthly newsletter
Animal health and breeding is covered with the focus on
R&D in industry and universities.

BioEngineering News
Deborah and Thomas Musiewicz
109 Minna Street, Suite 304
San Francisco, CA 94105
Telephone: (415) 777-4572
   Subscription: $295 per year for weekly newsletter
The title says it; the focus is on news items such as patents,
stock prices, conference digests, financings—information of
interest mainly to entrepreneurs and investors.

Biotechnology Newswatch
McGraw-Hill, Inc.
1221 Avenue of the Americas
New York, NY 10020
Telephone: (212) 997-4462
   Subscription: $417 per year for semimonthly newsletter
Newswatch ranges from cell genetics to legal, governmental and commercial aspects of using one cell organisms in fuels, chemicals, medical and agricultural products.

Chemical and Engineering News
American Chemical Society (ACS)
1155 Sixteenth Street, NW
Washington, DC 20036
Telephone: (202) 872-4600, (614) 421-3776 for
   subscriptions
   Subscription: $30 per year to non-ACS members for
                 weekly periodical
This publication covers technical and business developments in the chemical process industries.

Chemicalweek
McGraw-Hill, Inc.
P.O. Box 430
Hightstown, NJ 08520
Telephone: (609) 426-7294
   Subscription: $30 per year for weekly periodical,
                 controlled circulation for industry
                 management
Chemicalweek covers the chemical process industries with management-oriented news and analyses of business and technical developments.

Genetic Engineering News
Mary Ann Liebert, Inc.
(For address and telephone, see *Agricultural Genetics
   Report*, above)
   Subscription: $75 per year for bimonthly newspaper
Written for an industry which feels a need to have Wall Street developments monitored in one of the departments of the magazine, *Genetic Engineering News* covers the usual

range of patent news, personnel changes, R&D developments, etc.

MAJOR MEETINGS

American Association for Clinical Chemistry Annual
    Convention
1725 R Street, NW, Suite 903
Washington, DC 20006
Telephone: (202) 857-0717
Usually held in late July or early August in a major city, this convention features medical analytical instruments and reagents and includes bioengineering developments.

In addition to this professional convention, a number of brokers sponsor meetings on medical and genetic advances for their clients. Check with yours. Three such sessions are offered by the following firms.

Alex Brown and Sons
135 East Baltimore Street
Baltimore, MD 21202
Telephone: (301) 727-1700
Alex Brown's seminar on developments in medicine and genetics is held each May in Baltimore.

F. Eberstadt and Company, Inc.
(For address and telephone, see Richard Emmitt and Scott
    King, under *Leading Analysts,* above)
The Eberstadt medical seminar is usually held in the spring of every year in New York.

Hambrecht and Quist Medical/Genetic Seminar
(For address and telephone, see Annette Campbell White,
    under *Leading Analysts,* above)
Hambrecht and Quist's seminar is offered in San Francisco every January.

VII

Robotics: Will the Real Workers Please Stand Up

Robots are movie stars, robots are pitchmen on television, robots are comic-book heroes. Yet in reality, there's not even a consensus as to what qualities something needs to have in order to qualify as a card-carrying robot. The Robot Institute of America (RIA) defines the beast as "a programmable, multifunctional manipulator designed to move materiel, parts, tools, or specialized devices through variable motions for the performance of a variety of tasks"—which pretty well knocks the wind out of anyone's imagination. The Japanese Industrial Robot Association (JIRA) doesn't do much better with its definition. It even includes manual manipulators which perform only fixed sequences. By the Japanese definition, robots need not even be programmable.

This more inclusive vision of the robotic world in part explains why Japan has over three times as many installed robots as the United States has. Most of the Japanese automatons simply don't qualify as robots under the more stringent American definition. The other reason for the disparity in robot population is that the Japanese embrace robotics technology much more readily than Americans do. Considering that robots originated in the United States, this psychological difference seems rather odd.

The term "robot" is Czechoslovakian, originating in a 1922 play, *R.U.R.*, by Karel Capek. R.U.R. stands for "Rossum's Universal Robots." Etymology aside, at the time the word reached these shores, there was nothing more substantial than imagination behind Capek's coinage.

The first actual robot is much harder to trace than the name. However, a fair case can be made for placing the birthdate of at least the primordial version sometime in 1952. That was the year MIT's Servomechanisms Laboratory introduced the numeric-control milling machine. Although the reaction of representatives of the aircraft industry, for which the machine had been developed, was less than enthusiastic—according to James McDonough, one of the machine's originators, "They came and saw it, and they went away"—numeric-control machine tools were to sweep through industry beginning in the mid-fifties.

Using digital technology as their cousin the computer, which began its ascendancy at the same time, was doing, numeric-control tools employed a punch tape instead of IBM-style punch cards for the entering of information. "We considered punched cards, but some were expensive," McDonough explained, "and it would have meant a fairly large number of cards. And we worried about sequencing problems —what happens when you drop a deck of cards on the floor?"

That was one of the few times the numeric-control industry and computers took somewhat separate roads. Today, computer technology and numeric control, as well as other means of industrial production control such as lasers, are completely intertwined.

As the revolution launched by numeric control continues, its original front will be replaced more and more by "intelligent" microchips more versatile than the programmed numeric-control tools could ever be. And as this occurs, industry will come closer and closer to producing the public's image of a real robot.

What sets even the elementary robot of today—which is usually no more than a manipulative arm or two—apart from the automatic machine is the fact that its electronic control system can be reprogrammed, and the nature and sequence of the robot's motions redefined, for each new task. For another thing, today's robot is general-purpose in nature. Robots are designed to manipulate tools, which do the actual work, rather than being themselves the implementing tools.

Robots have a number of practical aspects that make them attractive compared to human labor. The initial cost of hiring them may be extremely high, but their hourly rate is lower; unemployment and social security taxes are eliminated; overtime is no problem; paid vacations are nonexistent; and robots do not tire, complain, or suffer from the Monday-morning blues. They can work under inhuman shop conditions, and they can do the job in exactly the same way each and every time around.

Does this mean the elimination of manual labor in the foreseeable future? Far from it. The workerless factory is not going to arrive in the eighties. Those factories that are automated are small ones.

Mr. Iguchi of Tokyo is a golf enthusiast. He also owns a small plastic-injection-molding plant specializing in toy parts. He leases four robots from Japan Robot Leasing Company (yes, that's for real, and the cost is only $167 per worker per month). He has no other employees.

Every morning, Mr. Iguchi checks in at his plant, empties the bins of finished parts, and loads them into his car. Then he fills the materials tanks by the robots, locks up the plant, and sets off to deliver the parts to his customers. Whatever time he has left over he devotes to playing golf. It may be noted that since the arrival of the robots his handicap on the green has been declining steadily.

Mr. Iguchi's plant represents a very special situation, using not particularly sophisticated robots to churn out simple parts by means of a simple process. Still, it's an example of the progress made in factory automation.

In spite of such examples, and in spite of the impressive potential for the use of robots in manufacturing, the technology of robotics and, more important, its applications have developed very slowly. One retarding factor has been the high cost of the prerequisite computer memory. Even for simple robotic tasks, a large memory is needed. However, memory prices are plunging, while at the same time memory capacity is expanding exponentially.

A second and more substantial brake on any real robot explosion has been the industry's inexperience in defining the basic problems and parameters involved in robotics applications. Consider, for instance, a task as simple as picking a bolt out of a bin, inserting it into a hole, and tightening it up. The number of possible variables that must be considered in preparing a robot to perform this task successfully is amazingly large—no bolts in the bin, the position of the bolt in the bin, a damaged thread, a damaged head, and so on. Robotics, while familiar in tales twice told, is so revolutionary in actual application and development that much of the research is perforce still at the trial-and-error stage that other technologies were going through in the 1700s and the 1800s.

The third factor impeding the growth of robots is that, outside of spray-painting and welding applications, there are as yet no economies of scale in their production. Most robots are close to being one-of-a-kind devices. In the second half of the eighties, however, volume can be expected to pick up dramatically.

If the acceptance of robots in the workplace has come slowly, the actual development and implementation of robotic technology has barely kept abreast. Robotics, except perhaps for specialized devices, is not a tinker's bailiwick. Massive amounts of capital are required to support the necessarily long-term engineering endeavors—which is why there will probably be a major shakeout of robot manufacturers over the next couple of years. At the moment, although it may not seem that way once you peruse the list of manufacturers at the end of the chapter, there are far too many firms, with products far beyond their needed sophistication, chasing a market far too small.

This is beginning to dawn on some of the companies in the industry. For instance, Kulicke and Soffa recently announced that it is shelving earlier plans to manufacture industrial robots. After evaluating the current situation in robotics, the company decided there would be no significant return on investment in the field for some time to come.

Companies currently involved in robot manufacture are taking one of two approaches. Some, like Prab Robots, have primarily continued with lines in which they already had an existing advantage—thus improving the odds for success. The Prab robot was designed as an offshoot of the company's original conveyor-belt business. Materials handling, the old Prab Conveyors specialty, became the robot's specialty as well. However, on acquiring AMF's Versatran line of robots, which had previously met with a turkey's reception in the marketplace, Prab also began pursuing a second strategy, namely, one of making a broad line of products in order to become big and profitable fast.

Most robot companies today are pursuing this latter strategy. When it works, it leads to a vastly bigger company than the specialty strategy does, of course. But the company's chances of falling by the wayside are also greatly increased.

The more diverse a robot's applications, the more likely it is to fail, at least initially, because of events beyond the manufacturer's knowledge or control. Yet the robot's single most important feature is reliability. The mean-time-between-failures rate for a robot needs to be in the hundreds of operating hours—better yet, thousands. In a familiar specialty situation, the application design and the anticipation of problems can be complete enough to approach these standards consistently. But the more sophisticated and generalized the application becomes, the lower the mean-time-between-failures reliability falls. Current technology is simply not capable of producing a sophisticated general-purpose robot.

The widely broadcast 1982 Japanese media story "Robot Murders Worker" illustrates the problem in its extreme. What actually happened was that the unfortunate worker entered an unauthorized area at the wrong time and was simply run over by the robot, which could not sense the worker's presence. The state of the art is such that no manufacturer can devise a robot that is able to deal with all the myriad unforeseeable events. But if a company has been manufacturing spray-painting robots and suddenly branches out into parts-sorting robots, unexpected production problems of a very basic nature are bound to arise. The impossibility of anticipating every exigency is what makes the grow-big-and-profitable-fast strategy so risky.

To a large extent, our human ability to anticipate is based on what our senses perceive. Sensing is crucial to the development of intelligent robots as well, for without it they cannot interact with the environment. Yet the sensory mechanisms of robots are, except in such highly specialized cases as laser-guided welding, extremely crude.

Human vision, which is a passive, noncontact, receptive medium, has extraordinary sensitivity. It can detect location, motion, shape, size, color, and texture without making any physical contact with the objects whatsoever. To duplicate this sensitivity electronically in even rudimentary form would take an immense amount of memory and programming, far beyond what is affordable. Software, the usual rescuer in computer-related difficulties, cannot possibly cover all the possibilities in the real three-dimensional, full-color world with adequate decision rules for the poor dumb robot.

On a lower level of perception, there's the problem of perspective. Almost all manufactured products, from precision turbine blades to Rubik's cubes, are derived from a few simple geometric shapes—blocks and cones, cylinders and spheres and doughnut-shaped toroids. Human engineers working with blueprints see solidity in the two-dimensional drawings of these parts. They know which lines will disappear from view as a drawn object changes its orientation. Traditional computers can't deal with this problem, which in turn means that the robots those computers drive can't either.

As complex as the "hidden line" problem is, however, work is progressing toward its solution. The University of Rochester has developed a computer language called PADL-1, acronymic for "Parts and Assembly Design Language," which at least handles right-angle blocks and cylinders for the computer, although hundreds of thousands of instructions must implement the process. Try to visualize how many instructions it would take to delineate a plate of spaghetti (without the sauce).

A Fifth Avenue sculpture company called Solid Photography, Inc., recently switched its name to Robotic Vision and is now tackling the same problem, using a visual three-dimensional interpretation technique. Other firms working in the crucial area of image sensing are Object Recognition Systems and Automatix—every cognoscente on the Street was eagerly waiting for this last one to go public. Machine Intelligence originally had its sights set on producing a series of machine-vision products for robots, but scaled that effort back in favor of becoming more of an importer of Japanese robots.

This latter approach probably sums up robotics for the next couple of years—lots of grand plans, some leaps forward, and numerous strategy changes, with many cash-starved companies standing in the wings waiting to go public in order to finance the research and development that may eventually make it all possible. Advanced Robotics, Octek, Perceptronics, R-2000, Thermwood, and U.S. Robots are all companies that may cross your financial horizons on their way to public ownership. Then again, considering the unlikely short-term possibilities of large-scale robot sales, some of them may vanish before they get that far.

In projecting the long-term future of robotics, however, a close parallel between the future evolution of manufacturing and what has occurred in the agricultural sector of the economy should be noted. Today all of 3.8 percent of the United States work force is engaged in producing the nation's food—and generating a vast surplus in the process. Less than a hundred years ago, agriculture was the nation's dominant form of employment. The change was brought about by the substitution of capital, in the form of sophisticated equipment, for labor. Arguably, that may not have been in the best long-term interests of agriculture. Nevertheless, it's the direction in which the marketplace led the food-production industry.

The percentage of the work force employed in manufacturing has been decreasing dramatically in turn. Currently 28.6 percent of this country's workers are engaged in manufacturing. But the percentage has been declining for twenty-five years, and the decline is accelerating. Some extreme predictions foresee only 1 percent to 3 percent of the overall work force employed in manufacturing in the next century. While this figure is probably well on the low side, there can be no doubt that electronics, lasers, software, telecommunications, and systems design are all falling into a symbiotic relationship which, through the integration of computer-aided design (CAD), computer-aided engineering (CAE), and robotics, will lead to computer-aided manufacturing (CAM), a market projected to be worth $25 billion by 1990.

Robots will not be serving coffee in bed soon. But they will be making the coffeepots—and, for some astute and lucky investors, money.

INDUSTRY INVESTMENT DIRECTIONS

Most of the buyers in the robotics market are also buyers of heavy machinery and/or machine tools. When they don't have the money for one, they probably don't have the money for the other either. So keep an eye on the business indicators in the machinery industry as well as staying informed about the robotics market. Watch the producers' durable orders

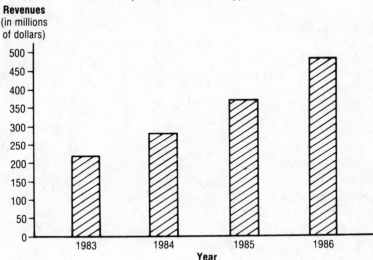

Projected Market Growth of Robotics

(U.S. Producers Only)

Expected compound annual growth rate: 30 percent (after the 1982–83 recession)

and machine-tool orders. When they rise, robot sales will, too.

There's a hint of adolescent lust about the way some investors view robotics. But robotics can't be rushed. The waiting game is probably the best strategy to follow for a couple of years, say until 1984 or 1985, unless an unexpected major breakthrough occurs in software control and/or sensing devices. Although such premature advances are not likely, anything is possible in this sci-fi industry.

Meanwhile, the activities to start watching most closely are those of the related industries, which are more likely than robotics itself to do well at first. Sensors and artificial intelligence will probably be the next facets of robotics technology to show promise, then peripheral equipment and components. These more specialized manufacturing areas will afford small companies more profitable means of entry to the market than will the "body-building" systems, the complete prepackaged robots that dominate the popular perception of robotics today.

KEY COMPANIES

Analogic, Inc.
Audubon Road
Wakefield, MA 01880
Telephone: (617) 246-0300
Contact: Frederick Young
        Market: OTC
        Symbol: ALOG

Analogic is the possible beneficiary of a robotic-vision system that might be developed through its board-level array processors. That's not a reason to buy the company, but it could be a boost later on.

Automatix, Incorporated
1000 Tech Park Drive
Billerica, MA 01821
Telephone: (617) 667-7900
Contact: John Diaz, Treasurer
        Market: OTC
        Symbol: AUTX

Automatix manufactures industrial robotic systems and artificial vision subsystems. It is still losing money, though growing rapidly in revenues.

Boston Digital
86 South Street
Hopkinton, MA 01748
Telephone: (617) 435-6871
Contact: Ara Aykanian, President
        Market: OTC
        Symbol: BOST

A manufacturer of ultra-precision, multiple-axis computer-controlled machine tools, Boston Digital is likely to be a supplier-beneficiary of robotics growth. It's a small, well-run company.

Brock Hotel Corporation
2209 West 29th Street
Topeka, KA 66611
Telephone: (913) 266-7021
Contact: R. L. Brock, Chairman
      Market: NYSE
      Symbol: BHC

Showbiz Pizza Palace Restaurants may seem a long way
from factory-floor robots, but robot entertainers are packing in
the crowds and making lots of money, at least for the moment.
Robots and pizza contribute only a third of its income, but
they are Brock Hotels' fastest-growing segment. A big rival of
Pizza Time Theater, it settled that competitor's infringement
suit out of court.

Computer Products
1400 Northwest 70th Street
Fort Lauderdale, FL 33309
Telephone: (305) 974-5500
Contact: David Yoder, President
      Market: OTC
      Symbol: CPRD

As an original equipment manufacturer (OEM), Computer
Products is a leader in power conversion and conditioning
devices for process-control manufacturing, which is prerequisite to the development of the automated factory of the future.

Electronic Modules
P.O. Box 141
Timonium, MD 21093
Telephone: (301) 666-3300
Contact: Robert Vogel, President
      Market: OTC
      Symbol: EMOD

Here's a leader in process-control devices with a technological jump on the competition. Data gathering and control are
key building blocks in factory automation.

Hurco Manufacturing Company, Inc.
P.O. Box 68180, 6602 Guion Road
Indianapolis, IN 46268

Telephone: (317) 293-5309
Contact: Alan McLean, Vice-President of Finance
    Market: OTC
    Symbol: HURC

This company supplies high-precision machine-tool centers.

Mobot Corporation
980 Buenos Avenue
San Diego, CA 92110
Telephone: (714) 275-4300
Contact: Carol Dunn
    Market: OTC
    Symbol: MBOT

Mobot's robots are modular, designed for specific tasks. They provide 100 percent of the company's revenues. But the firm is very small, with approximately 1 percent of the market. It has little capital and little profitability.

Moog, Inc.
Proner Airport
East Aurora, NY 14052
Telephone: (716) 652-2000
Contact: Geraldine Bayler
    Market: ASE
    Symbol: MOGB

Moog is a well-run company manufacturing high-precision servo valves for hydraulic robots. Most of its sales are to aerospace. The problem is, hydraulic robots are expected to be a declining percentage of the robotic population.

Object Recognition Systems
521 Fifth Avenue
New York, NY 10017
Telephone: (212) 682-3535
Contact: John Artley
    Market: OTC
    Symbol: ORSI

This small company, which is in the developmental stage, makes pattern-recognition vision systems. It's not yet clear whether the firm is better at quality control, production packaging, or robotics applications. Profitability is also a problem.

Pizza Time Theater
1213 Innsbruck Drive
Sunnyvale, CA 94086
Telephone: (408) 744-7300
Contact: William Koenig, Vice-President and Treasurer
Market: OTC
Symbol: CHKY

Chuck E. Cheese's Pizza Time Theaters use proprietary Cyberamics robot characters in their family entertainment centers, which peddle pizza and coin-operated video-game amusements. The company is growing fast, but watch out if new store openings slow down.

Prab Robots
5944 East Kilgore Road
Kalamazoo, MI 49003
Telephone: (616) 349-8761
Contact: Bill Fulkerson, Assistant Comptroller
Market: OTC
Symbol: PRAB

Basically, Prab Robots is, or rather was, a small manufacturer of specialized conveyor belts that saw a market niche where robots could augment or supplement the belts. Now the robots are supplying 50 percent of the revenues. Prab's robotic devices are hydraulic and stand alone. The company has about a 6 percent share of the overall robot market and ranks fifth in the country (after Unimation; Cincinnati Milacron, whose robots account for only 6 percent of its revenues; ASEA, an American division of the Swedish company; and DeVilbiss, a division of Champion Spark Plug). It's still a relatively small and low-technology company.

Robotic Vision Systems
536 Broad Hollow Road
Melville, NY 11747
Telephone: (516) 694-8910
Contact: Paul DiMatteo
Market: OTC
Symbol: ROBV

Robotic Vision is a very speculative company, with an interesting technology whose profitability for robotics applications is dubious because it's too expensive. Formerly Solid Photography, the company moved into robotics to design three-dimensional vision systems for robots. Government development contracts and past military connections on the part of management may offer an entree into the crucial and growing field of military sensing and reconnaissance applications.

Unimation, Inc.
Shelter Rock Lane
Danbury, CT 06810
Telephone: (203) 637-6337 or (203) 744-1800
Contact: Edward Kelly
     Market: OTC
     Symbol: RBOT

Unimation is 100 percent robots—hydraulic, electric, and portable. Apprentice, Puma, and Unimate are all Unimation brands. With heavy sales to the automobile industry and heavy debts on the balance sheet, the company has agreed to be acquired by Westinghouse. It's the largest producer of robots in the country, with a 42 percent share of the market.

LEADING ANALYSTS

Laura Conigliaro
Prudential/Bache
100 Gold Street
New York, NY 10038
Telephone: (212) 791-4872

There's a robotics-news mailing list available—if you generate a lot of commissions for your broker.

Nathanael Greene, Jr.
Hambrecht and Quist
235 Montgomery Street
San Francisco, CA 94104
Telephone: (415) 986-5500

Eli Lustgarten
Paine Webber Mitchell Hutchins, Inc.
140 Broadway

New York, NY 10005
Telephone: (212) 437-2765
Eli Lustgarten comes to this field with the background of a machinery analyst.

Timothy Reiland
Robert Baird and Company
777 East Wisconsin Avenue
Milwaukee, WI 53202
Telephone: (414) 765-3990
The Baird Machinery Service mailing list originates here—again for due consideration.

Richard Schwarz
L. F. Rothschild, Unterberg, Towbin
55 Water Street
New York, NY 10041
Telephone: (212) 425-3030

PERTINENT PUBLICATIONS

American Machinist
McGraw-Hill Publications
1221 Avenue of the Americas
New York, NY 10020
Telephone: (212) 997-2061
    Subscription: $35 per year for monthly periodical
Edited for managers and engineers in the metalworking industries, *American Machinist* covers trends, technology, and economic outlook, as well as relevant government, labor, and international market developments. Special issues are devoted to the International Machine Tool Show and such topics of interest as management, quality assurance, controls, and materials.

Machine Design
Penton/IPC
Penton Plaza
1111 Chester Avenue
Cleveland, OH 44114
Telephone: (212) 696-7000
    Subscription: $42 per year for twenty-eight issues

Basically a semimonthly periodical, *Machine Design* publishes four extras each year: a CAD/CAM review (mid-April), an electrical/electronics issue (mid-May), a special on ELECTRO (the general IEEE meeting) a week or two later, and an issue on the WESCON convention, a general industry show (late August).

Manufacturing Engineering
Society of Manufacturing Engineers (SME)
P.O. Box 930, 1 SME Drive
Dearborn, MI 48128
Telephone: (313) 271-1500
  Subscription: $4 per year (included as part of the Society
               of Manufacturing Engineers membership
               dues) for monthly periodical
Manufacturing Engineering is edited for engineers and managers concerned with procurement and management of manufacturing equipment and systems. Typical special issues have covered robotics, composites, and shows (the Society of Manufacturing Engineers meeting in April and the International Machine Tool Show in August).

Production Engineering
(For address and telephone, see *Machine Design*, above)
  Subscription: $30 per year for monthly periodical
Special feature issues cover computers in June, testing and inspection in July, materials in August, input/output controls in November, and material handling in December. This publication also covers roughly four major trade shows, on design engineering, manufacturing, machine tools, and fluid power. Regular issues feature articles on manufacturing, technology, trends, legislation, and current developments.

Robotics Today
(For address and telephone, see *Manufacturing
  Engineering*, above.)
  Subscription: $24 per year for bimonthly periodical
Robotics Today covers industrial robot technology, emphasizing manufacturing operations. The magazine offers industry news, a calendar of events, product reviews, and case histories of new applications.

MAJOR MEETINGS

AUTOFACT
(For address and telephone, see *Manufacturing
Engineering,* under *Pertinent Publications,* above)
Held late in November or early in December each year in a
major city, AUTOFACT (abbreviation for "automated factory") is a trade show with both a factory automation orientation and CAD/CAM coverage (see chapter 12 on Computer
Graphics).

Bache Robotics
Bache Halsey Stuart Shields, Inc.
(For address and telephone, see Laura Conigliaro, under
Leading Analysts, above)
This meeting is for the big spenders. Every year, usually in
October, industry and institutional investors participate in a
"Where are we, and where are we going, and when?" symposium.

ROBOTS
Society of Manufacturing Engineers
(For address and telephone, see *Manufacturing
Engineering,* under *Pertinent Publications,* above)
Held in March each year, usually but not always in Detroit's
Cobo Hall, ROBOTS is the trade show with all the information and customers (human ones) you could hope to find.

PROFESSIONAL ASSOCIATIONS

Robotics International of the Society of Manufacturing
Engineers
(For address and telephone, see *Manufacturing
Engineering,* under *Pertinent Publications,* above)
Robotics International brings together all the aspects of this
multidisciplinary industry and acts as a translation and information exchange center for individuals as well as providing a
forum for ideas.

VIII

Cellular Mobile Radio: A Honeycomb of Potential Profit

There's a classic science fiction story in which the characters suddenly begin hearing decade-old radio broadcasts on their receivers. That's all they hear, because there's no room for new broadcasts, the available airwaves being altogether occupied. There is no possibility of such a time warp, of course. However, overcrowding of the airwaves and congested radio channels are very real problems today. Congestion is particularly obvious in the realm of mobile phones, where demand is so high that potential users in some areas have been waiting up to ten years for a line of their own.

That's about to change, however. The overload problems will be eliminated by simply dialing 900 megahertz—the frequency location of a juicy watermelon of a market that lots of hungry companies are already nibbling.

It all started back in 1968 when the Federal Communications Commission (FCC) called for a new technology to increase the availability of mobile telephone service. Traditional mobile systems work through high-powered central base stations. Under such an arrangement, only one call at a time can be handled on each communications channel. The same channel cannot even be used in cities nearby because of signal overlap. The channel-reuse distance, the minimum distance that must separate two base stations in order for them to operate without interference, is seventy-five miles. With only forty-four channels allocated by the FCC for this form of communication, then, a maximum of fifty channels are available to cover some five thousand square miles if the base stations are spaced the requisite distance apart.

According to the revised FCC rules, however, a total of 666 channels are provided, on the newly allocated 900 megahertz band, primarily for car and portable telephones. When the cellular solution is implemented, the number of communicators able to use the channels simultaneously will be expanded exponentially.

Under the cellular solution, there will still be a large communications central, or base station, for a given region. However, instead of spreading its powerful signals over its full range of transmission, it will be linked to numerous small cell transmitters by means of microwave transmitters or by wires. With 333 channels allocated for radio common carriers (RCC), the other 333 on the 900 megahertz band being reserved for the local telephone company, up to 83 channels can be used by the low-powered base station in each cell, and the 83 channels can be reused by any cell site one cell over. Sophisticated computer-controlled automatic switching will move the caller from one radio frequency to another as the caller drives from cell to cell, without interrupting communications.

The possibilities for growth in the mobile-telephone industry offered by such a honeycomb arrangement are immense. Some estimates project a million and a half subscribers to the system by decade's end, compared to 160,000 users of mobile telephones today.

The real question for you is which companies are going to profit from all of this. Basically, they are to be found in two categories, the hardware manufacturers and the transmission operators. Unfortunately for investors, however, the break is not so clean, there being a lot of industry overlap. For instance, in 1977 venerable old AT&T opened the first experimental cellular system through its Illinois Bell Telephone subsidiary in Chicago. AT&T considers itself a supplier of service, yet for the most part it makes its own equipment. So here the two functions are combined in one company. On the other hand, during the same year the FCC granted American Radio-Telephone Service (ARTS) a trial license to run a cellular-radio-based mobile system designed by Motorola in the greater Baltimore-Washington area. In this case there is a distinct double play: ARTS for operation, Motorola for equipment. Motorola also sells hardware to AT&T.

Cellular mobile radio is a most fitting new area of expansion for an old-line diversified high-tech company that began with a single product, to wit, the car radio. Motorola's name, in fact, derives from "motor" and "victrola." Being in the forefront of mobile communications, the company has its sights set far beyond mobile telephones as we know them today, for as large as the market might be for automobile-based phones, it's still limited. "People need to communicate with people, not vehicles," John Mitchell, Motorola's president, points out, "and that's key to the marketability of portable phones."

What Motorola has in mind is another product made possible by the introduction of the cellular-transmission concept, specifically, a true pocket phone to replace the pocket pager, the "beeper" occasionally heard to emanate from a doctor or a plumber on the golf course or at a party. While the present Motorola "pocket" phone would require a cantilevered, pigskin-lined pouch to support its bulky mass, it does fit into a briefcase with space left over. The truly portable telephone, slim and lightweight, or, better yet, Dick Tracy's wrist television with telephone, is not all that far away.

Currently, considerations of cost rather than technological feasibility are probably the largest deterrent to the development of the true pocket phone. Cellular mobile radiophones will probably cost $700 to $1,000 for the next couple of years. Portables, even those larger and heavier than pocket size, are expected to range from $150 upward initially, according to industry estimates. As with all electronics products, of course, the learning curve can be expected to cut prices and increase quality sharply once cellular systems get off the ground nationally.

Not much of this will get off the ground, however, until the FCC completes processing of the applications from the mobile radio companies for territories. AT&T alone has some $200 million invested in cellular already and plans to spend up to $1 billion on the field by 1986. But it can't do so until the 57,600 pages of license applications it has delivered to the FCC are processed. Similarly stalemated are Cox Broadcasting, Graphic Scanning, GT&E, LIN Broadcasting, MCI Communications, Metromedia, Westinghouse, and the many smaller companies springing up around the edges of the industry. Meanwhile, until the final all-clear is sounded above the regulatory turmoil, more miniature legal delays may cause flurries of frustration in the field. Several smaller vendors are objecting to the proposed allocation of one license in each market to a local telephone company as being too favorable to the AT&T network.

Such uncertainties present real problems for investors. The earnings impact of cellular radio on a company as mammoth as AT&T obviously cannot be considered significant enough to justify an investment in such a behemoth on the basis of what is, for it, a minor, albeit profitable, diversion. Motorola, which has traditionally dominated the mobile-radio and pocket-pager markets, will attempt to continue to do so. But even if it succeeds, cellular mobile radio together with its adjunct hardware could probably not add more than 5 percent to Motorola's revenues and profits for several years. The companies most likely to boom—or collapse under the high capital costs of cellular radio—include Communications Industries, Graphic Scanning, and some as yet undiscovered or unfounded companies.

Any new unknowns in the field, however, will include only hardware manufacturers, whose products will be standardized by the FCC and thus easy to replicate—by, among others, the Japanese and the tiny dragons. The operational end of cellular radio is simply too capital-intensive for small companies. The preliminary feasibility study for a license application alone can run to over $100,000 and a small urban system itself to $10 million in venture money.

A kindred question is suggested by these considerations. Does the about-to-be-born cellular-radio boom—whoever its still-to-be-determined beneficiaries are—spell doom and disaster for the plain pager? Far from it. A tremendous technology overlap exists in companies such as Communications Industries, Graphic Scanning, Mobile Communications Corporation of America, and Radiofone, firms which are involved in both directions of communications research.

There are three significant recent developments in the pager market. The first of these is the formation of comprehensive satellite-interconnected paging systems with nationwide communications capabilities. In July 1982, Mobile Communications Corporation of America announced a joint venture with National Public Radio called National Satellite Paging. Three frequencies have been allocated by the FCC for such satellite networks, and national—perhaps even international —beeping will soon be a market force.

Pagers themselves are becoming more sophisticated, which is another development significant for the investor. Digital transmission, now allowed by the new FCC rules, adds limited message-transmission capabilities. One drawback remains. Paging channels—however sophisticated the message transmittable becomes—allow for only one-way communication, from the base station to the receiver. Thus, as the FCC regulations presently stand, they cannot compete directly with cellular mobile radio.

The third development the investor should keep in mind is one that is common to all electronics technology: Price is declining, while quality and versatility are on the upswing.

You won't even be able to get away from cellular mobile radio and expanded-capability pagers in an airplane. Airfone, Inc., 50 percent owned by Western Union, has just about taken care of that eventuality. American, Delta, Eastern, Pan Am, and TWA, to name but a few of the pertinent airlines, have already made plans to install Airfone's radiotelephones aboard their planes. The cost to the customer is projected to be $7.50 per three minutes of conversation.

Initially, at least, the plan is to have only passenger-to-ground calling. The airlines don't want to be bothered with paging passengers for incoming calls. However, there are electronic solutions to this problem as well. The only real question remaining to be asked about such communication, as about cellular mobile radio in general, is: Will it fly—for the investor?

INDUSTRY INVESTMENT DIRECTIONS

The cellular-mobile-radio market, like so many others in high technology, is not yet really in existence. So what the investor must bet on initially is companies which are successful in the pager equipment and services market—an area less well publicized than that of cellular-radio transmission, but very attractive nonetheless. Then, with a few of his chips, the courageous investor might try a few cellular-mobile-radio long shots.

The real lay of the land for cellular-radio competition is not going to be evident until at least 1985, because it takes two years to build the systems. For all we can tell, in advance of the awarding of licenses and the setting of tariffs, those poor old whipping boys of telecommunications, the local tele-

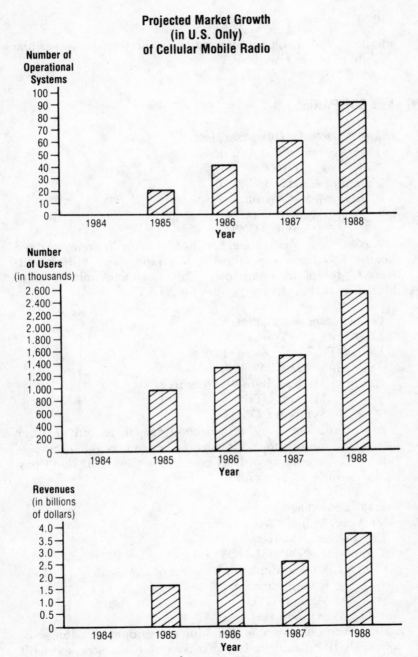

**Projected Market Growth
(in U.S. Only)
of Cellular Mobile Radio**

Number of
Operational
Systems

Year

Number
of Users
(in thousands)

Year

Revenues
(in billions
of dollars)

Year

Estimated compound annual growth rate: 30 percent

phone companies, may turn out to be the winners in cellular mobile radio. Beeper Bell, anyone?

KEY COMPANIES

Auxton Computer Enterprises, Inc.
1345 Avenue of the Americas
New York, NY 10019
Telephone: (212) 489-7620
Contact: J. P. Croxton, President
      Market: OTC
      Symbol: AUXT

Auxton's forte is management consulting in computerized business systems—specifically, toll rating and billing software for telephone companies. They have a toehold in cellular radio via their Chicago work for AT&T.

Communications Industries, Inc.
1100 Frito-Lay Tower
Dallas, TX 75235
Telephone: (214) 357-4001
Contact: Michael Barnes, Treasurer
      Market: OTC
      Symbol: COMM

A well-run company with a good growth record in other areas, Communications Industries is currently pursuing cellular mobile radio as well. It could be a plus. Just don't pay up for cellular mobile radio.

Graphic Scanning
99 West Sheffield Avenue
Englewood, NJ 07631
Telephone: (800) 631-1608, in New Jersey (201) 569-7711
Contact: Marvin Raphael, Director of Corporate
      Communications
      Market: OTC
      Symbol: GSCC

Barry Yampol, Graphic Scanning's president, is a long-ball hitter. He'll either score big or strike out. Right now he's a bit extended, with lots of debt.

MCI Communications Corporation
1133 19th Street, NW
Washington, DC 20036
Telephone: (202) 887-2172
Contact: Wayne English, Chief Financial Officer
        Market: OTC
        Symbol: MCIC
Yes, the terrible telephone upstarts are moving into cellular mobile radio! Watch out, everybody.

Metromedia, Inc.
One Harmon Plaza
Secaucus, NJ 07094
Telephone: (201) 348-3244
Contact: D. C. Brainerd, Vice-President
        Market: NYSE
        Symbol: MET
Normally, a company as large as Metromedia should not be included in a list of prospects such as this. Cellular mobile radio isn't likely to have a big impact on its revenues. But three pager-company acquisitions (Beep Communications, Radiofone, and Zipcall) in three months says Metromedia is serious. With its record, that means something. The company is very leveraged financially.

Millicom, Incorporated
153 East 53rd Street, Suite 550
New York, NY 10022
Telephone: (212) 355-3574
Contact: Orhan Sadik-Khan, President
        Market: OTC
        Symbol: MILL
Millicom is a 1982 high-flyer with developmental prospects in cellular radio, paging and digital message systems.

Mobile Communications Corporation of America
Capitol Towers, Suite 1500
Jackson, MS 39201
Telephone: (601) 969-1200

Contact: Richard Weatherholt, Vice-President of Finance
Market: OTC
Symbol: MCCA

A bit more fragile than something like Communications Industries, Mobile Communications Corporation is still a possible acquisition target. It has a pager business which is attractive in its own right.

PageAmerica Communications Inc.

228 East 45th Street
New York, NY 10017
Telephone: (212) 286-8901
Contact: D. A. Post, President
Market: OTC
Symbol: PAGE

Nationwide daily rental of pocket pagers to travelers and monthly pager rental to corporate field service users is Page's activity. Profits have been a problem.

Phone-Mate, Inc.

325 Maple Avenue
Torrance, CA 90503
Telephone: (213) 320-9800
Contact: John Morris, Vice President of Finance
Market: OTC
Symbol: PHON

From a base of telephone answering machines, Phone-Mate is trying to leap into cordless, or portable, telephones. The product looks good, better than the company's record so far.

Western Union

One Lake Street
Upper Saddle River, NJ 07458
Telephone: (201) 825-5000
Contact: Warren Bechtel, Vice-President
Market: NYSE
Symbol: WU

Western Union is the opposite of Metromedia: its track record leaves you wondering. But the company is after something in telecommunications. Maybe cellular mobile radio is the base hit. Watch out for phantom earnings resulting from items like no taxes, unfunded pension liabilities, and capitalized costs. A kicker is Western Union's 50 percent ownership of Airfone.

Leading Analysts

John Bain and Winston Himsworth
Lehman Brothers Kuhn Loeb
55 Water Street
New York, NY 10041
Telephone: (212) 558-1500
Wide coverage of telecommunications services and equipment companies is offered by Bain, on the regulatory angles, and Himsworth, on the technology involved. Their focus is on the larger companies.

Mary McCaffrey and Charles Reid
Alex Brown and Son
135 East Baltimore Street
Baltimore, MD 21202
Telephone: (301) 727-1700
Wide coverage of the smaller companies in particular is offered by this team of analysts. They also hold a seminar in Baltimore every spring on broad telecommunications topics.

Glenn Pafumi and James Samuels
Merrill Lynch, Inc.
One Liberty Plaza, 165 Broadway
New York, NY 10080
Telephone: (212) 637-8245
These two analysts have written *pounds* on the telecommunications markets and technology, of which they have a good grasp.

PERTINENT PUBLICATIONS

Telocator
Telocator Network of America
1800 M Street, NW, Suite 1020N

Washington, DC 20036

Telephone: (202) 659-6446

Subscription: $30 per year for eleven monthly issues

In this monthly publication of the radio common carrier trade association are published reports on mobile-phone and pager operations, pertinent government regulations, financial studies, trends, a calendar of events, and reviews of new technologies.

W. R. Young, "Advanced Mobile Phone Service: Introduction, Background, and Objectives," in *The Bell System Technical Journal* (January 1979)

Bell Laboratories

Room 1J-319

101 John F. Kennedy Parkway

Short Hills, NJ 07078

Telephone: (201) 564-2000

Single-issue sales price: $2 (subscription: $20 per year for monthly periodical)

For that matter, the whole January 1979 issue of this company periodical is devoted to cellular mobile radio as viewed from AT&T's vantage point.

IX

Fiber Optics, Lasers, and Microwaves: The Dance of the Light Fantastic

From the signal fires high atop the hillsides of ancient Troy to the coastal lighthouses that lit the way home for the cargo-laden schooners of the eighteenth and nineteenth centuries and on up to the flashing semaphores of today's naval vessels, light has been used to transmit information throughout the ages. The earliest signal lights predated written messages by millennia, and light as a means of instantaneous long-distance communication grew with the civilizations.

Then suddenly, a hundred years ago, light signaling was almost totally overshadowed by twin siblings on the same electromagnetic spectrum, namely, radio and electrical transmission. Today, through man's restructuring of light with lasers and the purification of sand into superglass, light waves may once again become a frontrunner in communications. If so, it will all be done with mirrors—almost literally.

In fiber-optics communications, messages are transmitted by means of light pulses zipping along glass fibers thinner than human hair. The technology offers distinct advantages over traditional electronic wire and radio transmission. It is immune to interference from electrical-radiation sources such as transformers, microwave devices, and standard transmission wires, as well as from electrical storms. On the security front, it is, at least currently, immune to eavesdropping—have you ever tried to listen to a light beam? It's faster. It's able to handle much more information at a potentially lower cost, since it uses materials lighter in weight and precautions such as grounding are not necessary.

For all its allure, fiber-optic communication still uses the same four building blocks as other communications systems

115

do. It needs transmitters/receivers; the transmission cables themselves; repeaters, or amplifiers; and connectors.

Receiving devices in optical-fiber communication owe their development largely to the military's electronic-weaponry research. The darkness of night having always been a handicap in warfare, much research has gone into overcoming the limitations of an unlit battlefield. Among the more notable advances was the development of detectors called photodiodes, which can sense, for instance, the glowing end of a cigarette a mile away at night.

The transmitting devices of fiber-optics communications are based on laser technology and the development of light-emitting diodes, those familiar LEDs used for handheld-calculator display. Which light source will ultimately dominate optical communications depends in large part on further developments in the manufacture of the fibers themselves. LEDs and laser-generated light sources currently employ two distinct types of fibers.

LED-based transmissions traverse multimode optical fibers. Multiple light beams carry the messages through fibers with a glass core 30 to 50 microns in diameter—about the thickness of a human hair. Lasers transmit messages in a single mode, through fibers with a core diameter of only 5 microns.

In technology, smaller means more difficult, though not impossible. Single-mode fibers are also currently much more expensive to produce than the multimode variety. Thus they have not been widely accepted as yet. Monomode fibers have a distinct advantage, however, in that they can carry more information in less time. This benefit points toward a growing use of the single fibers once fabrication techniques are mastered. Keep your investment eyes open for any companies developing efficient monomode-fiber-production techniques. They could be real winners.

Another advantage of monomode fibers is that light traversing them bounces around less than it does in multimode links. That's why it doesn't lose so much energy in transit. Traveling ten to fifteen times farther before needing amplification, it makes possible an equivalent reduction in the third component of fiber-optic communication, the repeaters. Amplification in this field is expensive, using as its means an optical-to-electronic-and-back-to-optical conversion. The strengthening of light signals can only be achieved electronically, not optically. Its partial elimination could thus well compensate for the other, higher costs of a single-mode system.

There is currently no way to eliminate repeaters completely when dealing with long-line fiber-optic transmission. Nor is there a way to get around connectors, the unglamorous fourth component of this type of communication. In fact, however unalluring and low-tech-looking something as basic as splicing and coupling wires may seem, these devices constitute one of the major hurdles—and one of the areas of greatest potential gain for the investor—facing fiber-optics communications. The hurdle is twofold, a result of the previously mentioned light-loss bugaboo plus the alignment problem. If you have trouble successfully sighting a ten-foot putt on the golf course, imagine trying to line up a couple of 5-micron wires end to end.

Yet precisely such minutiae are the stuff of which investment riches are often made. In terms of overall investment strategies for fiber-optics communications, the fibers themselves are not the way to go. It's true that the financial and popular media focus on the big fiber producers like Corning Glass, Times Fiber, and Western Electric, but for the most part these companies are either so large or so diversified that their optical-fiber-generated revenues won't be significant in terms of overall earnings. Also, once the technology is mastered, the fibers will be churned out like so much spaghetti—and bulk items, with commodity status, aren't a high-tech investment, no matter how high-tech their end use may be.

Proprietary designs for detectors and connectors, on the other hand, stand a good chance of developing unique and profitable market niches for their companies. At the moment, the detector industry is the one furthest along in its development. The crucial connector effort is still waiting for its multi-million-dollar breakthrough.

Another major investment area, one easily overlooked, is tools and training. Field splicing and cable repair are not going to be done with pliers, wire strippers, and a "that looks about right" technique. They're going to require high-resolution, microprocessor-based fusion splicers and the skills to use them properly. Here's a wide-open area for the play-off of the small, as yet private companies expected to step forward with a new maintenance-and-repair technology—perhaps using laser-guided optical fiber splicers, which would fittingly complete the optic circle.

Telecommunications can be expected to dominate optical-fiber use well into the nineties, taking perhaps 85 percent of the product. Military applications will consume probably 9 percent. Nevertheless, there are some intriguing other future uses for the investor to track.

One spillover from military technology is the optical gyroscope already being installed aboard some commercial aircraft. Without going into all the technical wonders of this device, which lie beyond the scope of an investment-oriented book, the key advantage of the laser gyro is readily discerned: using laser-generated light as its "motion," it has no moving parts. It is thus mechanically simpler, more reliable, and less power-hungry than its traditional counterpart—all very powerful inducements to the adoption of laser gyros in future navigational systems, both military and commercial.

As sensing devices, gyroscopes are not unique in their adaptability to electrooptics technology. Far from it, sensing devices as a whole promise to become a major market for this technology. Kessler Marketing Intelligence estimates that the overall market for optical-fiber sensors will reach $40 million by 1986 and $180 million by 1991. The products will range from instruments for measuring building stress, internal temperatures of nuclear reactors, and vital signs in hospital patients to oil-exploration technology and missile-control devices. Even electrocution-proof amplified fiber-optic guitars are in the works. In every case, fiber optics will bring with it reduced costs as well as greater reliability and sensitivity.

Lasers, like optical fibers, have a broad range of applications outside the telecommunications field. In fact, the communications and information-handling field currently ranks fourth as a market for lasers. Weapons research, metalworking, and inspection/control applications, in that order, are the largest dollar volume generators for the laser industry.

The wide spectrum of laser applications is based on the very physics of laser light itself. The word "laser" derives from the term "light amplification by stimulated emission of radiation," a term that is perhaps less than edifying to the uninitiated, and that also leaves out the quality of laser energy that sets it apart from light as we normally conceive of it.

Light emitted by such sources as stars, candles, and electric lamps is incoherent, composed of energy in a chaotic form, somewhat resembling the between-stations static on your radio. Lasers, by contrast, emit coherent light, regular and continuous waves of concentrated energy quite like the "At the tone, the time will be six o'clock" signal heard on radio stations before the evening news.

Concentrate light and you can control it. Control light and you control energy. Add precision, and you have a semiuniversal tool.

A laser beam can easily drill holes 0.0005 inch across, either in metal, for precision toolwork, or in flesh, for microsurgery. Welding of either material requires only a change in procedure. The same optical precision applied differently can be used for continuous alignment, as in, say, leveling a field with a bulldozer so it slants one inch every five thousand feet. Lasers can be utilized in microphones, contact-lens fitting, fingerprint identification, mapping systems, printing, velocimeters, optical computer memories, and pollution measurement. A laser-equipped cane for the blind has even been designed by Bionics Instruments, Inc. Using laser sensors, the cane produces a poking sensation in the blind person's fingers warning of obstacles ahead and auditory notice of obstacles above and below.

But somehow lasers remain a product in search of a major market, akin to personal computers in the early days when they were still called home computers. As the microcomputer market suddenly exploded, so should the laser market—eventually. When it does, probably the company with the best marketing force will be the one that emerges as the big investment winner. After all, nearly anyone can make a laser these days—Codenoll Technology, Coherent, Inc., Control Laser Corporation, and Spectra-Physics are a few of the companies that do. It's selling them that's the problem.

The forerunner of the laser was the maser, acronymic for "microwave amplification by stimulated emission of radiation." When it was discovered that light waves could be amplified in the same way as microwaves, the resultant device became known as an optical maser. Only later did the term "laser" evolve.

While most people have heard of lasers, masers are virtually in the Scrabble realm. But for investors that should not remain the case. The market for microwave components is seven times the size of that for optical fibers, four times that for lasers, and it's growing rapidly.

For the most part, companies such as Anaren Microwave, Avantek, and Narda Microwave are oriented toward the military and telecommunications. This is both good and bad. Being a dependable, growing market is one thing. But much of microwave's application for the military falls under the C^3 category—communications, command, and control—which puts the products in the classified drawer. How do you measure progress in a company's products if you aren't allowed to know about them, much less check them out? It's tough, but the sources in this chapter should help you make the most of that portion of activity which is unclassified.

Technological breakthroughs can be monitored, and they will precede any growth leaps in the industry. Gallium arsenide (GaAs) semiconductor technology is a case in point. GaAs devices cram more electronic circuits onto a chip than ever before possible. Newly formed ventures such as Gigabit Logic and old-line Hughes, Texas Instruments, and Varian, among others, hope to be selling GaAs semiconductors by 1984, or 1986 at the very latest. If and when they do actually put their semiconductors on the market, the cost of manufacturing microwave components, some of which already use GaAs technology, should drop dramatically, new markets should emerge—and earnings should accelerate rapidly.

GaAs semiconductors, which operate at higher frequencies than do the traditional silicon chips, may well also open the door for the microwave companies to enter the digital (read computers and computer linkage) market, boosting the industry's earnings even further. Currently the Japanese giant Nippon Electric Corporation is betting on GaAs as the candidate most likely to win in the digital computer switching game. IBM is on the side of the faster but more expensive Josephson Junction. It's definitely a scrimmage to scrutinize in the struggle for investment profit.

Projected Market Growth of
Optical Fibers and Components

(U.S. Producers Only)

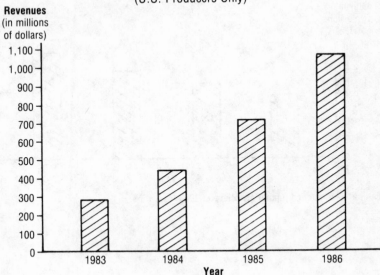

Estimated compound annual growth rate: 50 percent

Projected Market Growth of
Lasers

(U.S. Producers Only)

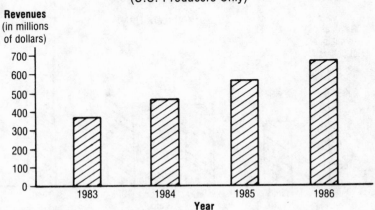

Estimated compound annual growth rate: 19 percent

**Projected Market Growth of
Lasers and Related Products Combined**

(U.S. Producers Only)

Revenues
(in billions
of dollars)

3.0
2.5
2.0
1.5
1.0
0.5
0

1983 1984 1985 1986

Year

Estimated compound annual growth rate: 20 percent

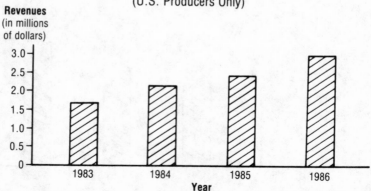

**Projected Market Growth of
Microwave Components**

(U.S. Producers Only)

Revenues
(in millions
of dollars)

3.0
2.5
2.0
1.5
1.0
0.5
0

1983 1984 1985 1986

Year

Estimated compound annual growth rate: 20 percent

INDUSTRY INVESTMENT DIRECTIONS

Military and telecommunications budgets are the financial key to growth in the fiber-optics, laser, and microwave industries. Both budgets should be healthy in the eighties, and given the benefits of optical and microwave products for military and telecommunications users, such growth appears inevitable.

Which industry segment you invest in is less important to your success in the field than is the quality of the particular company. Market choices and opportunities abound, and the various technologies, while hardly trivial, need not be of overriding concern, because the markets will pull along the technologies of their successful suppliers. That is to say, winning companies will have available the capital necessary to fund the improvement of their products. So buy the currently successful marketeers with good profit records.

KEY COMPANIES

Alpha Industries, Inc.
20 Sylvan Road
Woburn, MA 01801
Telephone: (617) 935-5150
Contact: Anne Hughes, Manager of Investor Relations
        Market: ASE
        Symbol: AHA

Alpha's revenues are 70 percent defense-related and stem primarily from the sale of microwave components. A potential sizzler is millimeter-wavelength microwave products hitting the market by the middle to late eighties.

Anaren Microwave
185 Ainsley Drive
Syracuse, NY 13205
Telephone: (315) 476-7901
Contact: C. W. Gert, Jr., Executive Vice-President
        Market: OTC
        Symbol: ANEN

Anaren concentrates its efforts in the radar surveillance equipment sector of the electronic countermeasures field.

Avantek, Inc.

3175 Bowers Avenue
Santa Clara, CA 95051
Telephone: (408) 727-0700
Contact: Gary Harmon, Chief Financial Officer
      Market: OTC
      Symbol: AVAK

Components and subassemblies account for 60 percent, equipment and systems for 40 percent of Avantek's revenues in microwave-frequency products, sold mainly to United States military and telecommunications users worldwide.

Codenoll Technology Corporation

1086 North Broadway
Yonkers, NY 10701
Telephone: (914) 965-6300
Contact: M. H. Coden, Chief Executive Officer
      Market:OTC
      Symbol: CODN

A development-stage company working with semiconductor lasers to be used in office-equipment products, Codenoll is an investment long shot.

Coherent, Inc.

3210 Porter Drive
Palo Alto, CA 94304
Telephone: (415) 493-2111
Contact: J. L. Donovan, Senior Vice-President of Finance
      Market: OTC
      Symbol: COHR

Over a third of Coherent's product line is medical, the rest is scattered. So are the profits, which go up and down.

Control Laser Corporation

11222 Astronaut Boulevard
Orlando, FL 32809
Telephone: (305) 851-2540

Contact: James Felcyn, Chief Financial Officer
                Market: OTC
                Symbol: CLSR

Control Laser is the largest solid-state laser manufacturer for machine tools. It also makes gas lasers and has a tie-in with high-powered CO_2 laser system producers.

DBA Systems, Inc.

1135 West NASA Boulevard
Melbourne, FL 32901
Telephone: (305) 727-0660
Contact: T. B. Willmann, President
                Market: OTC
                Symbol: DBAS

Providing mostly software and custom computer services, DBA Systems concentrates on U.S. government agencies as customers in the satellite-tracking and digital-communications fields.

EIP Microwave, Inc.

4500 Campus Drive
Newport Beach, CA 92660
Telephone: (714) 540-6655
Contact: G. D. Clark, Chief Financial Officer
                Market: OTC
                Symbol: EIPM

EIP has a history under various names going back to 1961. It designs and manufactures microwave test equipment.

M/A-Com, Inc.

South Avenue
Burlington, MA 01803
Telephone: (617) 272-9600
Contact: Joseph Bothwell, Jr., Vice-President
                Market: NYSE
                Symbol: MAI

MAI supplies microwave components and fiber-optic and coaxial cable, mainly for cable television.

Narda Microwave Corporation

435 Moreland Road
Hauppauge, NY 11788

Telephone: (516) 231-1700
Contact: H. S. Laver, Vice-President of Finance
    Market: ASE
    Symbol: NRD

Primarily a component manufacturer, Narda also makes test equipment. Half of its sales are in electronic warfare, a third in radar. A poor fiscal 1983 will probably provide a buying opportunity.

Newport Corporation

18235 Mount Baldy Circle
Fountain Valley, CA 92708
Telephone: (714) 963-9811
Contact: E. C. Berry, President
    Market: OTC
    Symbol: NEWP

Recently popular with analysts and investors, this company has carved a niche for itself as the support resource for laser users. Its specialty alignment tables have cornered the market.

Spectra-Physics, Inc.

3333 North First Street
San Jose, CA 95134
Telephone: (408) 946-6080
Contact: M. R. Gaulle, Vice-President of Finance
    Market: NYSE
    Symbol: SPY

Concentrated in lasers, for a wide variety of markets, Spectra-Physics is hard hit whenever there is a recession. Investors seem to forget this fact just before each periodic earnings collapse.

Times Fiber Communications, Inc.

P. O. Box 384, 358 Hall Avenue
Wallingford, CT 06492
Telephone: (203) 265-8500
Contact: Kirk Evans, Treasurer
    Market: OTC
    Symbol: TFCI

The sex appeal here is optical fibers, but the profits so far are made in coaxial cable.

LEADING ANALYSTS

Phillip Brannon
Merrill Lynch, Inc.
One Liberty Plaza, 165 Broadway
New York, NY 10080
Telephone: (212) 637-8237

Cliff Higgerson and Bruce Seltzer
Hambrecht and Quist, Inc.
235 Montgomery Street
San Francisco, CA 94104
Telephone: (415) 986-5500

Charles Hill
Kidder, Peabody and Company
100 Federal Street
Boston, MA 02110
Telephone: (617) 357-6762

Herb Klieman
Prescott, Ball and Turben
1331 Euclid Avenue
Cleveland, OH 44115
Telephone: (216) 574-7411

PERTINENT PUBLICATIONS

Fiberoptics Report
Advanced Technology Publications, Inc.
P.O. Box 1111
Littleton, MA 01460
Telephone: (617) 244-2939
    Subscription: $140 for monthly newsletter
Intensive coverage of fiber-optics technology and applications is offered by this newsletter, along with an annual economic review and forecast.

International Fiber Optics and Communications
Information Gatekeepers, Inc.
167 Corey Road
Brookline, MA 02146
Telephone: (617) 739-2022
   Subscription: $48 per year for bimonthly periodical,
                 controlled circulation
Written for the user of telecommunications products,
IFO&C is a mix of news, tutorials, new-product announce-
ments, etc. for telephone, CATV, military, and similar user
areas.

Laser Focus (with *Fiberoptic Technology*)
(For address and telephone, see *Fiberoptics Report*,
   above)
   Subscription: $38 per year for monthly periodical
Technical articles and news on applications, personnel,
new products, and coming events in the fiber-optic/laser field
are provided by this specialty publication. *Laser Focus* is edited for specialists with tutorial articles and news of industry
developments.

Laser Report
(For address and telephone, see *Laser Focus*, above)
   Subscription: $140 for monthly newsletter
Coverage similar to that of *Laser Focus* is provided by this
newsletter, but it's more intensive. One issue every year is
devoted to economic trends and outlook.

Microwave Journal
Horizon House-Microwave, Inc.
610 Washington Street
Dedham, MA 02026
Telephone: (617) 326-8220
   Subscription: $36 per year for monthly periodical
This publication covers industry developments broadly and
specialized technical advances in detail. Edited for managers
in companies using or producing products in the microwave
spectrum, the *Journal* covers radar, electronic warfare, communications, instrumentation, and components areas.

MAJOR MEETINGS

EASCON
The Institute of Electrical and Electronics Engineers, Inc.
345 East 47th Street
New York, NY 10017
Telephone: (212) 644-7555
Sponsored by the Washington, DC, section of the Institute of Electrical and Electronics Engineers (IEEE) and the IEEE Aerospace and Electronic Society (AES), the Electronics and Aerospace Systems Conference is held annually in September. It covers developments in microwave, fiber optics, and laser technology pertinent to the military forces.

INTERFACE
Interface Group
P.O. Box 927, 160 Speen Street
Framingham, MA 01701
Telephone: (800) 225-4620, in Massachusetts
    (617) 879-4502
INTERFACE is a large telecommunications exposition, featuring vendors in all phases of the technology and industry along with tutorial sessions, held every March in a major city.

PROFESSIONAL ASSOCIATIONS

Association of Old Crows
2300 Ninth Street, S, Suite 300
Arlington, VA 22204
Telephone: (703) 920-1600
This is the society of professionals involved in defense electronics and electronic warfare, including C^3 (communications, command, and control) and microwave applications. It publishes the *Journal of Electronic Defense* (available to members, who must be United States citizens, for $15 a year).

X

Applications Software Packages: Fuel for the Computer

Mr. X was a skilled programmer writing specialized applications software for a medium-sized manufacturing firm. Good at his job but rather oddball and opinionated, as programmers often are, he was fired. The episode, a simple matter of personality conflict, would probably have ended then and there had it not been for the company's modern-day dependence on its computers and a presentiment on the part of Mr. X that he might be dismissed someday.

Two months after his discharge, the firm was in chaos, heading toward unexpected bankruptcy. Payrolls were not being met, inventory control was shot, taxes couldn't be filed—and the IRS is the sternest taskmaster of them all. The reason? Mr. X had planted a simple bomb in his software. He had hidden some instructions in the main operating system of the computer directing it to erase all memory and self-destruct if for two consecutive weeks a paycheck was not issued to him. His ploy could be as simple as that because, when you get right down to the nitty-gritty, software is what computing is all about. Computers without software are books without print.

Software comes in essentially two forms: applications programs, which tackle specific tasks such as running inventory control, payroll, or even the ubiquitous video games; and systems programs, which run the computer itself as it processes the applications software. Systems software runs the disk drives, telling the computer how and where to access, say, the payroll data on the disks; the payroll applications program then calculates the actual payroll data, with all its numerous variables.

Computer software was once relegated to the industry's back burner. A company bought its machines bundled, that is to say, as complete systems—hardware, software, and maintenance all in one package deal—and was then locked in to the original supplier. If the applications programs turned out not to do exactly what the firm needed done—and almost always a wide gulf yawned between what was promised and what was delivered—well, then programmers had to be hired to tailor the programs to the company's needs. As to the systems software, there one was usually stuck with whatever came with the machine. After all, how many people do you know who, when the oil crunch came, had the gasoline engines removed from their cars so that they could be retrofitted with diesel power? They went out and bought new diesel cars instead. A lot of people have ended up with new computers that way.

The main force behind the computer companies' marketing strategy was the assumption that software simply couldn't be profitable. But in fact, with the advent of inexpensive personal computers, software has become necessary and accessible. There's no more locking it away in the corporate data-processing-department temples, no more "We can't handle your project for another three months" pronouncements from the high priests of the new religion. Now the dictum is "I think I'll step out at lunchtime and buy that new accounting package."

The overall software market is expected to have four times as many users in 1985 as it had in 1980. Total sales, meanwhile, will go from $2.4 billion to $8.4 billion. An average annual growth rate of 28 percent is nothing to sneeze at. In this projection of sales volume, incidentally, applications software is on a slightly slower track, with an estimated 25 percent growth rate, systems software running ahead at 30 percent.

The key to the marketplace for emerging software companies lies in discovering a supply vacuum, an area no one else is providing programs for, and then simply filling the void. Dan Fylstra, president of VisiCorp, began marketing VisiCalc, the first electronic spread sheet, way back in 1977. All of a sudden, a businessman with access to a personal computer could enter, for example, basic company projections, then change any of the variables and instantly see the results. Instead of hours, days, or even weeks of manipulating data with a pencil, it now took no longer than a game of Space Invaders to answer the crucial "What if . . . ?" questions.

Once the product was there, so were the customers, particularly since you could almost pick up VisiCalc at the corner drugstore. As Dan Fylstra comments, "We sell software packages in much the same way RCA sells phonograph records—through thousands of retail outlets." The need had been there all along. All it took was one person to realize it.

Some 500,000 copies of VisiCalc—it has a unit price of $250—have been sold to date, making it the software industry's first "golden floppy"; and those figures represent only part of VisiCorp's growing software sales. Actual totals are hard to come by, since the company remains private. But whatever the total, the bottom line almost has to be golden, inasmuch as the packaged-software industry is not capital-intensive.

Packaged software is being priced to sell in the hundreds of thousands of units, its development cost being spread over a base of users tenfold, twentyfold, or even a hundredfold larger than the relatively limited markets of the traditional minicomputers and the mainframes, those room-sized machines which we all used to think of as the true computers and which we watch in sci-fi movies and, televised, on election night. With its new low-price profile, packaged software sells. As it does so, volume increases even faster, because development costs are more quickly written off, and the per-unit return after that is almost pure gravy. Even price slashing—which occurs only if competition appears on the video-screen horizon—does not noticeably affect the sometimes preposterously high margins, which leave plenty of cash for new-development expenditures and excellent profits. So who needs money? That explains why packaged software is often a difficult pie for investors to partake of.

On the other hand, software is time-intensive. This feature works both for and against the numerous small programming companies springing up. The relatively long lead time required to develop a software package and establish it in the marketplace, plus the almost mandatory CIA-like clandestineness of the industry, means never knowing who is one step ahead of whom. A software supplier two steps ahead can often consolidate his position to the point of dominance. Consider VisiCorp, distributor of VisiCalc. Although there are now so many "calc" programs to choose from that their merchandising is referred to as the "calc wars," VisiCorp, with an ever-expanding, integrated-product base, is clearly a superpower in its software niche, while most of the other purveyors remain emerging nations. Sure, David beat Goliath—but how often?

A subset of packaged software, and an area in which investor participation is more feasible, is industry-specific software. Instead of, say, a general ledger sequence that can be used equally well, if perhaps with slight modification, by the Hampton Chicken Factory, Sticky Zippers, Inc., and the Hampshire Ergonomic Emporium, these programs might offer Sticky Zipper a tooth-designing routine and the Hampton Chicken Factory a means of projecting plucking performance by age, breed, and ambient temperature.

Such software is often sold as a turnkey system, wherein the vendor designs the programs and then couples them with a particular manufacturer's hardware, delivering the final product to the customer's door. In theory, all that need be done in order to have everything humming smoothly is to turn the key, hence the term "turnkey."

While it resembles the traditional bundled approach to selling hardware, here the software holds sway. The customer is purchasing a very specific programming product, the hardware being more or less the box it comes in. The Hampton Chicken Factory isn't buying the new Peaches and Cream computer and then getting it to perform wonders. It's buying the plucking-performance program. The Peaches and Cream computer just happens to be what comes with it.

Specialized-applications software packages are particularly dominant in the personal computer field, where there are dozens of interesting and fast-growing software companies. The problem is, most of these enterprises are private, and lots of them are sold before they go public. The individual investor seldom has a chance to participate. Some of the more interesting privates to keep your eyes on—just in case—are Digital Research, McCormack and Dodge, Micro Data Base Systems, MicroPro International, Microsoft, SAS Institute, Solvation, and VisiCorp.

Unlike the software packaged for cross-industry markets, industry-specific software requires a very broadly based and thorough expertise in the field to be served. If you're developing an agricultural-land-management program, software for a life insurance company's financial analysis, or a bank operations system, expertise in writing software plus plucking chicken feathers simply won't do. This particularity limits a turnkey company's customer base. It also limits competition, however, since once a system is up and running, similar programs for other companies in the same field can be produced at a cost considerably lower than that for entirely new software.

A good packaged-software play may be a difficult investment to find. Once located, however, it can be a very profitable one, for several reasons, some of which you're familiar with by now. The applications-programs market is a large and fast-growing one, as we have seen, and packaged software is a robust technology with staying power. As yet in the early stages of the learning curve, it has its most spectacular growth still to come. Intrinsic profits in the industry are comparatively large, product costs being low and sales prices high. An unusually low assets-to-sales ratio means a possibility of explosive growth at the bottom line. In addition, packaged-software companies aren't followed closely by many analysts. This is particularly true for companies with industry-specific products that would require the analyst to be familiar with the user industry in order to discuss or evaluate the software effectively. This situation will eventually change as fear of technology dissipates among traditional industry analysts. But meanwhile you, with this book in hand, have an investment opportunity.

And what about Mr. X? He's currently a free-lance programmer—designing bombs for packaged-software companies. Thievery is on the rise, both in the form of illegal copying and as plain old nonpayment for services rendered. According to some industry observers, it's more than merely on the rise, it's already a monumental problem.

The market need for safeguards is evidenced by the fact that specialty companies such as American Integrity Systems, Inc., and Soft Link Corporation have developed custom bombs and encryption programs, which allow a customer to test-run a basic program but not to have access to the complete version until it's paid for, and subsequently decoded. Where there's a market need, a new packaged-software firm will usually find itself a niche—an explosively profitable niche, one might add.

Projected Market Growth of Applications Software

(U.S. Producers Only)

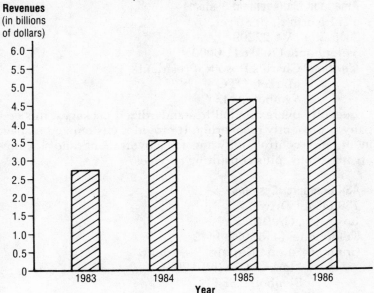

Revenues (in billions of dollars)

Year

Estimated compound annual growth rate: 26 percent

Note: These figures do not include captive production, or software developed for a company's own use.

INDUSTRY INVESTMENT DIRECTIONS

Paradoxically, for a new technological area, the things that count in the applications-software industry are the old-fashioned industrial and commercial virtues. Reliability, prompt and effective service, and the other traditional elements of good marketing and distribution are what distinguish a good company, and thus a suitable investment, from the also-rans.

There are so many customers with so many needs that success has to do primarily with not fouling up the golden opportunities. As in the entertainment world, there are numerous talents, but few stand out in the limelight unless they find the right showcase. In applications software, the showcasing consists in finding a cost-effective way to deliver the product to the user and then doing the details well.

KEY COMPANIES

American Management Systems
1777 North Kent Street
Arlington, VA 22209
Telephone: (703) 841-6000
Contact: Charles Rosotti, President
          Market: OTC
          Symbol: AMSY
Recently overextended in standardized packages, this company is presently recovering. It provides customized management and control software for government and business organizations, plus consulting services.

ASK Computer Systems
730 Distel Drive
Los Altos, CA 94022
Telephone: (415) 969-4442
Contact: Sandra Kurtzig, President
          Market: OTC
          Symbol: ASKI
ASK supplies turnkey systems to manufacturing management, using ASK software plus Hewlett-Packard and Digital Equipment computers.

BPI Systems, Inc.
3423 Guadalupe
Austin, TX 78705
Telephone: (512) 454-7191
Contact: Randall Ferguson, Treasurer
          Market: OTC
          Symbol: BPII
Accounting software packages are BPI's major product, supplied to manufacturers of minicomputer and microcomputer systems, to date primarily keyed to Apple computers.

CGA Computer Associates, Inc.
255 Route 520 East
Marlboro, NJ 07746
Telephone: (201) 946-8900

Contact: Edith Weinstein
        Market: OTC
        Symbol: CGAC

Insurance companies, banks, and other financial enterprises are the principal customers of CGA, which provides consulting and software services.

Computer Associates International

125 Jericho Turnpike
Jericho, NY 11753
Telephone: (800) 645-3003, in New York (516) 333-6700
Contact: Charles Wang (pronounced "Wong")
        Market: OTC
        Symbol: CASI

Offering computer utility and productivity programs for IBM users in a broad range of industries, this company has the largest international presence in the software industry.

Computone Systems, Inc.

One Dunwoody Park
Atlanta, GA 30338
Telephone: (404) 393-3010
Contact: William Robeson, Chief Executive Officer
        Market: OTC
        Symbol: CTON

Computone manufactures a portable terminal system used by life insurance agents to furnish prospective customers with on-the-spot financial analysis.

Comserv Corporation

1385 Mendota Heights Road
Mendota Heights, MN 55120
Telephone: (612) 452-7770
Contact: Richard Daly, Chief Executive Officer
        Market: OTC
        Symbol: CMSV

Comserv offers packaged manufacturing-management software to users with IBM installations. From a financial standpoint, its research and development accounting is more liberal than the industry norm.

The Continuum Company, Inc.
3429 Executive Center Drive
Austin, TX 78731
Telephone: (512) 345-5700
Contact: Michael Cheney, Chief Financial Officer
  Market: OTC
  Symbol: CTUC

Baldwin United owns nearly 60 percent of the common stock of this company, which supplies consulting and software services to the life and health insurance industry.

Cook Data Services, Inc.
6510 Abrams Road, Suite 410
Dallas, TX 75231
Telephone: (214) 349-6900
Contact: Kenneth Anderson, Chief Financial Officer
  Market: OTC
  Symbol: CDSG

Cook provides data-processing services to oil and gas industry companies, consultants, and investors. Proprietary software is concentrated in petroleum economics, reserves, and revenue forecasting.

Data Architects, Inc.
460 Totten Pond Road
Waltham, MA 02154
Telephone: (617) 890-7730
Contact: Martin Cooperstein, President
  Market: OTC
  Symbol: DRCH

The developer of BOSS, a bank operations system for large banks, Data Architects has seen its earnings depressed by a major customer's delays in implementing the program.

Hogan Systems, Inc.
14951 Dallas North Parkway, Suite 400
Dallas, TX 75240
Telephone: (214) 386-0020
Contact: Richard Baumgartner, Executive Vice-President
  Market: OTC
  Symbol: HOGN

Hogan sells applications software packages to banks, savings and loan associations, and savings banks—at snappy margins.

Instacom, Inc.
Instacom Centre
7610 Stemmons Freeway
Dallas, TX 75247
Telephone: (214) 631-1505
Contact: William Kennedy, Jr., Chairman
       Market: OTC
       Symbol: ICOM
Instacom features transfer services for truckers on the road, twenty-four hours a day.

Intermetrics, Inc.
733 Concord Avenue
Cambridge, MA 02138
Telephone: (617) 661-1840
Contact: J. E. Miller, President
       Market: OTC
       Symbol: IMET
A participant in the new Defense Department–sponsored computer-language ADA program, Intermetrics supplies computer software services to defense, aviation, and space users, along with custom programming and compilers.

ISC Systems Corporation
9922 East Montgomery
Spokane, WA 99206
Telephone: (509) 922-2623
Contact: J. Lindeblad, Financial Vice-President
       Market: OTC
       Symbol: ISCS
This company is closely watched and volatile. It provides turnkey computer systems to savings and loans, its historical customers, and banks, its new customers.

Management Science America, Inc.
3445 Peachtree Road, NE
Atlanta, GA 30326

Telephone: (404) 239-2000
Contact: John Imlay, Chief Executive Officer
        Market: OTC
        Symbol: MSAI

A major supplier of general ledger and other generic management applications software, the firm recently acquired Peachtree Software, through which it supplies programs for the IBM Personal Computer and other microcomputer models.

Monchik-Weber Corporation

11 Broadway
New York, NY 10004
Telephone: (212) 269-5460
Contact: John Weber, Chief Executive Officer
        Market: OTC
        Symbol: MWCH

An improving firm, Monchik-Weber provides software packages and services to brokerage firms, banks, and investment advisers.

NCA Corporation

399 Oakmead Parkway
Sunnyvale, CA 94086
Telephone: (408) 245-7990
Contact: Mark Ciotek, President
        Market: OTC
        Symbol: NCAC

Like Comserv and ASK, NCA provides manufacturing-management software—via Digital Equipment Corporation computers.

Pansophic Systems, Inc.

709 Enterprise Drive
Oakbrook, IL 60521
Telephone: (312) 986-6030
Contact: J. A. Wilkins, Vice-President of Finance
        Market: OTC
        Symbol: PANS

Pansophic equips large IBM installations with computer data center utility programs, repeatable routines for tasks the computer is required to perform over and over again, functions such as sorting lists of data and controlling library programs.

Policy Management Systems Corporation
1321 Lady Street
Columbia, SC 29201
Telephone: (803) 748-2000
Contact: G. L. Wilson, President
        Market: OTC
        Symbol: PMSC
The Siebels Bruce Group has a majority stock position in this corporation, which sells software to automate property and casualty insurance company functions on IBM equipment.

SEI Corporation
680 East Swedesford Road
Wayne, PA 19087
Telephone: (215) 687-1700
Contact: C. V. Raneo, Chief Financial Officer
        Market: OTC
        Symbol: SEIC
SEI is the leading supplier of packaged bank trust department accounting software.

SofTech, Inc.
460 Totten Pond Road
Waltham, MA 02154
Telephone: (617) 890-6900
Contact: Jerri De Kriek, Investor Relations
        Market: OTC
        Symbol: SOFT
Presently moving from custom software services to portable microcomputer software—currently representing about 10 percent of its business—SofTech has marketing and development rights from the University of California at San Diego for its version of Pascal. The company is also a contractor for the Department of Defense-sponsored ADA language.

Syscon Corporation
1054 31st Street, NW
Washington, DC 20007
Telephone: (202) 342-4000
Contact: J. Yglesias, Chief Executive Officer
      Market: OTC
      Symbol: SCON

Mainly a government contractor, Syscon provides software services in procurement, systems operation and training, systems development, and feasibility studies.

Systems and Computer Technology Corporation
Great Valley Corporate Center
4 Country View Road
Malvern, PA 19355
Telephone: (215) 647-5930
Contact: Charles Pollack
      Market: OTC
      Symbol: SCTC

This firm sells resource management services and software to governmental and educational users.

TERA Corporation
2150 Shattuck Avenue
Berkeley, CA 94704
Telephone: (415) 845-5200
Contact: M. J. Keaton, President
      Market: OTC
      Symbol: TRRA

Consulting and software services designed to enhance productivity and cut costs are offered by this company to energy industries such as utilities, petrochemical, and coal companies.

Triad Systems Corporation
1252 Orleans Drive
Sunnyvale, CA 94086
Telephone: (408) 734-9720
Contact: Rick Walter
      Market: OTC
      Symbol: TRSC

Triad manufactures and services turnkey computer systems, principally targeted toward automotive-parts jobbers and warehouse distributors. Its trick is low-cost, easy-to-use software, but it's been hurt by the recession.

LEADING ANALYSTS

Al Berkeley and Kenneth Burke
Alex Brown and Son
135 East Baltimore Street
Baltimore, MD 21202
Telephone: (301) 727-1700

Curt Monash
Paine Weber Mitchell Hutchins, Inc.
140 Broadway
New York, NY 10005
Telephone: (212) 437-2102

Dave Henwood
Prescott, Ball and Turben
1331 Euclid Avenue
Cleveland, OH 44115
Telephone: (216) 574-7411

Sy Kaufman
Hambrecht and Quist, Inc.
235 Montgomery Street
San Francisco, CA 94104
Telephone: (415) 986-5500

Carter Dunlop
Robertson, Colman and Stephens
100 California Street
San Francisco, CA 94111
Telephone: (415) 781-9700

David Wu
Montgomery Securities
235 Montgomery Street
San Francisco, CA 94104
Telephone: (415) 989-2050

PERTINENT PUBLICATIONS

EDP Industry Report
International Data Corporation
5 Speen Street
Framingham, MA 01701
Telephone: (617) 872-8200
  Subscription: $325 for biweekly newsletter
The International Data Corporation has separate letters
every two weeks on just about everything. The best and least
wasteful of your time and money is the "Gray Sheet," as the
EDP Industry Report is known in the trade. It covers the
entire electronic-data-processing industry.

Software Business Review
International Computer Programs, Inc. (ICP)
9000 Keystone Crossing
Indianapolis, IN 46240
Telephone: (317) 844-7461, (800) 428-6179 for
  subscriptions
  Subscription: Free if you qualify for the quarterly
                publication. Call for the prerequisite form
                to fill out. The publication is for people in
                the business, so you need some sort of
                business relationship to the field in order
                to qualify.
With great coverage of a wide range of topics in the field—
including insurance, banking, manufacturing, and administra-
tive editions˙as well as one geared to data-processing management—this publication sponsors an "Interface" review issue
for the industry as a whole every June.

Software News
Sentry Database Publishing
5 Kane Industrial Drive
Hudson, MA 01749
Telephone: (617) 562-9308
  Subscription: $20 per year for monthly newspaper
Applications, systems, and data-base software; industry per-
sonnel changes; legal issues; user ratings; and surveys are
featured in this monthly.

Transactions on Software Engineering
The Institute of Electrical and Electronic Engineers, Inc.
  (IEEE)
345 East 47th Street
New York, NY 10017
Telephone: (212) 644-7555
   Subscription: $6 per year for monthly periodical
Good, but technical, this publication is sponsored by the
IEEE's Computer Society. An annual technology review in
January surveys the major issues of the previous year and
forecasts the future.

MAJOR MEETINGS

Wang Institute of Graduate Studies
Tyng Road
Tyngsboro, MA 01879
Telephone: (617) 649-9731
The Wang Institute sponsors monthly lectures by experts
on software engineering in the first half of the year. The talks
make for heavy going, but they offer great insights—for free.

PROFESSIONAL ASSOCIATIONS

Association of Data Processing Service Organizations, Inc.
  (ADAPSO)
1300 North 17th Street, Suite 300
Arlington, VA 22209
Telephone: (703) 522-5055
An industry trade group formed to work on standards and to
lobby for favorable legislation, the Association of Data Processing Service Organizations has helped to advance industry
causes such as patent versus copyright protection. The association also provides seminars and study programs of industry
interest.

Institute of Electrical and Electronic Engineers (IEEE)
  Computer Society

(For address and telephone, see *Transactions on Software Engineering,* under *Pertinent Publications,* above)

This professional society focuses on individual concerns such as continuing education and the outlook on employment and salaries.

XI

Custom Circuits: Cashing In the Chips

Custom shops are part and parcel of the American way of life. If you want to take a plain old Chrysler sedan and turn it into a limousine, that's no problem. There are companies ready and willing to take a welding torch to your car, cut it in half, and add a new center section of however many feet you'd like. Do you want your suit lapels narrowed? A tailor will do it. Do you want wine bottled under your own label? A vintner will do it. Do you want a birdbath that whistles "Dixie" when a feathered friend lands? Someone will do it.

Socially, perhaps such made-to-order items reflect the individuality democracy makes possible. Economically, they usually fall into the luxury category. Custom work on the industrial level—the forges, package manufacturers, and tool-and-die shops serving the machine industry, for instance—is a different story, being an essential component of industry as a whole.

Probably in no manufacturing endeavor is this more true than in the freewheeling world of electronics technology. Essentially, there are four types of custom integrated circuits in the semiconductor industry: programmable memories; their logic-chip equivalents, field-programmable logic arrays (FPLAs); uncommitted chips, or gate arrays; and fully customized circuit chips. Standard, noncustom semiconductor integrated circuits are fully fashioned at the time of manufacture for various types of general use, much as hammers or screwdrivers are made. The field-programmable logic chips and the memories programmable in the field or in the course of by-product manufacture are more like speed-wrench sets with their changeable socket sizes. They are quasi-standard, quasi-custom.

The first stage in the sophistication of custom circuits is the alphabet soup of memories. These include PROMs, EPROMs, EAROMs, and EEPROMs (also called, for purposes of simplification, E²PROMs—yes, we agree with you, that's not much in the line of simplification, but so it goes in the electronics industry).

A typical application of PROM, or "programmable read-only memory," is video games. Here's a prime example of where semicustom circuits, or partially dedicated chips, as they are sometimes called, come in.

Suppose you have just invented a new video game called Strangle the Author (the object of which is obvious). You can't afford the millions of dollars needed in order to start making your own chips for this game. But luckily it can employ the same type of controls and the same display monitor as the popular Pac-Man does. So you buy some PROM game chips, since their programmability allows you to enter electronically into the existing chips whatever functions you want them to have.

PROM circuitry allows you to program a chip once and only once, as if it were a piece of paper on which you could write with an indelible pen. For your Strangle the Author game, it would be fine, because the rules of the game need not be altered once laid out. For other applications, however, PROM is too limiting. Thus EPROM was developed. EPROM stands for—you guessed it—"erasable programmable read-only memory."

Flexible during the manufacturing process, EPROM circuits do not retain this elasticity at the applications end of operations. They are erased by exposure to a heavy dose of ultraviolet light—something not readily achieved when the chips are mounted on a board inside the computer. Hence the development of E²PROMs, or "electrically erasable programmable read-only memories."

All of these programmable memories have a growing use in electronics technology. But it's the basic PROM that most small manufacturers still usually turn to when looking for a chip to customize as a short-run (fewer than five hundred) special-purpose device. The future of chips such as the E²PROMs seems to be in updates.

Presently, when a manufacturer wants to update a product, he must send a repairman out with a replacement PROM.

Were he to use E²PROMs, the changes could be transmitted over the telephone, and the computer could literally update itself. If that sounds like a neat idea, then it helps in explaining why companies such as Motorola expect E²PROM sales to hit $450 million by 1985.

Various programmable chips are used by manufacturers in a wide range of products, from single experimental test units to games turned out by the thousands. They may be regarded as user-programmable, rather than true made-to-order custom circuits. However, for special applications requiring quantities as low as five hundred to a thousand units per year, semicustom gate arrays, also known as uncommitted chips, can be used.

Uncommitted chips have on their silicon surfaces a number of individual gates, or signal circuits, capable of making electronic choices like and/or decisions. The signal circuits are not connected to each other. Customizing begins when the buyer orders these gates connected in the unique way called for by his particular application. The final product identity is established in the masking stage. A thin metal sheet defining the pattern of connections the customer wants is overlaid on the silicon wafer. Then a metal deposit is laid down, connecting those gates defined by the mask. It's like a template, the open spaces of the pattern being the part that is custom-designed.

There is no direct parallel in our liveaday world. But imagine a record company making blank discs and then having three hundred of them stamped with four different renditions of "My Old Kentucky Home" and another thousand of them with the theme from *Star Wars*, and you'll have the general idea. The disc is standardized, the spindle hole is standardized, the number of grooves allowable for recording is pretty well standardized. How many of these available grooves should actually be pressed into the blank, how much space should be left between cuts, and whether to utilize both sides of the record, as well as which actual music is to be recorded, are decisions open to the buyer.

Now if you are a phonograph manufacturer, and you decide to bring out a record player that for some reason uses 27-rpm cones instead of flat 33-rpm discs, you'll have to find a shop equipped to produce fully customized records. The equivalent in the semiconductor industry would be fully customized circuits, designed entirely from scratch for a specific purpose.

Being the most expensive integrated circuits (ICs) of all, these chips require a customer end use of at least 25,000 to 50,000 devices per year in order to be cost effective. However, there are plenty of potential customers with that range of demand, as the so-called silicon foundries are discovering.

Silicon foundry customizing is an activity many established companies like Motorola and Intel are pursuing with fervor. What it involves, essentially, is taking a customer's home-grown design and producing the actual part for him.

To the customer, one advantage of such an arrangement is that it obviates the highly capital-intensive business of setting up a fabrication line of one's own. A second benefit is expedited access to the technology of wafer fabrication. A third inducement is based on the fact that as microprocessors become more and more complex, they become at the same time more general purpose devices, incorporating more options for manufacturers and users. A given manufacturer thus finds it harder and harder to come up with unique features for his products not easily emulated by competing producers using the same basic microprocessor. However, a silicon foundry can design an optimized logic system for one customer's product that is difficult for the competition to copy utilizing standard circuits.

A final argument in favor of silicon foundries is time. From receipt of a customer's data-base tapes, or masks, defining the circuit, to actual production, turnaround time spans six weeks to six months, depending on the complexity of the part involved. That's faster than the customer could produce it on his own.

There are drawbacks, of course. The chief ones are lack of control and lack of standards.

Customers using silicon foundries have no real power. During periods of slack semiconductor activity, any chip company with excess capacity on the production line can turn around, advertise itself as a foundry, and solicit outside work. But what happens when business picks up? Will the buyer still have a foundry to deal with? Or will he be left foundering as regular production absorbs the capacity of the silicon foundry? Because of this peril, customers are looking for long-term commitments, and manufacturers are offering them as the only way to assuage the buyers' fears.

The second major drawback to silicon custom tooling is the lack of interface standardization. The best chip in the world isn't going to do a manufacturer any good unless it can interface, or connect, with the rest of his product. When you buy color film, you buy a certain size, say 35-millimeter, because you have a 35-millimeter camera. Things aren't that simple in the custom-circuit business. They'll sell you film, all right. But it may be 16-millimeter or 120-millimeter film. It will do what you want it to do. It will take a color picture. Unfortunately, you won't be able to use it in your 35-millimeter camera.

The growth of silicon foundries favors larger firms, since it allows them to leverage their expensive investments in production facilities. The foundries will not reach their full growth potential, however, until standards are worked out. When buying a custom circuit becomes as simple as buying film and having it developed, then the industry will explode. The original equipment manufacturers (OEMs) assembling electronics equipment will be able to concentrate on taking that special picture, or making their customized applications products; the foundries, like Kodak, can worry about producing the film and developing it—unless, of course, another Polaroid comes along.

Well might that happen, in point of fact. If it does, the nouveau Polaroid is apt to be that same gallium arsenide (GaAs) which is seeping into the microwave arena. The parallel between that field and the electronic technology of custom circuits is too obvious not to be drawn. Nobody has yet dared to suggest that Silicon Valley be renamed Gallium Gully. As Martin Lepselter, director of Bell Laboratories' Advanced LSI Laboratory, put it in a recent *Wall Street Journal* interview, "Even the Lord was bullish on silicon. The whole world is made of it."

It's true that up until now, all of the staggering advances in integrated circuit technology have been silicon-based. But circuitry based on gallium arsenide offers the advantages of greater speed, higher reliability, lower power consumption, and superior radiation resistance. Its major drawback is its higher cost compared to that of silicon-based circuitry ($25 to

$50 per square inch for the basic substrate of GaAs compared to $5 to $10 for silicon). The cost factor explains why it is currently confined to the microwave market, where its expense is secondary to its benefits. Even so, gallium arsenide is expected by many to become the second wave sweeping over circuit technology by 1985—in which case it should also mean a second wave of profits for investors.

Meanwhile, the next wave of investor profit may well rise in computer-aided design (CAD), a new master key in the manufacture of custom circuits. Consider VLSI circuitry, or very large-scale integrated circuits. VLSIs involve components whose density has been concentrated some twentyfold from the already extreme density of the chips of a decade ago, and whose individual etched transistors and connectors are now slightly larger than two microns apiece (a micron is thirty-nine millionths of an inch). Then consider that while the chips on the leading edge of technology have some 100,000 such components each, industry experts are predicting 100,000,000-component integrated circuits for the not-too-distant future. On reflection, you'll see why a computer is needed to cope with the complexity and accuracy implied in designing these circuits with the speed required. A computer is also needed to produce the intricate components and test them.

Computer-aided design has been a promise only partially fulfilled in the industry for over a decade now. It has simply pledged more for circuit development than it has delivered. But that disparity seems about to be overcome as computers finally prepare to displace a great deal of microelectronics engineers' manual design time—without any penalty in chip size.

Not only are the new CAD systems proving themselves capable of working accurately within the microminiature world of the integrated circuit chip, but they are providing, during the design stage, scrupulously precise simulations of the chip at work. What these dry runs mean, in effect, is that to a large extent the product can be tested before expensive manufacturing costs are outlaid. They also save time. Until now, it has been necessary to produce a prototype and iterate it—that is, to test, test, test it—for up to two months, making continual physical changes in the chip design as faults are discovered.

Paring two months or so from the lead time needed to introduce a new chip offers significant cost savings and a marketing advantage.

For small firms in particular, computer-aided design provides a very real strength. Expensive engineering talent can be leveraged by coupling it to computer-aided design for fast service in supplying unique customer products without having to compete with the silicon foundries of the larger firms. As more innovative software is produced for CAD, investment opportunities in these firms should proliferate. The production technology implementing computer-aided design entails transferring the final circuit design onto the silicon wafer. Present techniques for achieving this are quite similar to those used in silk-screening. First a mask of the circuit is laid over the wafer and the pattern is illuminated. Then the wafer is bathed in chemicals to remove the exposed surface film, remasked, exposed to light again, bathed again, and so on until a complex grid of transistors, resistors, capacitors, and other parts is built up on it.

However, as chip architecture calls for denser and denser packaging of electronic circuitry in the same amount of space, a point is reached where the lines are so thin that the natural diffraction of light begins to produce fuzzy lines. That point has nearly been reached.

The solution to the impasse is to use a medium less affected by diffraction—radiation in the form of X-rays or, better yet, an electron beam—to scribe the wafer directly. IBM already employs such a direct-write process, and commercial electron-beam writers are now becoming available for custom-circuit manufacturers. Produced by Electron Beam Corporation, GCA Corporation, and Varian Associates, these machines range in price from $1.5 million to $3 million. Solutions are not inexpensive in the electronics industry, a fact that can make them very profitable for the manufacturer—and the investor. The stock of GCA, the current frontrunner in direct-write technology, for instance, rose from $1.20 a share to $56 a share, adjusted for splits.

Another area of circuit-manufacturing technology that offers similar opportunity is testing. Consider the career of something like Teradyne's L200-series board testers. At this writing, thirty or so of these two-year-old systems have been sold

—at an average price of $800,000. Teradyne currently owns the lion's share of the tester market, predicted to rise at close to 50 percent per annum for the next couple of years. The long-term annual growth rate for integrated-circuit-manufacturing equipment as a whole, for that matter, is projected to remain steadfastly in the range of 25 percent annually for years to come.

The market for automatic testing apparatus is outpacing that for integrated-circuit-manufacturing equipment itself because the testers offer chip makers the advantages of automation from the very outset of the manufacturing process. Automated equipment in general has become the only truly cost-effective way to provide the precision required in the manufacture of the increasingly complex newer chips. The substitution of equipment for labor at any or all of the stages in the manufacturing process can increase the production volume for chips significantly, simultaneously augmenting unit growth and reducing unit costs, thus unit price. It's much cheaper and more efficient to run quality tests on chips during the early stages of production than when they are finished. At the same time, because the integrated circuits being developed today are so complex, an incredible number of tests must be run on each chip in order to check out all the various functions. Accordingly, automated test equipment is fast becoming a prerequisite for growth, or even survival, in an industry that now, in addition to its own internal competition, must continually battle the reputedly superior quality control of Japan, Inc.

Considering the crucial importance of automated circuit-testing equipment, the capital start-up costs for a new venture in the field can be amazingly low. The highly successful Megatest Corporation, for instance, was founded by Steve Bissett and Howard Marshal in 1977 with $20,000. Recently one of the fastest-growing automatic-test-equipment makers in the market, privately held Megatest had sales of $12.5 million in 1981 and probably topped $17 million in 1982. To support this growth, the entrepreneurs decided to sell 15 percent of their stock, for $2 million, to a small group of venture capitalists. Their next step may well be to go public—if the company isn't gobbled up by a larger, old-line company first.

That does happen. Another automated-test-equipment manufacturer, Millennium Systems, founded with less than

$10,000, was subsequently acquired by American Microsystems, in turn acquired by giant Gould. On the other hand, LTX Corporation, whose sales in the same field grew from $300,000 in 1977 to over $40,000,000 in 1982, took the public route. But whichever their eventual road to capital, public or corporate, it's companies like LTX, Megatest, and Millennium Systems, evolving from resolute start-ups to established firms, that you will be looking for if you choose this particular electronic slice of the high-tech market.

A last facet of the custom-circuit industry to keep a watchful investment eye on is interconnect products, or packaging. Modern integrated-circuit chips are so complex that trying to connect them efficiently to anything is next to impossible on an assembly line. From this dilemma of lots of computing power and no ready way to access it arose the dual in-line package. Looking somewhat like a centipede, the dual in-line package is a small flat parcel containing the chip plus a row of pins along each of two parallel sides. The pins are connected to the integrated circuit during the manufacturing process, and all a computer assembler on the production line need do is to plug the centipede into a socket.

Unfortunately, the centipede is developing too many legs as chips continue to gain in complexity. The connecting points needed are increasing in number to the point where assembly-line work with them is becoming difficult, and the package itself is growing too large within otherwise shrinking electronic equipment. This problem together with those of furnishing heat dissipation and radiation protection for the superchips is leading to a proliferation of new package types. Packaging may not seem a very exciting product. But as an investor you must define excitement, at least in part, as where the money is.

INDUSTRY INVESTMENT DIRECTIONS

Growth in the semiconductor business is leading to segmentation of the industry as the various technologies involved become more complex and as capital demands increase. This phenomenon forces all but the very largest companies to focus their efforts in specialty niches. Opportunities are thus contin-

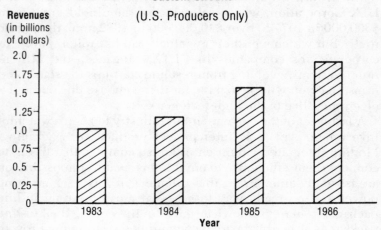

Projected Market Growth of Custom Circuits

(U.S. Producers Only)

Estimated compound annual growth rate: 22 percent

Note: These figures exclude production for a manufacturer's own use.

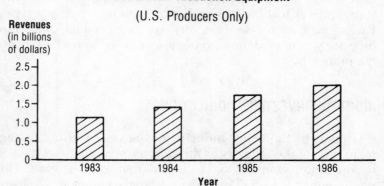

Projected Market Growth of Semiconductor Production Equipment

(U.S. Producers Only)

Estimated compound annual growth rate: 22 percent

Projected Market Growth of
Automated Semiconductor and Circuit Test Equipment

(U.S. Producers Only)

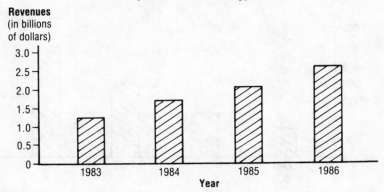

Estimated compound annual growth rate: 22.5 percent

Projected Market Growth of
Semiconductor Interconnect Products

(U.S. Producers Only)

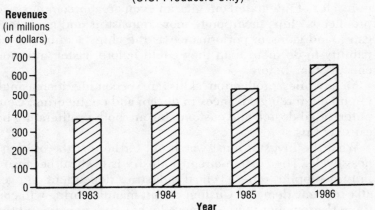

Estimated compound annual growth rate: 20 percent

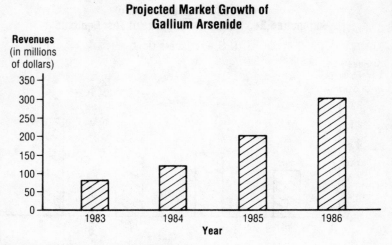

Projected Market Growth of Gallium Arsenide

Revenues (in millions of dollars)

Estimated compound annual growth rate: 55 percent

Note: The production process for gallium arsenide is still problem-plagued, so the market projections are tentative at best.

ually opening for new ventures in small, fast-growing segments of the industry. We have included five market projections for areas that are attractive from an investor's viewpoint, although gallium-arsenide technology will not offer much of an investment opportunity for another year or two. The projected markets depend for their growth on an increase in the unit sales of integrated circuits, an even greater complexity of product as chips incorporate more transistors and more logic gates, and gains in performance as the chips acquire the capability to do more than they could before, faster and more cheaply than before.

Meanwhile, production skills are becoming increasingly important, forcing advances in design and engineering. Computer-aided design and customizing are both proliferating because of this.

What the investor must watch out for here is the old business cycle. The custom-circuit industry is cyclical because it in turn supplies other cyclical industries dependent on overall economic demand. Custom-circuit manufacturing will continue to grow, but there will be a lot of oscillation around that upward curve.

Invest in the financially strong companies with good track records. Management skills are crucial in the custom-circuit industry. The production-equipment companies tend to be the cheapest buys in relation to earnings, the interconnect suppliers are the runners-up, and the automatic-tester firms are the most expensive. Keeping this perspective on the industry, the high-risk investor may see good opportunities for profit at times when the differences among these three market segments are temporarily exaggerated or, alternatively, inverted by the marketplace. For example, in a strong market, if the stocks of production-equipment and interconnect companies have risen smartly while those for automatic-test-equipment suppliers have not kept pace, the latter might be a good buy. Overall company and economic conditions must also be considered, of course, before a final purchasing decision is made.

KEY COMPANIES

Applied Materials, Inc.
3050 Bowers Avenue
Santa Clara, CA 95051
Telephone: (408) 727-5555
Contact: Gary Robertson
        Market: OTC
        Symbol: AMAT
Specializing in production equipment, Applied Materials leads in chemical-vapor deposition systems for semiconductor manufacture. It has had indigestion since the 1981 acquisition of Cobilt, but should look less bilious in 1983.

Augat, Inc.
P.O. Box 448, 89 Forbes Boulevard
Mansfield, MA 02048
Telephone: (617) 543-4300
Contact: Gerald Barrett, Executive Vice-President
        Market: NYSE
        Symbol: AUG

Augat has stayed on top of the evolving semiconductor-circuit-interconnect field better than anyone. Even its earnings setbacks are graceful.

Cherry Electrical Products Corporation
3600 Sunset Avenue
Waukegan, IL 60087
Telephone: (312) 689-7600
Contact: W. L. Cherry, Chief Executive Officer
     Market: OTC
     Symbol: CHER
This company is a manufacturer of electronic and electromechanical components, mostly switches. Its custom-circuit operations are small in relation to its total production.

Data I/O Corporation
10525 Willows Road, NE
Redmond, WA 98052
Telephone: (206) 881-6444
Contact: Larry Mayhew, Chief Executive Officer
     Market: OTC
     Symbol: DAIO
Data I/O, an automatic-test-equipment supplier, is the leader in programmable read-only memory (PROM) integrated-circuit test and programming systems. It shares the market with Pro-Log, a private company.

GCA Corporation
209 Burlington Road
Bedford, MA 01730
Telephone: (617) 275-9000
Contact: W. R. Davidson
     Market: NYSE
     Symbol: GCA
GCA led the production equipment field in wafer-stepping devices for semiconductor manufacture. It's had trouble finding an encore in the recession.

GenRad, Inc.
300 Baker Avenue
Concord, MA 01742
Telephone: (617) 369-4400

Contact: R. F. McNulty, telephone (617) 890-4900
       Market: NYSE
       Symbol: GEN

An automatic-test-equipment leader, GenRad has been trying to do a lot at once, and it was showing the strain during 1980 and 1981. Things look better now.

KLA Instruments Corporation

2051 Mission College Boulevard
Santa Clara, CA 95054
Telephone: (408) 988-6100
Contact: Kenneth Levy, President
       Market: OTC
       Symbol: KLAC

KLA Instruments, a production-equipment manufacturer, specializes in automated electro-optical photomask inspection systems, used in the making of very large-scale integrated circuits (VLSIs).

Kulicke and Soffa Industries, Inc.

507 Prudential Road
Horsham, PA 19044
Telephone: (215) 674-2800
Contact: Martin Weiss, Senior Vice-President
       Market: OTC
       Symbol: KLIC

Another production-equipment supplier, this one leads the world in the manufacture of the wire bonders used to connect semiconductor chips to the package leads. Changes in circuit packaging will give this company opportunity and risk.

LTX Corporation

145 University Avenue
Westwood, MA 02090
Telephone: (617) 329-7550
Contact: Barbara Katzen
       Market: OTC
       Symbol: LTXX

LTX concentrates on linear-circuit automatic-test equipment. The modularity and flexibility of its product line have given it an early market lead.

Machine Technology
20 Leslie Court
Whippany, NJ 07981
Telephone: (201) 386-0600
Contact: Gary Hillman, Chief Executive Officer
        Market: OTC
        Symbol: MTEC

Machine Technology makes the Omnichuck, a quite successful high-productivity silicon-wafer handling station used on the production line. The firm's main competition is from Silicon Valley Group, which recently went public.

Matrix Science Corporation
455 Maple Avenue
Torrance, CA 90503
Telephone: (213) 328-0271
Contact: John MacQueen, Vice-President
        Market: OTC
        Symbol: MTRX

A supplier of interconnect devices, Matrix specializes in connectors for aerospace and other demanding environments where the use of custom circuits is increasing.

Micro Mask, Inc.
695 Vaqueros Avenue
Sunnyvale, CA 94086
Telephone: (408) 245-7342
Contact: Joseph Ross, President
        Market: OTC
        Symbol: MCRO

Photomasks and hard-surface photoplates, used in the manufacture of integrated circuits, are Micro Mask's forte in semiconductor production equipment.

Molex, Inc.
2222 Wellington Court
Lisle, IL 60532
Telephone: (312) 969-4550
Contact: J. C. Psalts, Treasurer
        Market: OTC
        Symbol: MOLX

The growing sophistication of consumer electrical and electronic products plus timely entry into the Japanese market have made investors happy with the controlling Krehbiels' domination of this interconnect-devices producer.

Monolithic Memories, Inc.
1165 East Arques Avenue
Sunnyvale, CA 94086
Telephone: (408) 739-3535
Contact: William Wall
            Market: OTC
            Symbol: MMIC
Two-thirds memory and one-third logic products, this company is still three-thirds risk as it tries to build to economic size for its programmable-array logic and other custom-circuit goodies.

Silicon Systems, Inc.
14351 Myford Road
Tustin, CA 92680
Telephone: (714) 731-7110
Contact: L. J. Alves, Vice-President of Finance
            Market: OTC
            Symbol: SLCN
Silicon Systems has a proprietary computer-aided design (CAD) system, which is its primary competitive weapon in the custom-circuit business.

Silicon Valley Group, Inc.
3901 Burton Drive
Santa Clara, CA 95054
Telephone: (408) 988-0200
Contact: Gerald Starek, President
            Market: OTC
            Symbol: SVGI
Silicon Valley Group is a semiconductor production equipment manufacturer specializing in automated wafer handling and production processing stations.

Siltec Corporation
3717 Haven Avenue
Menlo Park, CA 94025

Telephone: (415) 365-8600
Contact: T. M. Hansell, Treasurer
    Market: OTC
    Symbol: SLTC

A player on high-volume demand for semiconductor wafers, Siltec has plenty of competition from other semiconductor-production-equipment companies.

Standard Microsystems Corporation

35 Marcus Boulevard
Hauppauge, NY 11788
Telephone: (516) 273-3100
Contact: Paul Richman, President
    Market: OTC
    Symbol: SMSC

This custom-circuit supplier has lots of proprietary technology, which is starting to pay off.

Teradyne, Inc.

183 Essex Street
Boston, MA 02111
Telephone: (617) 482-2700
Contact: Fred Van Veen
    Market: NYSE
    Symbol: TER

Teradyne has more competition than it had before in the field of automatic test equipment for electronics manufacturing, but it still leads in several areas.

Tylan Corporation

19220 South Normandie Avenue
Torrance, CA 90502
Telephone: (213) 532-3420
Contact: E. A. Maginnis, Jr., Vice-President of Finance
    Market: OTC
    Symbol: TYLN

A production-equipment manufacturer, Tylan is a leading supplier of the controllers used on semiconductor diffusion furnaces. It also makes the furnaces.

Varian Associates, Inc.

611 Hansen Way
Palo Alto, CA 94303

Telephone: (415) 493-4000
Contact: C. A. Tabor, Treasurer
Market: NYSE
Symbol: VAR

Contrary to the rest of the semiconductor-production-equipment manufacturers in particular, and electronics manufacturers in general, Varian had a swell 1981–1982. Will its success continue?

VLSI Technology, Inc.

1101 McKay Drive
San Jose, CA 95131
Telephone: (408) 942-1810
Contact: Kenneth Goldman, Chief Financial Officer
Market: OTC
Symbol: VLSI

This custom and semi-custom chip designer sells chips and software for chip design. It was heavily dependent on the home video game market in 1982, and was in the red.

XICOR, Inc.

851 Buckeye Court
Milpitas, CA 95035
Telephone: (408) 946-6920
Contact: Raphael Klein, President
Market: OTC
Symbol: XICO

XICOR started as an EAROM producer (electrically alterable read-only memories) and sales have been on a steep climb. Profits are planned to follow.

LEADING ANALYSTS

Timothy Allen and Jay Cooper
F. Eberstadt and Company, Inc.
61 Broadway
New York, NY 10006
Telephone: (212) 480-1391 and (212) 480-0892

Timothy Allen specializes in semiconductor-production-equipment suppliers, Jay Cooper in automatic-test-equipment manufacturers.

Richard Chu and Alan Rieper
Cowen and Company
28 State Street
Boston, MA 02109
Telephone: (212) 785-6000 and (617) 523-3221
Richard Chu covers interconnect products; Alan Rieper covers semiconductor-custom-circuit producers.

Blake Downing
Robertson, Colman and Stephens
100 California Street
San Francisco, CA 94111
Telephone: (415) 781-9700
    Blake Downing is a custom-circuits expert.

John Gruber
Montgomery Securities
235 Montgomery Street
San Francisco, CA 94104
Telephone: (415) 989-2050
John Gruber follows production-equipment companies.

Mike Krasko and Tom Kurlak
Merrill Lynch, Inc.
One Liberty Plaza, 165 Broadway
New York, NY 10080
Telephone: (212) 637-8144 and (212) 637-8146
Mike Krasko and Tom Kurlak keep track of a broad list of electronics companies, including semiconductor-custom-circuit, production-equipment, and connector-product suppliers.

    John Lazlo and Garry Stone
Hambrecht and Quist, Inc.
235 Montgomery Street
San Francisco, CA 94104
Telephone: (415) 986-5500
John Lazlo follows custom circuits and interconnection products. Gary Stone covers automatic test equipment.

PERTINENT PUBLICATIONS

Electronics
McGraw-Hill
1221 Avenue of the Americas
New York, NY 10020
Telephone: (609) 448-8110
    Subscription: $19 per year to qualified subscribers
                (check with the publisher) for 26 issues
This more general publication provides some coverage of
the status of circuit development.

The Rosen Electronics Letter
Rosen Research, Inc.
200 Park Avenue
New York, NY 10166
Telephone: (212) 586-3530
    Subscription: $395 per year for irregular publication of
                roughly 25–30 issues per year
The Rosen letter provides broadly based and detailed coverage of the electronics industry, with special in-depth reports
on emerging industry segments. It also reports the proceed-
ings of the personal-computer and semiconductor-industry
forums sponsored in conjunction with the investment banking
firm of L. F. Rothschild, Unterberg, Towbin.

Status
Integrated Circuit Engineering Corporation
15022 North 75th Street
Scottsdale, AZ 85260
Telephone: (602) 998-9780
    Subscription: Not usually sold separately from the
                company's consulting service
Issued as *Status 1982, Status 1983,* and so on, the year
appearing as part of the title, this report on the integrated-
circuit industry is made available to institutional clients by
several brokers, and you may be able to wheedle a copy. It
offers a good summary of the entire industry and trends, both
technical and business.

VLSI Design
Redwood Systems Group P.O. Box 50503
Palo Alto, CA 94303
Telephone: (415) 966-8340
   Subscription: $19.95 per year for quarterly periodical
Technically oriented, *VLSI Design* covers all aspects of integrated circuits—computer architecture, design, strategies, costs, and so on—and their interrelations.

MAJOR MEETINGS

International Electron Devices Meeting
Courtest Associates
1629 K Street, NW
Washington, DC 20006
Telephone: (202) 296-8100
This assembly on electronics devices meets each December in a major Eastern city. Melissa Widerkehr of the sponsoring firm can give you details.

International Solid State Circuits Conference
The Institute of Electrical and Electronic Engineers, Inc.
345 East 47th Street
New York, NY 10017
Telephone: (212) 644-7555
Held in a major city, usually an Eastern one, in February of each year, the International Solid State Circuits Conference (ISSCC) is the one to attend if you want to find out about new developments in integrated circuits, including custom chips. But it's fairly technical.

Semicon/East and Semicon/West
Semiconductor Equipment and Materials Institute
625 Ellis Street, Suite 212
Mountain View, CA 94043
Telephone: (415) 964-5111
Semicon/East convenes every September, usually in Boston. Semicon/West is held each March, in the Los Angeles area. These conventions provide good insight into the automatic-test-equipment and production-test-equipment end of the semiconductor business.

PROFESSIONAL ASSOCIATIONS

Semiconductor Industry Association (SIA)
20380 Town Center Lane, Suite 155
Cupertino, CA 95014
Telephone: (408) 255-3522
Periodic meetings on topics of industry interest such as out-look, Japanese competition, and so on will cost you a few dollars. But they give you a chance to meet industry biggies over drinks, dinner.

XII

Personal Computers: Looking Beyond the Razor and Blade Market

One of the hottest high-tech fields around is the revolutionary realm of personal computers. In some ways, this one may be a field too hot to handle. Besides, IBM recently joined the fray, which may signal the end of the revolution—at least for investors. But there are numerous ongoing peripheral skirmishes well worth looking into.

Historically—and the history of personal computers begins in 1975—manufacturers did what they could to prod consumers into buying home computers. Their efforts were unsuccessful. Price, chaotic distribution, and an inevitable "What can I do with it?" challenge kept microcomputers behind the starting gate. Then suddenly, between 1980 and 1982, video-game mania swept the nation, and the notion of a personal computer no longer seemed farfetched. After all, one of the new low-price computers didn't cost much more than one of the high-priced video-game systems. At the same time, the business applications, and thus the acceptance of personal computers, broadened from the domain of stockbrokerage to the affairs of accountants, attorneys, farmers, and even the local automobile-parts supplier.

The microcomputer race broke into full stride when prices dropped and mass marketers like J. C. Penney, Sears, Toys "R" Us, and the stereo-equipment stores, whose sales were being hurt by video games, began to promote the new computers—as if they were toasters or portable radios. Computers aren't, of course, and in the long run, the intervention of these sales outlets may well mean a lot of machines joining the CBs and radio scanners gathering dust in the nation's closets.

For now, the unit growth of personal computer sales is over 100 percent per year in the under-$3,000-retail-price category. As the market explodes, moreover, competition and price slashing are eroding the market shares of Apple, Commodore, and Tandy, the early leaders.

Part of the initial dominance of this triumvirate was due to the availability of their software. Software, the programs that actually make computers do something, is machine-specific. That is, Apple programs can't run on, say, a Commodore computer without being modified. But all three of these leaders in the microcomputer cabal had a reasonably strong software base, with Apple the clear commander in that it encouraged outside vendors to develop programs for its machines.

Software houses have undergone a success explosion of their own. They're now busy matching their existing materials to all of the most popular computers, including any newcomers that appear to be on their way to volume sales. At the same time, of course, they are continuing to develop further applications software for home, education, and small business, all of it matched to most of the large new entries as well as the old leaders.

This means that the software edge Apple, Commodore, and Tandy had can no longer be counted on, particularly considering the entry into the micro field of big blue IBM and other heavies such as Digital Equipment Corporation, Hewlett Packard, and Wang. Furthermore, as well as these large, old-line computer makers may do in this particular market segment, personal computers will not add enough to the bottom line in their case to justify a buy by investors on that basis alone.

The other side of the competition coin is the hardware emulators like Franklin Computer Corporation. Franklin's ACE 1000 is an unabashed imitation of an Apple; not only is its hardware and software compatible with the Apple, but it is equipped with more memory as well (64K to the 48K of the Apple II Plus). It features lowercase in addition to uppercase letters, VisiCalc keys, and a separate numeric pad. It has the same general shape and tan color that the Apple has. It's more performance for the same money.

With this kind of fierce—some would say "rotten to the

core"—competition, there's bound to be a hardware shakeout and consolidation in the personal-computer industry by 1984. More than a hundred personal-computer manufacturers, with seventy-three brand-new models to introduce, exhibited their wares at the big Hanover Fair in 1982.

Odds, as usual in the marketplace, favor the strong, the aggressive, the clever. Apple, Digital Equipment Corporation, Hewlett Packard, IBM, Tandy, and Wang are among the most likely to survive in the personal-computer field. Slightly weaker but still apt to make it, at least in specialized niches, is a much larger group of companies, including Altos, Convergent Technologies, Commodore, Corvus Systems, Cromemco (a privately held company), NorthStar (another private company), Osborne (also private), Sinclair (private), and Texas Instruments.

Looking at the number of enterprises in this industry segment that are still private, you'll no doubt sniff opportunity. And it's there. Some of these companies, like Osborne, may have already sold stock by the time you read our list. Fortune Systems, GRID Systems (private), and TeleVideo are other lights radiating opportunity—if, like so many of the private software suppliers, they aren't bought out first. Commanding a continuing market share in the face of ever-increasing competition is a real problem, since resolving distribution difficulties brings new problems of service and maintenance. Personal computers are now fighting for shelf space in the stores like so many brands of dog food.

About the only bright light in the competitively over-crowded personal-computer picture is shining from Japan. Japan, Inc.'s juggernaut has so far been unable to conquer the world of personal computers in the way that it conquered television, stereo equipment, watches, and cameras. In fact, the first wave of its microcomputer invasion never got up the beach. Japanese personal computers, for the moment at least, are software-poor and lack distribution and innovation.

The situation could change, of course. NEC, which controls 40 percent of the almost-$400-million-in-sales Japanese personal-computer market, is launching its second-wave attack complete with lots and lots of applications software—IBM's, in fact. NEC has designed its new machine to be "completely compatible" with the IBM Personal Computer, with a few added bells and whistles.

If it is risky to invest in razors (the computers) and razor blades (the software), where is the money to be made? Most likely in shaving soap, kit bags, and mirrors (the support equipment). Even here the competition is fierce, albeit much less publicized overall.

The one area that seems to be garnering at least mild media attention is the opening of software-only stores to complement the hardware retailers such as ComputerLand. In fact, ComputerLand plans to have its franchise holders open satellite shops specializing in software.

The market comparison usually made has been between hardware versus software vendors and stereo equipment versus record shops. That analogy may be less than accurate, in that software stores will probably need a lot more customer support than a record shop does. Sure, there will be "Top Fifty" charts of software—*Variety* even now is listing the best-seller computer games each week—but for complicated business systems such ratings will not be enough to sell the product.

Customers in search of specific solutions to particular problems will need handholding, which means that something will have to be done about the personnel shortage. Bookstores and record shops depend on cheap, not particularly savvy sales clerks. Software shops are going to need skilled workers. Not only will such a staff be difficult to find, but payroll costs will be very high for a retail type of operation.

Nonetheless, Future Computing, Inc., a Texas-based consulting firm, predicts the opening of some 1,600 software-only stores by 1986, and Wall Street has not let this possible trend pass it by. Programs Unlimited, a software-specialty-store company that went public at $1 a share in 1979, more than doubled in price during the span of one month—with only two stores in actual operation.

The software market is difficult to define. But annual sales are projected to reach nearly $5 billion by 1986, according to some, perhaps overly optimistic, sources. That means someone, somewhere, is going to delineate both the market and the distribution process properly. One possible form already in evidence includes software wholesalers such as privately owned Softsel, and publishers such as Software Publishing (also private). Keep your eyes open, as the growth of software distribution can only be explosive.

Computer support goes beyond software and its distribution, of course. Buyers can be expected to upgrade their personal computers on an almost continual basis. In a way, personal computers are adult Barbie dolls, and peripherals the available wardrobe accessories. Once you have one outfit, you need another and another and another. . . .

First the customer buys the basic computer, with its keyboard, video monitor, and probably a disk drive. Soon thereafter the indispensability of a printer becomes obvious, as does the usefulness of a telephone modem, the nicety of upgrading the monitor for color, the fun of a speech synthesizer, the necessity for a second disk drive, and the convenience of a hard-disk drive. Then there's . . . but you get the idea.

Without covering all the myriad accessory categories, let's look at what may well be the most important one, namely, memory—not the processing memory contained in the computer itself, although even there the basic rule is that you never have enough memory, but archival memory, the auxiliary memory in which programs arrive and data is stored. Archival memory for the personal computer falls primarily into three categories: tape, floppy disks, and hard disks.

Tape, via cassette recorder, the storage medium generally used by the lowest-price-range computers (the under-$300 models such as Commodore's VIC 20), is dying because of its poor-quality recording and agonizingly slow speed. It will linger on for a while longer, but don't expect any new companies to make money in this shriveling market.

Floppy disks, those soft little plastic platters people shove into their personal computers' disk drives, are another story. Small disks record information more densely these days. Their storage capacity is thus actually greater than that of their larger and older counterparts—a strange situation in the normal world but par for the course in electronics. Increased capacity, of course, means that buyers want the latest, most compact and capacious memory system. Add to this the fact that the incredible shrinking disk points an unmistakable finger toward a truly portable, pocket-sized personal computer, and future demand seems certain to repeat today's 30 percent growth rate for disk drives and greater than 100 percent growth rate for the disks themselves.

At the same time, hard-disk prices, once a multiple of the price of the computer itself, are tumbling. A $4,000 system in 1981 was $2,000 in 1982 and will be under $1,000 by the end of 1983. Winchester disks, the most common form of hard memory media, have become a major market force, and a new breed of cartridge Winchester disks, each equivalent in memory capacity to thirty or more floppy disks, may be ready to pick up the pace once standard Winchesters have made their mark in the personal-computer marketplace.

A number of public companies are making their mark in the mass-memory-storage area. Another host of still-privates, including Iomega, Morrow, Priam, and Rand Systems in the disk-drive field and Archive, Dastek, and Data Electronics in Winchester-related systems, are about to make their splash—perhaps going public as they do.

The personal-computer field needs to be watched in its entirety. After investigating it, you may decide that software is the arena of the future. But that doesn't mean you can stop following the game of the hardware manufacturers or the peripherals. Computers, after all, are where the software is going to be used. Conversely, even if your primary investment focus is on hardware, you need to keep an eye on software development, or you may end up investing in something like the fabled Sol—an excellent machine, from now-defunct Processor Technology, with nothing to do.

INDUSTRY INVESTMENT DIRECTIONS

The market for personal computers is going to be a huge one, measured in tens of billions of dollars. There will be plenty of ways to make money. The worst pitfall for an investor is to have tunnel vision, to assume there's only one way to invest, and thus miss many opportunities.

Marketing will be the key company skill to look for, since the basic technology is already well established. What a company needs to do is to expand its market share by making its computers attractive to the largest possible number of potential users. Invest in companies dominated by business people

Projected Market Growth of
Personal Computers

(Priced Under $10,000 Retail)

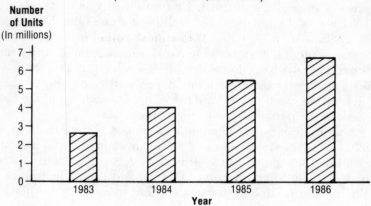

**Number
of Units**
(In millions)

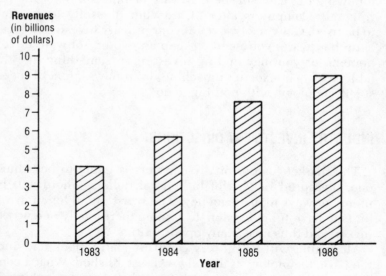

Revenues
(in billions
of dollars)

Estimated compound annual growth rate: 30 percent

Note: These figures exclude separate disk drives, printers, and software, but include monitors and integral drives.

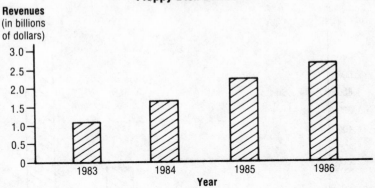

**Projected Market Growth of
3½-Inch and 5¼-Inch Winchester and
Floppy Disk Drives**

Revenues
(in billions
of dollars)

Year

Estimated compound annual growth rate: 35 percent

who do all the mundane things right—planning, financial control, service, and so on—and who focus their products and sales on manageable target niches.

The personal-computer market as a whole will become more and more segmented. The hardware will become cheaper, but the cost of acquiring a computer system won't, because the concomitant software, increasing in complexity and performance, will keep prices for business solutions in the range of $1,000 to $3,000 for the next few years. Software, unlike most high-tech products, continually becomes more expensive as it is refined and improved. An additional reason why systems prices won't plummet is that the costs of distribution will remain high. Distribution is both crucial and not easily subjected to cost cutting. It may also be an area of likely investment profit, particularly if the software distributors now evolving go public.

The largest individual markets—those for the portable and desktop general-purpose computers, printers, drives for the 5¼-inch disks, and the media, or the disks themselves—will attract a lot of competition. In these market areas, low-cost production will be important, if not vital. Watch out for the Japanese in such manufacturing-oriented markets. Eventually they will become better and tougher.

Projected Market Growth of Magnetic Media, Hard and Floppy Disks

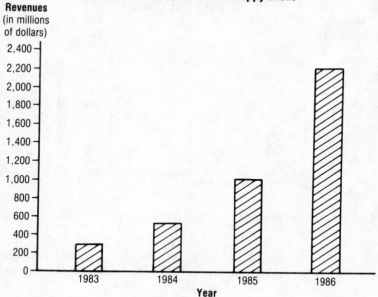

Revenues
(in millions
of dollars)

Estimated compound annual growth rate: 100 percent

KEY COMPANIES

Altos Computer Systems
2360 Bering Drive
San Jose, CA 95131
Telephone: (408) 946-6700
Contact: David Zacarias, Vice-President of Finance
Market: OTC
Symbol: ALTO

Altos makes a multiterminal microcomputer system which competes with those of Convergent Technologies and Corvus Systems.

Apollo Computer, Inc.
15 Elizabeth Drive
Chelmsford, MA 01824

Telephone: (617) 256-6600
Contact: David Lubrano, Chief Financial Officer
     Market: OTC
     Symbol: APCI

They aren't priced as low as personal computers, but Apollo's scientific- and engineering-oriented systems could have a major impact on minis and a significant networking potential.

Apple Computer

10260 Bandley Drive
Cupertino, CA 95014
Telephone: (408) 996-1010
Contact: Fred Hoar, Vice-President of Corporate
     Communications, telephone (408) 973-3446
     Market: OTC
     Symbol: AAPL

The successful introduction of new products in 1983 is Apple's lever in reestablishing its winner image. Advance news indicates that it's doing the job well. The company has a full line of personal computers from top to mid/low in price and performance.

Cipher Data Products, Inc.

10225 Willow Creek Road
San Diego, CA 92131
Telephone: (714) 578-9100
Contact: Robert Wall, Vice-President of Finance
     Market: OTC
     Symbol: CIFR

A manufacturer of backup storage systems for Winchester magnetic disk drives, Cipher Data Products also makes other tape drives. The company looked like a solution in search of a problem for a while, but it is coming along well under new management.

Commodore International

3330 Scott Boulevard
Santa Clara, CA 95050
Telephone: (408) 337-7100
     and

950 Rittenhouse Road
Norristown, PA 19403
Telephone: (215) 666-7950
Contact: S. A. Greenberg, telephone (212) 246-1000
　　　　Market: NYSE
　　　　Symbol: CBU

Commodore is strong in Europe, weak in the United States. However, its newer personal computers, particularly those on the lower end of the price scale, are becoming stronger in the United States marketplace. Distribution is the company's weak point, and management turnover is a potential problem.

Computer and Communications Technology

495 South Fairview Avenue
Santa Barbara, CA 93017
Telephone: (805) 964-0771
Contact: Everett Bahre, President
　　　　Market: OTC
　　　　Symbol: CCTC

One of the three main manufacturers of magnetic heads for computer disk and tape drives, this company is developing a removable Winchester drive (the Winchesters presently in use are nonremovable). But it's always tough to innovate. Computer manufacturers are conservative.

Convergent Technologies, Inc.

2500 Augustine Drive
Santa Clara, CA 95051
Telephone: (408) 727-8830
Contact: M. E. Newman, Treasurer
　　　　Market: OTC
　　　　Symbol: CVGT

Strictly a seller of computer systems to other manufacturers such as Burroughs and NCR, Convergent Technologies sells at a very fancy price considering that it has such wobbly customers.

Corvus Systems, Inc.

2029 O'Toole Avenue
San Jose, CA 95131
Telephone: (408) 946-7700

Contact: C. W. Dougherty, Vice-President of Finance
Market: OTC
Symbol: CRVS

Networking personal computers together is a cherished dream of organizations that have more than one or two. It would facilitate interoffice electronic memoranda and peripheral and data-base sharing and control. The early network prototypes are interesting, and one public play is Corvus's personal-computer workstation plus magnetic storage peripherals and networking products. The company's reliance on distributors for coverage is a departure from the practice of its main competitors, and that dependency may limit volume economies.

Dysan Corporation

5440 Patrick Henry Drive
Santa Clara, CA 05050
Telephone: (408) 988-3742
Contact: George Farinsky, Treasurer
Market: OTC
Symbol: DYSN

Suffering from an earlier overdose of research and development, Dysan needs to establish a consistent profit record in its chosen field of magnetic media. Otherwise, it's a promising company. Dysan has expanded its profit horizons by investing in several related private firms plus Seagate, a Winchester-disk-drive company.

Emulex Corporation

2001 East Deere Avenue
Santa Ana, CA 92705
Telephone: (714) 557-7580
Contact: Malcolm Green, Executive Vice-President
Market: OTC
Symbol: EMLX

Emulex manufactures high-performance magnetic-disk storage systems and controllers for Digital Equipment and other manufacturers' minicomputers. It's a good idea, so long as Digital Equipment and the others can't or won't meet demand for these products. Emulex has prospered because of a shrewd blend of technology and marketing.

National Micronetics
5600 Kearny Mesa Road
San Diego, CA 92111
Telephone: (714) 279-7500
Contact: Ned Buoymaster, President
   Market: OTC
   Symbol: NMIC

Another major manufacturer of magnetic heads for computer disk and tape drives, National Micronetics vies with Computer and Communications Technology for the attention of the market. Applied Magnetics is traditionally first in the field, but supplies slower-growing users.

Onyx + IMI
25 East Trimble Road
San Jose, CA 95131
Telephone: (408) 946-6330
Contact: Michael Spies
   Market: OTC
   Symbol: ONIX

Formerly Dorado Microsystems, Onyx + IMI supplies personal-computer manufacturers with drives, as well as offering a personal-computer system of its own. The company shares a common ownership with Corvus Systems.

Quantum Corporation
1804 McCarthy Boulevard
Milpitas, CA 95035
Telephone: (408) 262-1100
Contact: Joseph Rodgers, Vice-President of Finance
   Market: OTC
   Symbol: QNTM

Quantum makes 8-inch and 5¼-inch rigid-disk drives used with office automation systems and computers.

Seagate Technology
369 El Pueblo Road
Scotts Valley, CA 95066
Telephone: (408) 438-6550

Contact: Richard Certo, Vice-President of Finance
　　　　　Market: OTC
　　　　　Symbol: SGAT

The leading supplier of Winchester disk drives for personal computers, Seagate Technology employs a middle-of-the-product-line strategy that looks vulnerable over time, given its lack of real product differentiation.

System Industries, Inc.

525 Oakmead Parkway
Sunnyvale, CA 94086
Telephone: (408) 732-1650
Contact: R. L. Henander, Vice-President of Finance
　　　　　Market: OTC
　　　　　Symbol: SYSM

System Industries has the same script as Emulex Corporation, but Emulex has done it better.

Tandon Corporation

20320 Prairie Street
Chatsworth, CA 91311
Telephone: (213) 993-6644
Contact: Gerry Lembas, Senior Vice-President
　　　　　Market: OTC
　　　　　Symbol: TCOR

A leader in floppy-disk drives for personal computers, and coming up fast in Winchesters, Tandon employs the strategy of penetrating a large original equipment manufacturer (OEM) base with high volume in order to retain its position as a dominant supplier.

Televideo Systems, Inc.

1170 Morse Avenue
Sunnyvale, CA 94086
Telephone: (408) 745-7760
Contact: Richard DuBridge, Chief Financial Officer
　　　　　Market: OTC
　　　　　Symbol: TELV

Televideo makes video terminals and microcomputer systems in large quantities and at low prices. Its forte is manufacturing for distributors and OEMs.

Vector Graphic
31364 Via Colinas
Westlake Village, CA 91362
Telephone: (213) 991-2302
Contact: Loré Harp, President
  Market: OTC
  Symbol: VCTR

Management turmoil and the crunch of being crowded by IBM hurt Vector Graphic badly in 1982. Can it stage a comeback? Its personal computers are right in the middle of the price/performance spectrum.

Verbatim Corporation
323 Soquel Way
Sunnyvale, CA 94086
Telephone: (408) 245-4400
Contact: W. L. Carter, Chief Financial Officer
  Market: ASE
  Symbol: VRB

A major floppy-disk producer, Verbatim had quality-control problems a while ago, but it's back on track. Whether its innovation and new-product development are adequate is unclear, but it leads the industry now.

Wespercorp
14321 New Myford Road
Tustin, CA 92680
Telephone: (714) 730-6250
Contact: John Karsten, Executive Vice-President
  Market: ASE
  Symbol: WP

Describing itself as a supplier of "betweenput" devices, Wespercorp makes controllers for computer peripheral storage devices.

Xidex Corporation
2141 Landings Drive
Mountain View, CA 94043
Telephone: (415) 965-7350

Contact: Gary Filler, Vice-President of Finance
　　　　Market: OTC
　　　　Symbol: XIDX

Dominant in duplicating microfilm, with the majority share of the market worldwide, Xidex is now entering the disk-media-coating market. That's risky indeed. But it looks as if the company will pull it off. What Xidex really needs is a faster-growing market in which to invest all the microfilm cash.

LEADING ANALYSTS

Donald Brown
Prudential/Bache
100 Gold Street
New York, NY 10038
Telephone: (212) 791-2946
　　Mini- and microcomputers are the focus of this analyst.

Joan McKay
Kidder, Peabody and Company, Inc.
10 Hanover Square
New York, NY 10025
Telephone: (212) 747-2732
Joan McKay covers large personal-computer companies only.

Michele Preston
Cyrus J. Lawrence, Inc.
115 Broadway
New York, NY 10006
Telephone: (212) 962-2200
　　The focus is on the consumer.

Dan Reeve
Cowen and Company
28 State Street
Boston, MA 02109
Telephone: (617) 523-3221
　　Dan Reeve covers the large personal-computer companies.

Bruce Seltzer
Hambrecht and Quist
235 Montgomery Street
San Francisco, CA 94104
Telephone: (415) 986-5500
   Peripherals, mainly magnetic, are Bruce Seltzer's specialty.

Peter Wright
Gartner Group, Inc.
72 Cummings Point Road
Stamford, CT 06902
Telephone: (203) 964-0096
   Peter Wright follows the whole personal-computer field.

PERTINENT PUBLICATIONS

Computer Business News
CW Communications, Inc.
Box 880, 375 Cochituate Road
Framingham, MA 01701
Telephone: (617) 879-0700, (800) 343-6474 for
   subscriptions
   Subscription: $25 per year for 50 issues
Targeted for original equipment manufacturers (OEMs) in
orientation, *Computer Business News* isn't a bad publication
to peruse if you are an investor, since so many other periodicals are *user*-oriented; this one gives more information on big
developments and trends.

Computerworld
(For address and telephone, see *Computer Business News*,
   above)
   Subscription: $36 per year for weekly newspaper
Computerworld is the weekly analog of *Datamation*. It runs
to 150 pages, with wall-to-wall coverage. You don't really
need it if you get all the others—but maybe you'd rather have
this one and skip the others.

Datamation
Technical Publishing Company
875 Third Avenue

New York, NY 10022
Telephone: (212) 489-2588
   Subscription: $40 per year for 13 issues
The granddaddy of the field, *Datamation* is, like the National Computer Conference (NCC), overwhelming. A survey issue comes out in June, and the publication as a whole covers a wide range of issues, concerns, and topics, from personal computers to telecommunications-related developments.

Infoworld
Popular Computing, Inc.
Box 880, 375 Cochituate Road
Framingham, MA 01701
Telephone: (800) 343-6474, in Massachusetts
   (617) 879-0700
   Subscription: $25 per year for 51 issues
A weekly focused on microcomputer users and interests, *Infoworld* carries software-review articles plus news on hardware and technology.

Mini Micro Systems
Cahners Publishing Company
221 Columbus Avenue
Boston, MA 02116
Telephone: (617) 536-7780
   Subscription: $35 per year for monthly periodical
Mini Micro is good for personal computers and office automation. Special issues in 1982 were devoted to office automation (May), small-business computers (June), graphics (July). The magazine's coverage is aimed at users and sellers of minicomputer- and microcomputer-based systems.

Rosen Electronics Letter
Rosen Research, Inc.
200 Park Avenue
New York, NY 10166
Telephone: (212) 586-3530
   Subscription: $395 per year for roughly 25–30 issues
                  (irregular)
The best topical gossip sheet in the trade, Rosen's letter is also the most fun to read.

In addition to these publications, check your newsstand for the general-interest personal-computing magazines: *BYTE, Creative Computing, Interface Age, Personal Computing,* and *Popular Computing. BYTE* is the biggest and most technical; the ads give you an idea of where the market is going. Every upcoming personal-computer company advertises in *BYTE.* Vendor-dedicated magazines are available, too: IBM, Apple, etc.

MAJOR MEETINGS

COMDEX
Interface Group
166 Speen Street
Framingham, MA 01701
Telephone: (800) 225-4620
Now that it's on a twice-a-year schedule, COMDEX convenes late in November or early in December in Las Vegas and again in Atlantic City in the late spring. Geared towards distributors, retailers, and third parties (systems integrators who put together vendor systems), COMDEX has rapidly become *the* personal-computer show, because this is the place to sign up distributors.

National Computer Conference
American Federation of Information-Processing Societies
   (AFIPS)
1815 North Lynn Street
Arlington, VA 22209
Telephone: (703) 558-8617
The National Computer Conference (NCC) boasts an overwhelming crush of more than eighty thousand attendees. It takes several days just to walk around and look at it all. Here you can find everything computer-related, from big/little to hard/software, from hotdogs to magazines. Don't go if you tire easily. Worthwhile tutorial sessions provide relief from the walking. The convention rotates among major cities and lasts four days or so.

Personal Computer Forum
(For address and telephone, see *Rosen Electronics Letter,*
   under *Pertinent Publications,* above)

PROFESSIONAL ASSOCIATIONS

Association of Computer Users (ACU)
4800 Riverbend Road
P.O. Box 9003
Boulder, CO 80301
Telephone: (303) 443-3600
The Association of Computer Users has different sections by which it orients itself to its members according to the type of computer (large, small, home, hobby, word-processing, and so on) that they have. The association publishes *Interactive Computing*, the ACU bulletin, bimonthly. Membership is $60 per year per section. Additional sections cost $10 each.

Boston Computer Society
Three Center Plaza
Boston, MA 02108
Telephone: (617) 367-8080 or (617) 227-9178
Regular membership is $15 per year. Aimed at computer users, with interest groups classified by vendor, the Boston Computer Society also has robotics, education, and language sections. It's a good place to hear about trends, meet production people, find help. Nearly all large cities have groups like this—Boston's is just the best.

Institute of Electrical and Electronic Engineers (IEEE)
    Computer Society
345 East 47th Street
New York, NY 10017
Telephone: (212) 644-7555
Computer, published by the IEEE Computer Society twelve times a year, runs sophisticated articles on technical development.

XIII

Computer Graphics: A Picture Is Worth a Billion Bits

Computer graphics is an industry to which most people were first exposed with the release of the Walt Disney Productions' film *Tron* in 1982. The film turned out to be a box-office disappointment, but for computer-graphics buffs—and some unkind Hollywood observers maintain that they composed half the movie's audience—*Tron* was a triumph.

Computer-aided special effects had made an impression on Hollywood earlier, in such blockbusters as *Star Wars* and *Close Encounters of the Third Kind*. But never before had they been the single most essential ingredient of a film. *Tron* was filmed with the actors playing their minor parts on a darkened soundstage at Disney's Burbank studios. Then the Mathematical Applications Group and Information International computers took over, filling in the background and details. It took between five and twelve million digital calculations to generate a single frame. Multiply that by the 1,240 frames needed to produce but one minute of film, and you have some idea of the immense amount of computer time, energy, and memory involved in the project.

Memory and software are the particularly strategic components of any graphics system—including that of human perception. The precipitous price decline of computer memory over the past few years and its expected continuation on the same course for the foreseeable future augurs well for the graphics industry, particularly when one considers the degree to which computer graphics is a craft spawned by necessity. Data processing is currently spewing out so much information that the human mind—intended, after all, to be the end user—simply can't see the forest for the trees, or, in this particular instance, the facts for the information. By concentrating data into more readily accessible and assimilable pictures, graphics makes the information utilizable in less time.

A recent Wharton School of Business study on graphics showed that business managers could cut company time spent on meetings by 28 percent through data-to-graphics conversion. Graphics-supported presentations also reduced the time involved in the corporate decision-making process by 11 percent.

Even so, computer graphics has so far not reached the growth curve envisioned for it by the pundits. Labeled "a tool too useful to ignore" by developers, it has been ignored by buyers nonetheless. Currently, it trails the mainstream computer industry by somewhere between five and fifteen years, because graphics take up so much computer memory, which until recently was so expensive.

With the decline in memory prices, however, new graphics products should start making their way to market, which in turn should foster development of the requisite software lacking heretofore for want of hardware to run it on. Sometime during the electronic eighties, computer graphics will find its potential market. The decade will also witness the eventual market dominance of those companies which develop at least de facto standards and better systems integration. That dominance can spell great profits for investors who spot the emerging trend setters.

The lead area in computer graphics to date has been computer-aided design and computer-aided manufacturing (CAD/CAM). Here is where, fueled by inflation and productivity concerns, computer graphics began to make major inroads in the electronics, aerospace, and process industries, enterprises whose digitized data could be readily converted into computer-terminal screen pictures and drawings. The formerly highly labor-intensive representations could be continuously altered on the screen, rather than being painstakingly hand-drawn over and over again, as the designers' crucial "What if?" questions were iterated and the data changed. Unfortunately, the capital equipment spending markets dried up, parched by the no longer bearable interest rates levied on loans during the first years of the eighties. Buying withered likewise. Prices in the CAD/CAM sector of the graphics industry declined markedly, putting additional pressures on the established members of this infant industry segment.

Technology rushes on, however, and new approaches come

to the fore. Video-graphics-hardware companies and the crucial supporting software vendors are beginning to pop up faster than summer reruns do on the tube. So while sales are only crawling upward, customer equipment choices are exploding. Venture capitalists have funded nearly eighty companies in the video-graphics field over the last three years, and a host of not-yets waits in the wings, prepared to upstage the present industry leaders at the first opportunity. Some of the most interesting of these private graphics firms to keep your eyes on as they draw closer to going public include Chromatics, Integrated Software Systems, Summagraphics, and Vector General.

All video-graphics systems currently use one of three primary display technologies. Each of these technologies has its own cost/quality tradeoff in terms of price versus image detail, or resolution. The sharpness of an electronically produced image is defined in pixels, an abbreviation for "picture elements," the smallest units that can be turned on or off electronically on the screen. The more pixels the screen displays, the higher the quality of the image.

The maximum number of pixels to be found on an ordinary television set is 256 by 192, or a total of 49,152, give or take a couple around the edges of the screen. Something like IBM's Personal Computer, on the other hand, has a display of 640 by 200 pixels in its high-resolution mode, for a total of 128,000. Its visuals thus have much greater clarity. Ikonas' Raster Display System 3000, used for interactive three-dimensional modeling, seismic analysis, image processing, and animation, can be purchased with a screen accommodating 2,048 by 2,048 pixels, 4,194,304 altogether, while Vector Automation's Graphicus-80, employing what is known as vector refresh technology, displays a staggering 4,096 by 4,096 or 16,777,216 total, pixels per image.

The difference between the actual display technologies in use can be pictured in terms of the way an automobile windshield wiper works. The faster a windshield wiper sweeps across the windshield, the less you notice it. In most of the electronic display equipment used today, an electron beam sweeps horizontally across the screen in much the same way, pixel by pixel, line by line, "refreshing" the image. Hence the term "refresh technology." As in the case of the windshield wiper, the faster the refresh rate, the less likely the observer is to be distracted by it.

The least expensive means of achieving a high-resolution display, the direct-view storage tube (DVST), uses no windshield wiper at all. First introduced by Tektronix in 1967, its principal advantage is its ability to display sharp images without refreshing. Because it requires relatively little memory, needing only enough to activate the display, economies of cost and engineering come into play.

However, a storage tube cannot selectively erase parts of an image. In order to change the image, it must start all over again, from scratch. Another disadvantage is that the light output of this type of tube is relatively low. Furthermore, color displays are not possible. For a while, the low price of the tube and its high resolution compensated for its drawbacks. But as engineering sophistication increasingly demands color and more flexible display, the use of direct-view storage tube technology will be reduced to a few specialty applications.

Raster refresh tubes employ the same technology, albeit on a higher plane, as that utilized in the familiar television set. Images are formed by three electron beams, one each for red, green, and blue, sweeping back and forth across the screen from inside the tube. Raking it line by line many times a second, the beams illuminate corresponding phosphor dots on the screen, according to pattern instructions stored in computer memory. The number of possible colors, or gray levels in the case of black-and-white displays, is technically unlimited, determined simply by the number of memory planes in the system. However, as you can readily surmise, the more memory planes there are, the more memory is required.

Memory is expensive, as we have noted. But the fact that it is decreasing rapidly in price bodes well for further advances in raster refresh technology. The tubes, although still not cheap, are benefiting from overall declining prices, and they offer the advantages of high-quality color, selective erasure, and the ability to display photographic images clearly.

Vector refresh tubes, also called stroke writers, provide the highest resolution of all. The stroke writer, or random scan, is the Cadillac computer's windshield wiper. But the color display capacity of the vector tube is quite limited. This is not much of a drawback in engineering and design applications, where resolution is paramount. But most business users would rather have a little more color, a little less resolution. That preference more or less defines the different market paths these two technologies—raster and vector refresh—may be expected to take.

There are other things in computer graphics besides the method of visual display to be investigated by the prospective investor. One is hard copy—that is, printed-on-paper copies of computer-generated graphics. Another is input devices. Software and image enhancement are still other fields of profitable inquiry.

Hard copy is produced by various types of instrumentation. Pen plotters, as their name implies, use pens to produce the drawn image. Some plotting contrivances move pen across paper. Others employ a method equally practical, though less familiar to mankind, for drawing out computer data. The pen remains fixed, at least in one axis. The paper moves, and having been writ upon, moves on.

Then there are, of course, impact, or letterpress, printers—some of them capable of surprisingly sharp images and high-quality color resolution. One such printer is Ramtek's 4100, which uses four ribbons, one black, the other three each a primary color. The resolution of this particular printer is 3,600 dots per square inch—a lot finer than someone unfamiliar with halftone technology might expect.

Special color cameras such as those developed by Dunn Instruments, Image Resources, and Matrix Corporation use Polaroid film to take, quite literally, photographs of the display tube. These aren't exactly in the One Step or Pronto price range, by the way, costing as they do $10,000 to $20,000 apiece, with individual pictures amounting to $5 or more per shot. But one of their big advantages, for now, is the feasibility of permanent hard-copy slides for business presentations. Now there's a $1 billion market in and of itself.

Other hard-copy devices include ink-jet, electrostatic, dry-silver, and thermal printers. However, the most exciting potential development is to be found in the field of photocomposition, where already the image resolution has been brought up to an amazing two million individual dots per square inch. Several companies are exploring this frontier, among them Integrated Software Systems and Scitex, which has a number of laser-controlled photocomposition systems up and working, producing color separations for graphics suppliers to the print industry.

Input accessories for computer graphics come in many forms. The four most common ones are data tablets, digitizers, joy sticks (which are not unlike those used in video games), and light pens.

Data tablets have a surface sensitive to the imprint of a stylus. Images drawn on them are transferred electronically to the computer, thence onto the screen. Data tablets lend themselves to creative doodling. Digitizers, of which Summagraphics is a leading supplier, use cross hairs like those on a gunsight to target each point of a graphics image for the computer. Joy sticks move a cursor on the video image itself, as opposed to drawing offscreen. A data entry can be made or the image changed at any location by repositioning the cursor. A light pen works in the same way, except that the pen is used to actually "draw" on the screen itself. Which of these input technologies will eventually dominate depends on the future refinements of each—and on the availability of applications software geared to their specific capabilities.

Software, in general at the present time largely limited to the computer system for which it was originally developed, will eventually, once standards are agreed upon, become portable (read "computer-transferable"). Even as this transformation is occurring, the programs themselves will become more specialized. Interior-design systems, allowing an architectural firm, say, to populate the computer-generated layout of an office with equally imaginary furniture, are expected to develop a $200 million market all by themselves before the year 1990. To give but one example of this trend, Intergraph Corporation is drawing up its new Innovator CAD system to feature Steelcase office furniture. Not only will Innovator CAD decorate ghostly offices with images, but it will show the color and give the price of each individual piece available as well.

Specific software in the computer-aided design and computer-aided manufacturing (CAD/CAM) sector covers everything from mathematical solids modeling and renderings of parts assemblages to stress analysis and process development. Overall, CAD/CAM-involved companies have tended to specialize in particular markets as these have evolved. The electronics field was the first to open up, and so early video-graphics firms headed for this market segment, and stayed to develop dominance there. Manufacturing and mechanical engineering were the next large applications areas to avail themselves of computerized design assistance, and the second-wave CAD/CAM companies have focused their attention on the needs of these customers, which together represent the single largest family of users.

The future for computer graphics, and particularly for the adaptation of video graphics to the business and entertainment arenas, is wide open. However, given the volatile state of both the technology and the markets, manufacturers in this emerging industry have had an unfortunate, if understandable, record of pressing forward with product development to the neglect of financial controls. Auto-Trol Technology and Gerber Systems Technology have both borne witness to the delicate balancing act required in such circumstances. Both stumbled over management problems, and both saw their stock prices describe a very picturesque curve—over the cliff and straight down.

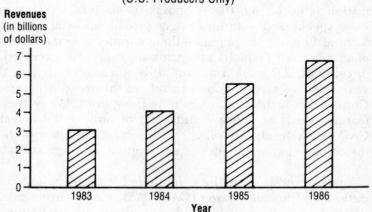

Projected Market Growth of Computer Graphics

(U.S. Producers Only)

Estimated compound annual growth rate: 30 percent

Note: These figures exclude hard-copy devices such as plotters and printers.

INDUSTRY INVESTMENT DECISIONS

Computer-graphics companies constitute three primary groupings. The first is the computer-aided design and computer-aided manufacturing (CAD/CAM) industry, composed principally of turnkey vendors, the suppliers of complete graphics systems which, like your car, need only the turn of a key to begin operating. The second group consists of manufacturers of specialized hardware components such as viewing scopes, plotters, and similar devices for displaying the graphics. The third category—potentially the most interesting to investors, but to date mostly privately owned—comprises the software companies. It is these firms which could really put business graphics, the largest latent graphics market, on the map.

The brake on business applications so far has been that graphics software has not been easy enough to use, a fault caused by the large quantities of cheap memory needed to effect pattern recognition. As that difficulty is overcome with diminishing memory prices, look for lots of new names in graphics software, some of which should develop into very profitable publicly traded companies.

More specialty manufacturers are entering, and thus segmenting, the CAD/CAM market as a result of the need for specialized expertise and product features in the various industries serviced by CAD/CAM. A well-executed business strategy and sound financial management are prerequisites to the future success of any company entering these fields. The contrasting business and stock histories of Intergraph (steadily up) and Computervision (up then slow) illustrate this.

Prices of the lower-cost products will be coming down further, thus stimulating new uses as well as turning up the competitive heat. This last effect will continue a much-honored tradition in high-technology industries, namely, that of acquisitions resulting from high-tech management that has made mistakes seeking financing from gullible low-tech buyers.

The bread-and-butter hardware suppliers in the computer-graphics industry will face a very competitive time in the eighties. More and more scopes, plotters, and printers will be cranked out in the low-labor-costs Far East, placing this mar ket segment in a low-markup-commodity category—accompanied by low investor profits.

KEY COMPANIES

Adage, Inc.

One Fortune Drive
Billerica, MA 01821
Telephone: (617) 667-7070
Contact: J. P. Cunningham, Chief Financial Officer
Market: OTC
Symbol: ADGE

Adage, a components supplier, has specialized in IBM-compatible computer-graphics workstations and done a good job of it.

Auto-Trol Technology

12500 North Washington Street
Denver, CO 80233
Telephone: (303) 452-4919
Contact: P. Jerde, Vice-President of Finance
Market: OTC
Symbol: ATTC

A turnkey manufacturer heavy with ex-IBMers, Auto-trol lost lots of them—and money too—in 1981 and 1982. It will be alluring if it pulls itself together.

Chyron Corporation

265 Bethpage-Spagnoli Road
Melville, NY 11747
Telephone: (516) 694-7136
Contact: L. Weissman, President
Market: OTC
Symbol: CHYC

Chyron provides television broadcasters with electronic titling-display equipment using animated computer graphics.

Computervision Corporation

201 Burlington Road
Bedford, MA 01730

Telephone: (617) 275-1800
Contact: F. J. Carr
>   Market: NYSE
>   Symbol: CVN

The leading manufacturer of computer-aided design (CAD) equipment, Computervision has been trying to maintain its share of the market by spending heavily during a recession-related slowdown of the industry. Some observers feel that the company has been spending its money on the wrong things.

Evans and Sutherland Computer Corporation

580 Arapeen Drive
Salt Lake City, UT 84108
Telephone: (801) 582-5847
Contact: Gary Meredith
>   Market: OTC
>   Symbol: ESCC

Pilot-training visual simulators and high-performance computer-aided design systems are the products, but the romance is Evans and Sutherland's top technology coupled with high margins.

Gerber Systems Technology

40 Gerber Road East
South Windsor, CT 06074
Telephone: (203) 644-2581
Contact: W. S. Mann, President
>   Market: OTC
>   Symbol: GSTI

Capital-starved under Gerber Scientific, this turnkey manufacturer is trying hard to catch up in computer-aided design and computer-aided manufacturing systems, but it's far behind and in the red. It's a real long shot with a good product.

Information Displays

28 Kaysal Court
Armonk, NY 10504
Telephone: (914) 273-5755
Contact: William Weksel, President
>   Market: OTC
>   Symbol: IDPY

All bootstrapped up, Information Displays seems ready to increase its share of the computer-aided design market.

Information International
5933 Slawson Boulevard
Culver City, CA 90230
Telephone: (213) 390-8611
Contact: Terry Taugner, Treasurer
           Market: OTC
           Symbol: IINT
Informational International makes the Cadillac of turnkey photocomposition systems, incorporating typesetting, pagination, and graphics. Belatedly, the company has moved after bigger markets.

Intelligent Systems Corporation
Intecolor Drive 225 Technology Park/Atlanta
Norcross, GA 30092
Telephone: (404) 449-5961
Contact: Charles Muench, Chairman
           Market: OTC
           Symbol: INTS
Medium-priced color-graphics terminals and desktop computer systems are this component supplier's forte, but competition is heating up and closing on its lead.

Intergraph Corporation
One Madison Industrial Park
Huntsville, AL 35807
Telephone: (205) 772-2000
Contact: R. E. Brown, Vice-President of Finance
           Market: OTC
           Symbol: INGR
Intergraph, a turnkey manufacturing concern, has flourished and gained market share thanks to its concentration in mechanical design and architectural engineering, the faster-growing sectors of computer-aided design and manufacturing.

Lexidata Corporation
755 Middlesex Turnpike
Billerica, MA 01865

Telephone: (617) 663-8550
Contact: Paul Murphy, Controller
Market: OTC
Symbol: LEXD

A late starter in computer graphics, components supplier Lexidata acquired new management and is catching up, but it's not easy.

Mathematical Applications Group

3 Westchester Plaza
Elmsford, NY 10523
Telephone: (914) 592-4646
Contact: P. S. Mittelman, President
Market: OTC
Symbol: MAGC

Famed for its *Tron* computer graphics, this supplier of components makes most of its money from direct-marketing software. The company has touched a match to lots of skyrockets. Maybe one will take off.

Matrix Corporation

230 Pegasus Avenue
Northvale, NJ 07647
Telephone: (201) 767-1750
Contact: Evelyn Bishop, telephone (516) 766-6565
Market: ASE
Symbol: MAX

It's a tossup whether Matrix's color cameras for digital information recordings make it a computer-graphics or a medical-components supplier, but its history is certainly worth studying.

Ramtek Corporation

2211 Lawson Lane
Santa Clara, CA 95050
Telephone: (408) 988-2211
Contact: T. J. Adams, Executive Vice-President
Market: OTC
Symbol: RMTK

Ramtek, another components supplier, can boast good technology and revenue growth, not so good strategy execution and profits. Management says they're changing that.

Scitex Corporation, Ltd.
P.O. Box 330
Herzlia B46 103
Israel
Telephone: (052) 53555
Contact: G. M. Dogon, Vice-President of Finance
 Market: OTC
 Symbol: SCIXF

Graphic arts, printing, and publishing are the main markets for this group with Itek and Boston University antecedents.

Visual Technology, Inc.
540 Main Street
Tewksbury, MA 01876
Telephone: (617) 851-5000
Contact: Thomas Foley, Chief Executive Officer
 Market: OTC
 Symbol: VSAL

A terminal for video displays that does it better is Visual Technology's game. Televideo is the tough competition. A large acquisition to gain volume is in the works.

LEADING ANALYSTS

Lydia Adelfio and Terry Carleton
Kidder, Peabody and Company, Inc.
100 Federal Street
Boston, MA 02110
Telephone: (617) 357-6762

Al Berkeley and Kenneth Burke
Alex Brown and Son
135 East Baltimore Street
Baltimore, MD 21202
Telephone: (301) 727-1700

Jay Cooper
F. Eberstadt and Company, Inc.
61 Broadway
New York, NY 10006
Telephone: (212) 480-0892

Tom Kurlak
Merrill Lynch, Pierce, Fenner and Smith, Inc.
One Liberty Plaza, 165 Broadway
New York, NY 10080
Telephone: (212) 637-8146

Larry Roberts
Hambrecht and Quist, Inc.
235 Montgomery Street
San Francisco, CA 94104
Telephone: (415) 986-5500

PERTINENT PUBLICATIONS

The Anderson Report
Anderson Publishing Company
P.O. Box 3534, Simi Valley Business Park
Simi Valley, CA 93063
Telephone: (805) 581-1184
 Subscription: $125 per year for monthly newsletter
General industry gossip about new products, trends, peo-
ple, trade shows and so on is written up in this newsletter for
industry participants.

CAD/CAM Technology
Society of Manufacturing Engineers
P.O. Box 930, One SME Drive
Dearborn, MI 48128
Telephone: (313) 271-1500
 Subscription: $24 per year, or $7.50 per year with
      Society of Manufacturing Engineers
      membership, for quarterly periodical
This is a new publication similar in format to the society's
Robotics Today. The magazine offers industry news and re-
views, a calendar of events, and case histories of new com-
puter-aided design and manufacturing applications.

Computer Graphics World
Penn Well Publications
P.O. Box 122

Tulsa, OK 74101
Telephone: (918) 835-3161
   Subscription: $24 per year for monthly periodical
Computer Graphics World contains the usual array of products, trends, calendar, analyses and book reviews for industry watchers and participants.

IEEE Computer Graphics and Applications
The Institute of Electrical and Electronics Engineers
   (IEEE) Computer Society/National Computer Graphics
   Association
10662 Los Vacqueros Circle
Los Alamitos, CA 90720
Telephone: (714) 821-8380
   Subscription: $23 per year to nonmembers, $8 per year
                 to members, for quarterly publication
Fairly academic and technical in presentation, this quarterly is nevertheless a good source of analysis and information on new developments and product directions.

The S. Klein Newsletter on Computer Graphics
Technology and Business Communications, Inc.
P.O. Box 89
Sudbury, MA 01776
Telephone: (617) 443-4671
   Subscription: $145 per year for semimonthly newsletter
The S. Klein letter covers industry developments, trends, technology and companies, besides providing a calendar of events. It approaches the industry generally from the standpoint of a participant.

MAJOR MEETINGS

Computer Graphics Week
(For address and telephone, see the *S. Klein Newsletter on
   Computer Graphics*, under *Pertinent Publications*,
   above)
Computer Graphics Week is held annually at the same time as the SIGGRAPH show or the NCGA show if one of these is being held in Boston. Check the S. Klein letter for news of this event.

NCGA Show
2033 M Street, NW, Suite 330
Washington, DC 20036
Telephone: (202) 466-5895
Held annually in June in a major city (Chicago in 1983), this show, sponsored by the National Computer Graphics Association, is vendor- and customer-oriented. For investors, it's a bit better than SIGGRAPH, but alternating shows might be best.

SIGGRAPH Show
111 East Wacker Drive
Chicago, IL 60601
Telephone: (312) 644-6610
The SIGGRAPH show is more technical and academic in orientation. Sponsored by the Association for Computing Machinery, it is held annually in July or August in a major city (Detroit in 1983).

PROFESSIONAL ASSOCIATIONS

Association for Computing Machinery
1133 Avenue of the Americas
New York, NY 10036
Telephone: (212) 265-6300
Associate membership is $40 per year, dues for the association's Special Interest Group on Computer Graphics (SIGGRAPH) are $10 per year additional. Members receive *Communications of the ACM,* the association's monthly magazine.

The Institute of Electrical and Electronics Engineers
    (IEEE) Computer Society
(For address and telephone, see *IEEE Computer Graphics and Applications,* under *Pertinent Publications,* above)

National Computer Graphics Association (NCGA)
(For address and telephone, see the NCGA Show, under *Major Meetings,* above)

XIV

Data-Base Services: What's Where, with Whom, and How to Find It Profitably

For most people, "data base" is one of those terms that make up the indecipherable newspeak of high technology. Like "documentation," which always comes with computers and software and simply means "instruction manual," a data base is an everyday thing all dressed up in a fancy new name and form. If the truth be known, your address book, that drawerful of canceled checks, and your recipe file are all data bases. A data base is any reasonably orderly collection of information arranged so that it can be retrieved, or found, and used by anyone who knows the system.

The piles of newspaper clippings, market forecasts, professional journals, research reports, and company propaganda flowing off the desk, over the credenza, across the chair and the stereo cabinet, around the corner, over the couch, onto the floor in the hallway, and into the next room are a data base—the data base for this book, as a matter of fact. However, should anyone move any of the various piles in an attempt to locate some specific item of information, chances are that not only would he fail to retrieve the particular datum in question, but he would destroy our power to do so as well. This data base, although it employs a form of file management, is very user-specific. As such, it is not a proper data base in the eyes of computer buffs.

A true computer data base is more than simply a classification of contents or a method of file management. First of all, it integrates every piece of available data into a single centralized unit that can be accessed by a multitude of users. And a multitude of users can access the information at the same time. This capacity for simultaneous use is the crucial component of data-base structures so greatly facilitated by computers.

Another attribute of a computerized data base is a logically organized master scheme by means of which important interrelationships between all the data to be stored, and retrieved, can be captured and pigeonholed as well. In noncomputerese, we would say that such a data base has an excellent cross-index. However you phrase it, this cross-referencing of the data eliminates costly redundancy, or duplication of information.

A third facet of a good computerized data base is that both the information input and the software controlling how it is stored and retrieved can be altered without affecting the overall data base. They can be modified independently of each other.

Access to the actual data in storage is provided by a data-base management system (DBMS). This is the computerized librarian, the software that handles all the details—the filing, the selective retrieval of data to answer information requests, and the providing of explanations as to how and why certain information is stored within the system. A large data-base management system can provide additional functions, but its basic operations are defining, or creating, files (that's like labeling file folders to let the staff know what's in them and what should be put in them in the future), modifying or deleting records and printing out responses to information requests based on those records, and sorting files according to specific parameters. (If this book was made into a data base, for instance, the DBMS for it could be set up to sort out the information within it by, among other things, companies whose stocks are listed on the New York Stock Exchange, those listed on the American Stock Exchange, those traded over-the-counter, and those still private.)

If all this sounds complex, you may be assured that it is, and the very complexity of an efficient data-base management system makes a large scale of operations mandatory if the system is to be economically viable. Data-base management of a small file such as the four or five thousand separate papers on which this book is based would be pure computer overkill. So, if only the largest data-base users need management systems, what are the market prospects for these services?

Accurate sales figures are difficult to determine, because data bases are often but one service among many provided by large information companies, which often don't break out earnings for this category separately, or because, like The Source, they are part of a private company. However, the overall market for data-base services, including electronic publishing and diversified media companies as well as the actual data-base management software companies and related computer services, generated aggregate revenues of $15.5 billion in 1980, a year during which electronic publishing and data bases as a whole were still barely off the ground. A lot of analysts feel that data-base management will be the major commercial product in the field of information processing, the ultimate software tool, of the 1980s.

There are currently three basic types of computer data-base design: hierarchical, network, and relational. Each uses a different organizational approach to the data, with its own advantages and disadvantages. A new form of data-base organization, were one to be developed—and there is no reason to suppose one won't be—could constitute a phenomenal industry breakthrough.

A hierarchical data base organizes and stores data according to what is known as a decision-tree pattern. In a corporate data base, for instance, your name and address might be filed under the name of the department for which you work, along with the names and addresses of the other employees in that department. So all the members of a department together would constitute one set of data. Decision trees are formed by various such sets of information linked together in different ascending hierarchies, the final iota, in this case your name and address, to be found at the tip of the tree. Obviously, an overall data base of this type is a veritable forest of information.

Hierarchical design is both rigid and complex, thus difficult for the user to deal with. It also provides less control over redundancy than the other data-base approaches do. On the positive side, it offers—once it's working—high reliability and performance. If a tractor-parts distributor needs to know what fuel injector to use for an Allis-Chalmers 5020 diesel, a hierarchical tractor-parts data base will give him the one and only correct answer, retrieved from the very tip of the decision tree.

Much of IBM's data processing is based upon hierarchical design. This has helped to make the decision-tree format the most prevalent in the industry.

Network data-base design is quite similar to the hierarchical approach, except for the crucial difference that each "member" of a set can belong to several other sets. Consider a college degree and the courses required for it. There are specific courses prerequisite to a major in, say, chemistry. Let's assume Chemistry 203 is one of them. But Chemistry 203 might also be required for a biology major, a physics major, and a geology major. The "member" Chemistry 203 then, unlike the fuel injector, would belong to a number of sets. So a hierarchical arrangement of data might be far less appropriate for a college curriculum than for tractor parts.

Cincom, Cullinet, Honeywell, and Sperry, among others, produce network data-base management systems. The network approach was particularly popular during the sixties and early seventies because it allowed complex relationships to be handled with limited computing power and memory, both of which were expensive at the time. Since then, however, computing power and memory alike have been plummeting in cost, which is why other forms of data-base management, even more complex, and thus more memory-intensive, may well come to the fore in the eighties.

One such advanced informational management structure already up and running is the relational system first developed by E. F. Codd at IBM in 1970. A relational data-base management system arranges the data in a tabular format. The information is situated in rows, called tuples, and columns, called attributes. The computer locates data by electronically slicing these rows and columns matching the tuples and attributes appropriate to the information for which it is searching. Unrequested information is dropped, and the remaining pieces are spliced into a new table. When the search process is completed, the resulting, finalized table is presented to the program user. The total number of tabular sequences required for a relational data base is usually exceedingly large, containing thousands upon thousands, perhaps even millions, of attributes and tuples, which, of course, means an immense memory capacity is also required.

A relational data-base management system affords much easier access to computer data by nonexperts. It's easy to learn to deal with and easy to query. The relational design can permit operators to query the data base without using any special computer language. The end user really need know nothing except what he is looking for.

The main drawbacks to relational data-base management to date have been its relatively slow operating speed and its huge memory demands, problems which should be alleviated over the course of the present decade. At the moment, very few commercial relational systems are available, but IBM has a prototype called System R in addition to its up-and-running SQL, Logica has Rapport, Relational Software has Oracle, and Tymshare has Magnum. All of these systems are on the leading edge of this promising information-management endeavor.

Whichever design eventually dominates in data-base management, there's no doubt that the market for management systems is tremendous. Currently less than 10 percent of the companies utilizing computers make use of such devices, in most cases because of the extra computer power and time involved. Yet some companies, of which Storage Technology Corporation is an example, have set apart separate computers whose sole function is to provide data-base management. With the declining cost of computing power and memory, the survey proportions are expected to do a complete flip-flop in less than a decade. That is to say, pundits predict that by 1990 only 10 percent of all the computer installations in the country will *not* have a data-base management system.

One should not forget what these great numbers of management systems will be managing, of course. Computerized data bases themselves constitute an industry not to be overlooked. We are living in the information age, after all, and the demand for information products and services can only keep growing.

Consider a few of the computer data bases available today. There's the Airline Fares Data Base, a comprehensive domestic and international tariff data base that includes calculations of the lowest possible constructed fares for connections throughout the North American market. The Carol Wright Data Base identifies 26 million American households of particular interest to packaged goods manufacturers. Dun's Corporate Family Data Base lists and links the branches, divisions, and subsidiaries of 4.7 million United States business establishments. The Trink Truck Fleet Data Base catalogs over 400,000 owners of trucks and tractors, classified by vehicle weight, fleet size, industry, and geographic area. The United States Universal Business Data Base provides an identification and information bureau on 4.7 million American business establishments, its data updated daily by 133,000 incoming transactions.

Twenty years ago these specialized electronic data bases wouldn't have been even conceivable. Today they exist, are used constantly—and make money. There are by now, in fact, well over twelve hundred data bases "on line," that is, up and running and waiting for customers to utilize them. That's a 300 percent increase in three years.

United States Department of Commerce figures indicate that information activity presently accounts for over 50 percent of the gross national product, as startling as that statistic may seem. The figure includes things like advertising, education, and printing plates as well as the books they are used to print. Even so, it's a staggering proportion when one thinks about it. And the fastest-growing segment of this already huge quota is that of computerized data bases and electronic information services.

Encyclopedia publishers are experimenting with electronic editions. The Bible is available in electronic form. The telephone company wants to put the Yellow Pages out on personal computers. A data base called Bambam keeps a running file on stolen books. One called Horse provides breeding—as well as track—records on equines.

The secret to building a successful and profitable data base is to be creative with existing sources of information. Anybody can gather data. The right presentation and ease of access for users are what effect a system with high demand. Incorporating these features into an information service that is expensive to duplicate is what keeps away the competition and assures a steadily growing customer base. Then too, interlocking products increase repeat sales. As customers using the system discover more and more peripheral information that could be helpful, they become addicted and dependent.

The credit, health-care, and insurance firms employing data-base technology and electronic publishing are particularly likely to increase the number of computer transactions they use once they adopt a system. This tendency makes them powerful money machines for the information-service companies, since once the high initial cost of establishing a data base is met, additional volume becomes very, very profitable.

The lower the cost of acquiring and continually updating information, the greater a company's potential profit on a data base becomes. This factor often gives a company already acquiring information for its own use a leading edge in the database market. After all, revenues generated from compiling that information into a base accessible outside the company then become almost gravy.

Another consideration bearing on the profitability of a data base is how quickly customers need the information. Speed must be worth a lot to the user in order to command a high price, a principle perhaps best exemplified by electronic stock quotes. A broker needs to know at what price a stock is trading when it is trading, not the day after, when its price is quoted in the paper. Newspaper quotes are worth a quarter to the average investor. The brokerage firms are willing to pay a lot more for instant quotes.

Software companies supplying data-base management and computer systems have one additional requirement for growth: They must key their products to the dominant computer brand used by large businesses. This means IBM. If the software doesn't play on IBM, it will never hit the top of the charts. Once it's running on IBM equipment, the task confronting a software concern trying to gain market share is a simple and clear-cut one, namely, to get the most feet on the street. The first with the most dominates the market.

As to computer-processing services, wherein a customer's own information, disbursement records and the like, as opposed to an established data base, provides the raw material, the road to success is mapped out by finding or creating a need and then getting customers to pay for solutions. Comdata Network followed this tack with the trucking industry, setting up a computerized system to provide truckers on the road with cash, available at the truck stops, for unexpected emergencies. Once the network was in place, the firm could build on a complete chain of extra services. Starting with a single basic service directed toward an untapped market source, dominating that market, and then expanding the services available is a much better way of making a debut in the field of information services than is the capital-intensive and problem-prone attempt to provide a broad range of services initially.

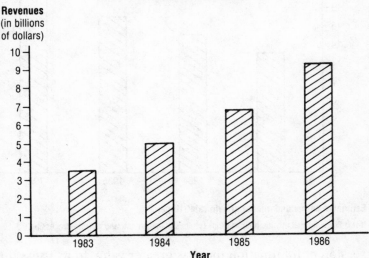

Projected Market Growth of Computer Systems Software

Estimated compound annual growth rate: 36 percent

Note: These figures include operating systems and data-base-management software.

INDUSTRY INVESTMENT DIRECTIONS

From the investor's viewpoint, there are three directions to watch among the various data-base companies. First, the vendors of data-base-management software products are a lot like applications-software companies. They sell software solutions to information-management problems. So any company that comes up with more efficient solutions or a radically different and better software approach, making a data base easier or more efficient to use, should provide a good investment.

Data-base services are furnished by companies which, often because of a related business activity, find themselves in pos-

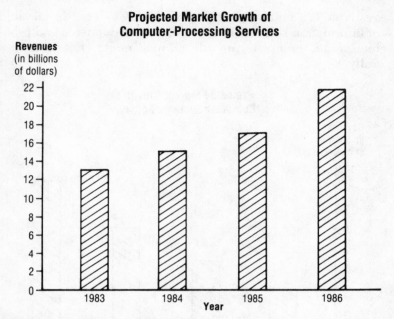

**Projected Market Growth of
Computer-Processing Services**

Estimated compound annual growth rate: 16 percent

Note: These figures include time sharing, facilities management, and custom processing.

session of information that has greater value to its users if the speed of access to it can be increased, or if the data can be cross-referenced or assembled in a new and more useful fashion. Frequently such companies are magazine or newspaper publishing firms. But remember, the fact that a company has a potentially large data base doesn't necessarily mean that it will have a large number of customers. General information, like that available to a newspaper, for instance, cannot command the high user price which a specialized data base, say one incorporating the latest research developments in genetic engineering, can command.

The most profitable data bases tend to feature business information such as that provided by Dun's Corporate Family Data Base, as opposed to consumer information like that provided by The Source. The reason for the difference in profitability is that businesses are willing to pay more for truly valuable information. Consumers must be convinced and cajoled, and it may be very hard for a company to build brand

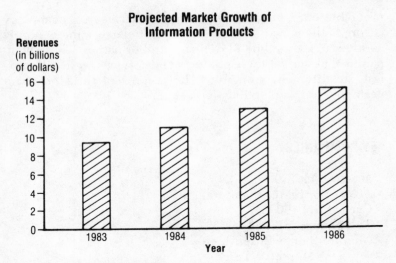

Projected Market Growth of Information Products

Revenues (in billions of dollars)

Estimated compound annual growth rate: 17 percent

Note: These figures include electronic and data-base publishing.

loyalty to an intangible product. (Ask your local savings and loan about customer loyalty!) The more proprietary the data or information, the more secure from competition and the more profitable a company's service will be.

The firms providing processing services make up the bulk of the computer service industry. As a group, they perform a miscellany of tasks for users of computers and computer-processed information, from check verification to facilities management of company data-processing centers. Theirs is basically a low-margin, high-volume business. Thus a successful company in computer processing will have long-term contracts with companies possessing a growing base of data in need of processing.

What all the diverse data-base firms have in common is their efforts to deal with our fastest-growing resource and problem, information. The market is one of almost unimaginably large size and can accommodate many successful companies. We have indicated a few of the keys to success, but the single most important element is the skillful identification and assessment of a large customer information need, followed by a profitable marketing strategy to meet that need. Technology is simply the way to get there, as a printed magazine is simply another, older method of delivering information. Those companies that market their products and services well will grow fast, steadily, and profitably. They represent the kind of investment you want to find and keep.

KEY COMPANIES

Anacomp, Inc.
11550 North Meridian Street
Carmel, IN 46032
Telephone: (317) 844-9666
Contact: James Rosensteele
        Market: NYSE
        Symbol: AAC

Chairman Palamara is very aggressive, smart, and promotional. If Anacomp does all it has set out to do with its bank operations-management products, it will become very big.

Applied Data Research, Inc.
Route 206 and Orchard Road CN-8
Princeton, NJ 08540
Telephone: (201) 874-9000
Contact: R. V. Smith, Treasurer
        Market: ASE
        Symbol: ADR

The oldest supplier of packaged software around, this company has great data-base-management products and a poor profit record, because of its lack of marketing orientation. One can have hope.

Automatic Data Processing, Inc.
405 Route 3
Clifton, NJ 07015
Telephone: (201) 365-7300
Contact: R. A. Patterson, Vice-President of Finance
        Market: NYSE
        Symbol: AUD

It should come as no surprise that the granddaddy of the computer-services industry plans to keep growing. But it's already pretty big.

Comdata Network
P.O. Box 15822, 2209 Crestmoor Road
Nashville, TN 37215
Telephone: (615) 385-0400
Contact: C. W. Harter, Jr., President
      Market: OTC
      Symbol: CASH

Comdata Network provides the trucking industry with computer-controlled cash-transfer services along truck routes.

Commerce Clearing House, Inc.
4025 West Peterson Avenue
Chicago, IL 60646
Telephone: (312) 583-8500
Contact: B. Elafros, Treasurer
      Market: OTC
      Symbol: CCLR

The revenues from information processing don't seem very profitable, but the record is steady.

Computer Network Corporation
5185 MacArthur Boulevard, NW
Washington, DC 20016
Telephone: (202) 537-2500
Contact: L. Johnson, Chief Executive Officer
      Market: OTC
      Symbol: CNET

Computer Network supplies facilities-management, time-sharing, and data-processing services primarily to the United States government.

Computer Task Group
800 Delaware Avenue
Buffalo, NY 14209
Telephone: (716) 882-8000
Contact: W. P. Adamucci, Treasurer
      Market: OTC
      Symbol: CTSK

Concentrating on minicomputers and minibusinesses, the Computer Task Group does a little of everything in the processing-services field. Its record is a bit erratic.

Cullinet Software, Inc.

400 Blue Hill Drive
Westwood, MA 02090
Telephone: (617) 329-7700
Contact: Phyllis Swersky, Treasurer
        Market: NYSE
        Symbol: CUL

The fastest-growing supplier of computer data-base-management systems, along with related utility programs, this company is moving into applications software. It has shrewd marketers who execute well.

Dow Jones and Company

22 Cortlandt Street
New York, NY 10007
Telephone: (212) 285-5000
Contact: L. A. Armour
        Market: NYSE
        Symbol: DJ

An information processor, Dow Jones, besides having a high P/E ratio, also provides a video play via its 25 percent interest in Continental Cablevision. Basically it's the same sort of show as Dun and Bradstreet, only smaller.

The Dun and Bradstreet Corporation

299 Park Avenue
New York, NY 10017
Telephone: (212) 593-6800
Contact: K. Bitter, Treasurer
        Market: NYSE
        Symbol: DNB

Data-base information services and publishing make for a high P/E ratio when done well this consistently. What's not yet clear is whether high technology will dominate this company.

Electronic Data Systems Corporation

7171 Forest Lane
Dallas, TX 75230

Telephone: (214) 661-6000
Contact: J. T. Walter, Jr.
    Market: NYSE
    Symbol: EDS
The business of Electronic Data Systems is mostly facilities management for medical agencies and government units. They do it nicely.

Harte-Hanks Communications, Inc.
40 Northeast Loop 410
San Antonio, TX 78216
Telephone: (512) 344-8000
Contact: L. Franklin, Vice-President
    Market: NYSE
    Symbol: HHN
Harte-Hanks Communications may look more like newspaper publishing and broadcasting than high technology, but there are high-tech stirrings within.

Informatics General Corporation
21031 Ventura Boulevard
Woodland Hills, CA 91364
Telephone: (213) 887-9040
Contact: Jerry Kalman
    Market: NYSE
    Symbol: IG
Spun out by the Equitable Life Assurance Society, Informatics General does a little of everything in software and services. The company is moving into packaged applications and tightening up. Its 1983 should be better than its 1982.

Mathematica, Inc.
12 Roszel Road
Princeton, NJ 08540
Telephone: (609) 799-2600
Contact: F. W. Daniels, Treasurer
    Market: OTC
    Symbol: MATH
Software revenues have been growing, thanks to the success of RAMIS, Mathematica's data-base-management system.

McGraw-Hill, Inc.
1221 Avenue of the Americas
New York, NY 10020
Telephone: (212) 997-1221
Contact: M. Cooper
            Market: NYSE
            Symbol: MHP
Data bases are growing and so are margins, but it's still hard to see the information processing in the total. Like Dun and Bradstreet, however, McGraw-Hill has a very consistent record.

National Data Corporation
One National Data Plaza, Corporate Square
Atlanta, GA 30329
Telephone: (404) 329-8500
Contact: H. Rootes, Treasurer
            Market: OTC
            Symbol: NDTA
National Data provides cash-management and credit-card-charge authorization services to corporate customers. Loss of the ARCO gasoline credit card business will slow 1982–83 profits.

Nielsen (A.C.) Company
Nielsen Plaza
Northbrook, IL 60062
Telephone: (312) 498-6300
Contact: J. Wennerstrom, Treasurer
            Market: OTC
            Symbol: NIELA
Research services (those famous television ratings, for example) are the staple here, but the use of advanced information-processing techniques is the way to growth. Slow but steady sums up Nielsen.

The Reynolds and Reynolds Company
800 Germantown Street
Dayton, OH 45407
Telephone: (513) 443-2000

Contact: Robert Dugan, Vice-President of Finance
Market: OTC
Symbol: REYNA

One of the earliest vertical-industry marketers, Reynolds and Reynolds supplies dealers with a variety of computer services and terminals. The automotive industry's multiyear slump has hurt.

Shared Medical Systems Corporation
Box 675
King of Prussia, PA 19406
Telephone: (215) 296-6300
Contact: James Kelly, Treasurer
Market: OTC
Symbol: SMED

Shared Medical Systems leads the field in providing information-processing services to large hospitals.

Software AG Systems Group
11800 Sunrise Valley Drive
Reston, VA 22091
Telephone: (703) 860-5050
Contact: John McGuire, President
Market: OTC
Symbol: SAGA

Technically elegant data-base-management software is easier to use than older types, but a late start with inadequate money has hurt. This one's a sleeper.

Systematics, Inc.
212 Center Street
Little Rock, AR 72201
Telephone: (501) 372-6141
Contact: V. D. Gosnell, Treasurer
Market: OTC
Symbol: SYST

Systematics provides a wide range of software and data-processing services for commercial banks using IBM equipment.

Telecredit, Inc.
1901 Avenue of the Stars
Los Angeles, CA 90067
Telephone: (213) 277-4061
Contact: D. Ingberg, Vice-President of Finance
          Market: OTC
          Symbol: TCRD

Telecredit supplies credit-card and check authorization services to point-of-sale users. The company is trying to make its facilities less labor-intensive.

Tymshare, Inc.
20705 Valley Green Drive
Cupertino, CA 95014
Telephone: (408) 446-8000
Contact: Vince Titolo, Senior Vice-President
          Market: NYSE
          Symbol: TYM

Tymshare's wide variety of processing services have, to the company's embarrassment, repeatedly evaded control. Maybe controls will catch up this time.

Wyly Corporation
UCC Tower, Exchange Park
Dallas, TX 75235
Telephone: (214) 353-7100
Contact: B. Carter, Treasurer
          Market: NYSE
          Symbol: WLY

This one provides the works: one-half computer services, one-quarter turnkey systems, one-quarter software programs. Controlled (58 percent) by Careal Holding, AG, Wyly has new management and is underfollowed.

LEADING ANALYSTS

Al Berkeley and Kenneth Burke
Alex Brown and Son
135 Baltimore Street
Baltimore, MD 21202
Telephone: (301) 727-1700

This team is tops in reviewing processing services and data-base-management software companies.

Victoria Butcher, Terry Cabot, James Dougherty, and
    Thomas Wong
F. Eberstadt and Company
61 Broadway
New York, NY 10006
Telephone: (212) 480-1342, 480-1389, 480-0896, 480-1393
Victoria Butcher and James Dougherty follow information processing, Terry Cabot and Thomas Wong follow processing services and software companies.

Edward Dunleavy
Salomon Brothers
One New York Plaza
New York, NY 10004
Telephone: (212) 747-7000
Data processing is the field in which Edward Dunleavy specializes.

Carter Dunlop
Robertson, Coleman and Stephens
100 California Street
San Francisco, CA 94111
Telephone: (415) 781-9700
Data-base management in particular and software companies in general are newly assigned to Carter Dunlop.

Joe Fuchs
Kidder, Peabody and Company, Inc.
10 Hanover Square
New York, NY 10005
Telephone: (212) 747-2796
    Joe Fuchs is a processing-services analyst.

David Henwood
Prescott, Bell and Tuben
1331 Euclid Avenue
Cleveland, OH 44115
Telephone: (216) 574-7411
This analyst covers both processing-service and data-base-management software firms.

Sy Kaufman
Hambrecht and Quist, Inc.
235 Montgomery Street
San Francisco, CA 94104
Telephone: (415) 986-5500
Sy Kaufman has good insights on data-processing and data-base-management software companies.

J. Kendrick Noble, Jr.
Paine Webber Mitchell Hutchins, Inc.
140 Broadway
New York, NY 10005
Telephone: (212) 437-2121
Kendrick Noble is well thought of as an information-processing-company analyst.

Sandra Plowman
Lehman Brothers Kuhn Loeb, Inc.
55 Water Street
New York, NY 10041
Telephone: (212) 558-1500
Sandra Plowman specializes in information-processing companies.

David Wu
Montgomery Securities
235 Montgomery Street
San Francisco, CA 94104
Telephone: (415) 989-2050
Data-base-management software and processing-service companies are this analyst's specialties.

PERTINENT PUBLICATIONS

EDP Industry Report
International Data Corporation
5 Speen Street
Framingham, MA 01701
Telephone: (617) 872-8200
  Subscription: $395 per year for semimonthly newsletter
International Data publishes nearly a dozen newsletters on the various aspects of the electronic-data-processing industry

—office automation, the Japanese market, and so on. Best of the lot is the "Gray Sheet," the general-coverage one.

ICP Software Business Review
International Computer Programs, Inc.
9000 Keystone Crossing
Indianapolis, IN 46240
Telephone: (317) 844-7461, (800) 428-6179 for
   subscriptions
   Subscription: Free to qualifying subscribers
The Interface Special Edition of this periodical is a great source of information. Once a year, it sums up the data-base-management software and processing-services companies, and it surveys the industry better than any of the other publications do. Five other special editions focus on separate subindustries.

IDP Report
Knowledge Industry Publications, Inc.
701 Westchester Avenue
White Plains, NY 10604
Telephone: (914) 328-9157
   Subscription: $225 per year for biweekly newsletter
The *IDP Report* covers data-base publishing and related video developments such as Videotext. It also includes digests and a calendar of meetings.

Software News
Sentry Database Publishing
5 Kane Industrial Drive
Hudson, MA 01749
Telephone: (617) 562-9308
   Subscription: $20 per year for monthly newspaper
Applications, systems, and data-base software, plus personnel changes, legal issues, user ratings, and surveys are all included in this monthly publication.

PROFESSIONAL ASSOCIATIONS

The Association of Data Processing Service Organizations, Inc. (ADAPSO)

1300 North 17th Street, Suite 300
Arlington, VA 22209
Telephone: (703) 522-5055

Designed for corporate membership, this association is liable to be a bit expensive for individuals, but it holds an annual meeting in New York every June for analysts and major investors. Call for details. A monthly newsletter plus an annual industry summary by INPUT, an industry consulting organization, are other services of the association. Call Cathy Colvard to join.

Information Industry Association
316 Pennsylvania Ave., SE
Suite 400
Washington, DC 20003
Telephone: (202) 544-1969

Designed for both corporate and individual membership, the IIA has workshops, publications, and meetings covering a variety of topics such as computer software, data-base producers and vendors, videotex, networking, teletext, etc. Membership is $275 a year, although publications may be ordered separately.

XV

Video and Advertising Technology: The Cyclops with Visions of Croesus

Telecasting technology is a broad category with ill-defined markets all tied together by the common denominator of the television tube. A whole generation has now grown up since the picture tube replaced the picture window as the central focus of American eyes. It's hard for these people to realize what the world must have been like without video. Yet the mighty Cyclops' reign has been so short!

Television as a concept was successfully demonstrated just before the Great Crash of 1929, but the idea long lay buried beneath the economic ruins, not to rise toward commercial availability until the early forties. Even then, another decade slipped by before the tube really flexed its cultural muscles. In 1946 there were all of ten thousand television sets in the United States. By 1951 the total had exploded to twelve million, and with Howdy Doody and Milton Berle as video media standard-bearers, the number of receivers had climbed over the fifty-million mark by 1958.

Today some 97 percent of all the families in the United States have at least one color television, never mind the old black-and-white sitting as a discarded and forlorn centerpiece in the living room. More than likely, for that matter, there's a palette of vibrant color in almost every room of the house, including, in many instances, the bathroom. Portnoy's father should have been so lucky.

Considering this overabundance of television sets—with twenty-four-hour programming to match—one might easily conclude that here is an oversaturated market if there ever was one. How could it possibly accommodate the exponential growth high-tech investors are seeking? Surprisingly, it does. The problem lies in solving the puzzle of direction.

The solid front of the network-dominated video industry has been shattered like a windowpane. A once predictable, secure market has been broken up into cable television, pay television, subscription television, low-power television, Teletext, and Videotext. The new technology of satellite broadcasting, of both the direct and the retransmission varieties, further complicates the issue. It's pretty hard to sort it all out. But what is clear is that a lot of companies with one or maybe two pieces of the puzzle put together see a lot of money in the picture if they can just lay their hands on another piece or so.

Basically, video and advertising are a numbers game. Even if you have millions of potential viewers, or customers, and a delivery medium, or the technology to reach the consumer, you still need to make money on the deal somehow. That somehow is the product, the programming, the part everybody is stuck on. To draw an analogy from the book business, the situation is somewhat comparable to having the bookstores, the editorial and production staffs, the printing and binding firms—and no writers. Can you sell blank-paged books? It's been done, but the market is limited. Can you sell reprints? That's done as well, and, to return to the video screen, reruns are the staple of many new video ventures. They draw audiences for a while, but only for so long.

With the cable market fragmented and, except for a few of the strongest pay television systems such as Home Box Office and Showtime, vastly underprogrammed, advertisers aren't yet sure that they should be spending their money in this direction, at least until the medium develops a more clear-cut identity. Few advertising dollars flowing in means not much cash filtering through to programming. Limited programming in turn reduces audience size. Small audience size reduces ad revenues, reduces programming budgets, reduces audience size still further, and so on, in classic chicken-and-egg circularity. Unless a breakthrough occurs eventually somewhere along the line, the whole show will go nowhere.

Companies possessing financial muscle, as do ABC, Getty Oil, and Time Inc., will have the marketing advantage in the capital-intensive video and advertising industry. But the advantage will provide no guarantees of fiscal success. Witness

CBS Cable's cultural network. Trying to break out of the small-time syndrome, CBS Cable initially refused to deal with advertisers that had less than $1 million to spend on video publicity. As the *Wall Street Journal* described the end result of this policy, "The advertisers are still in business, but CBS Cable isn't." The reporter writing up the story might have added that the experience cost CBS $30 million and that the advertising agencies are not only still in business, but doing just fine as well.

Looking at the figures, it isn't hard to see why. Among the largest cable-television advertisers, as reported by Broadcast Advertisers Reports, Inc., General Foods spent $4.5 million and Procter and Gamble some $2.7 million on cable-television advertising during the first half of 1982. During the same period, General Foods spent $144.5 million and Procter and Gamble $261.3 million on broadcast-television advertising.

The simple explanation of the difference in advertising dollars allocated to the two media lies in cable television's lack of a proven audience. It's easy enough for a cable-television company to show how many homes are wired up, but if no one is watching, what do the advertisers care? Whether even expanded programming can improve the situation remains to be seen. Consider Cable Health Network, whose shows, according to the enterprise's promotional campaign, cover "health and science, keeping fit, healthy relationships, human interest and life styles, self-help and medical care, growing up and getting older"—twenty-four hours a day, seven days a week. That's enough to make even a California hypochondriac swear off television after a while.

A whole new factor of tube fatigue may be affecting the video market. The number of people, from factory workers to business executives, who are spending at least part of their nine-to-five day staring at video displays is increasing, swiftly and tremendously. Perhaps these people don't want to come home and collapse in front of yet another screen. Perhaps the "good old days" nostalgia sweeping the entertainment world, from *Grease* to "Happy Days," will bring back quiet evenings of canasta and Mah-Jongg. Maybe a lot of people don't want the tube as their prime entertainment focal point any longer. Maybe cable television is the one screen too many. Stay tuned to tomorrow to find out.

Meanwhile, at this still confusing juncture, there are nevertheless a few determinable points of interest to the investor. First of all, cable-television companies may or may not be favorably positioned to take advantage of all those wired-up homes. Either way, it's going to take an awful lot of money for them even to find out where they stand. However well financed a cable-television venture is, it's still comparatively handicapped by the lack of advertiser acceptance to date. So the finances have to be superb.

For another thing, the video market is changing—undefined technologically as well as in terms of programming content. And there's no counting out AT&T, Western Union, and other old-line communications providers, for they may well end up dominating the video industry besides. Often it's companies that change rather than markets. They build on their developed expertise in one field to preside over another, especially if it happens to represent a new and capital-intensive market.

A third point to be remembered is that no matter how things turn out, there are two investment areas almost certain to be winners. Indeed, were it not for the possible management problems they involve, they would be sure, instead of all but sure, victors. The first of these prevailing spheres encompasses the suppliers of telecommunications transmission, reception, and distribution equipment for data and video broadcasting, and to a lesser degree voice broadcasting. Those involved with satellite transmission stand to do particularly well during the decade to come. Equipment manufacturers such as the Andrew Corporation and M/A-Com, if they continue to remain nimble in anticipating the direction broadcasting technology will take, are well worth watching closely.

Advertising agencies are a surprising second good bet for high-tech investors. While they themselves are only peripherally high-tech—they will certainly be using more video graphics and computer-aided design, for instance—the advertising media in the communications field somewhat parallel the software opportunities in the computer field. Their programming is not what the audience turns on the tube for, of course. Nevertheless, video broadcasting within the current industry structure is not going to get very far without the ads. Besides, as the video market becomes more and more fragmented, the opportunities for advertising agencies to increase their billings multiply right along with the increasing choices in video entertainment available to consumers.

Initially, this growth in placement alternatives could be a creativity-curbing and pecuniary drag on the agencies. But the long-term effect will probably be to stimulate the total demand for advertising. Look at the evolution of magazine publishing over the past few decades. General-interest magazines such as the *Saturday Evening Post, Look,* and the like (compare the networks) folded, but hundreds of new, specialized publications (compare the cable-television ventures) sprouted up to replace them—and one issue of *BYTE* magazine, for instance, carries ten times the advertising pages an issue of the *Post* ever did.

Among the public advertising agencies, the ones with the most consistent growth records are BBDO International; Doyle Dane Bernbach International; Foote, Cone and Belding; and Ogilvy and Mather International. They're all low P/E stocks, and while they may well remain so for quite some time, their growth potential affords certain investors—those who can't sleep at night holding stocks selling for twenty or thirty times earnings—a chance to benefit from the high-tech explosion.

At the other extreme of the investment-risk spectrum in video communications are the cable-television limited partnerships. What with everyone able to read a newspaper being aware of the "electronic cottage" and the information explosion, video technology has become an area so overtouted that it is difficult to discover an unexplored angle. It is also an area ripe for exploitation by salesmen more intent on pushing a commission-heavy product than is good for the investor's financial health.

Cable-television tax shelters have been around since the 1960s, but in those early years they were aimed at the well-heeled investor who could lay out a few hundred thousand dollars at a clip. Now, however, the cable-television industry needs to raise more cash—lots of it. So the fleet of former gold, diamond, oil, and gas shelter salesmen have had their original sights shifted by promises of new wealth in video. Today, cable-television shelters are available for a minimum investment of as low as $2,500. Investors do gain the extra plus of

tax write-offs. But they also lose control over their investments. There really is no secondary market for these partnerships. So an investor had better be prepared to endure ten
lean years or so before seeing any realized profits. Ten years
is a long time in this industry, both for management and for
the product. Cable-television partnerships are not something
to rush into.

That admonition perhaps best sums up the investment strategy for the field of video and advertising technology as a
whole. Don't rush into it. As an added precaution, don't become distracted by new and exciting gimmicks with great
press such as Videotex—it's hard to find anyone who is making money on it, except perhaps the media hype agent.

If technologies such as those of Teletext and Videotex are
not yet of profitable interest to the investor, there are three
high-tech telecasting areas that do offer current opportunities
for financial advancement. First there's cable television. A
recent technology, cable television is nevertheless already in
need of equipment updating, particularly in its most expensive component segment, that of the cables themselves. The
major thrust in upgrading here will lie in providing two-way
addressability, that is, in furnishing means by which the
viewer can signal responses back to the system, as opposed to
merely receiving signals. Numerous experiments in two-way
addressability are already underway, Warner Communications' Qube system in Ohio being the best known.

Two-way addressability in video telecommunication would
allow viewers to shop at home, to cast instant votes during
panel discussions, even to influence the outcome of programs
—in other words, to participate. It would make possible, for
instance, a revival of the old thumbs-up/thumbs-down Roman
circus, where the voting viewer could select between "She
decides to go ahead with a divorce" and "She decides to stay
with her crumbling marriage," and the soap opera plot would
continue along the line chosen by most viewers.

Whether in fact viewers really want options like that is open
to debate. But such features are currently considered marketing tools, and thus existing cable-television franchisers will
perforce upgrade their systems—at great expense.

Focused addressability is another broadcasting-industry
emphasis for the investor to watch. Cable television needs

new revenues, and one of its most promising sources of income is pay television. But in order to make pay TV pay, a broadcaster must be able to collect. People don't want to pay for something they don't watch. Pole-mounted or top-of-the-television-set converters can turn on or shut off a user's set depending on whether payment has been made or not. Reliability has been a problem for these converters. However, several companies are working on solving that problem. Texscan, TOCOM, C-COR, General Instrument, and Oak Industries, all part of the specialized cable-equipment industry, are worth following if you become interested in this particular segment of high-tech video development.

Another equipment area conducive to future growth is satellite reception antennas. Companies with large, as opposed to small, antennas and small, as opposed to large, price tags are the ones likely to succeed. But be wary of supplier situations too reliant on a single customer. Andrew Corporation, M/A-Com, Microdyne Corporation, Radiation Systems, and Scientific-Atlanta are all involved in antenna production. But their stock prices have been up and down and all around for the past couple of years. When no one else wants them and the company fundamentals still look good, that's the time to buy.

Overall, the novelty factor affects investors in video technology too much, causing prices to go up and down the fad yo-yo. A novel solution is offered, the public snaps up stock, the solution makes no money, so the public dumps the stock. Novelty does not necessarily generate profits. Find where the money is first. Then start looking for the companies raking it in.

INDUSTRY INVESTMENT DIRECTIONS

Because it is so highly visible to the public, the video and advertising industry tends to experience waves of overenthusiasm and despair out of proportion to its underlying progress. Among the industry segments, the future for cable projects looks a bit dull over the next couple of years. That industry will be consolidating its gains of the late seventies and adjusting costs to the recession's impact on subscribers—discon-

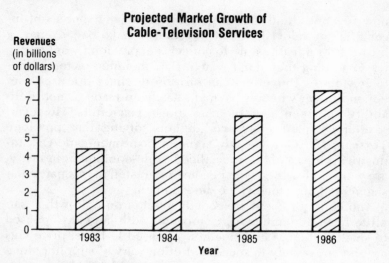

Projected Market Growth of Cable-Television Services

Revenues (in billions of dollars)

Year

Estimated compound annual growth rate: 20 percent

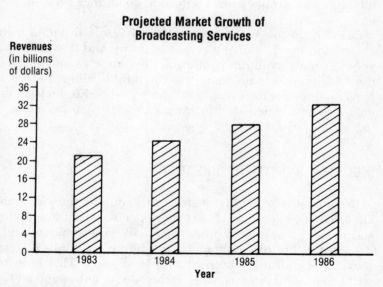

Projected Market Growth of Broadcasting Services

Revenues (in billions of dollars)

Year

Estimated compound annual growth rate: 15 percent

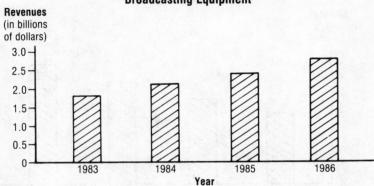

Projected Market Growth of Broadcasting Equipment

Estimated compound annual growth rate: 17 percent

nects are increasing. The favorable impact of pay cable on the industry is also fading.

It will be a while before addressability provides significant returns on cable-system-operator investments. Meanwhile, a continuing investment concern is the uncertain competitive impact of coming alternatives in broadcasting and transmission modes such as direct-broadcast satellites and Videotex.

The trick here is not to waste too much energy on crystal-

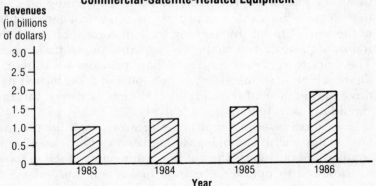

Projected Market Growth of Commercial-Satellite-Related Equipment

Estimated compound annual growth rate: 25 percent

Projected Market Growth of Video Users' Equipment

Estimated compound annual growth rate: 18 percent

Note: These figures include cable-television equipment, dish antennas, and other ancillary equipment.

ball gazing. What the investor must do is to try to buy cheaply enough not to have paid for any good news that does not materialize. Good news, should it come, will be a bonus.

Unlike many high-tech investments, video-technology stocks should not be bought strictly on the basis of growth. Investors should also evaluate them in terms of their resale potential. Examining their past, present, and likely future returns is a job for the experts, and a time-consuming one, but in the case of the cable companies you can gain a general idea of the market trends by keeping track of current prices in the industry's private transactions as reported in the trade press. The favorite yardstick used is dollars paid per subscriber, a figure which has ranged between $300 and $600 for the past three or four years. Like all rules of thumb, however, this one should not be relied upon exclusively.

In evaluating equipment manufacturers, look for proprietary niches where technological know-how affords an edge in competitive position. Many of the components of video transmission and reception are easy to make, and thus subject to foreign, particularly Japanese, cloning competition as well as to vigorous domestic rivalry. The field is relatively young and still evolving, so the investor cannot afford to be complacent about any of the companies' past records of success.

Federal Communications Commission regulatory whimsicality has been a problem for the cable industry in the past. So has the lobbying clout of the established broadcasters and networks, which for obvious reasons don't want cable to carve up what has until now been their exclusive pie. These factors seem likely to be much less crucial in the future, however, provided the pro-competitive mood prevalent in Washington continues. The AT&T breakup, apparently remote from the realms of cable and satellite broadcasting, could nevertheless have implications for these industries. So watch developments carefully as they unfold in 1983 and beyond.

KEY COMPANIES

American Satellite and Television, Inc.
900 Northwest Eighth Avenue
Gainesville, FL 32601
Telephone: (904) 371-7771
Contact: Mark Goldstein, President
       Market: OTC
       Symbol: ASTV/ASTVU
American Satellite and Television develops condominiums in southern Florida and operates cable-television (CATV) systems in northwestern Florida.

Andrew Corporation
1500 West 153rd Street
Orland Park, IL 60462
Telephone: (312) 349-3300
Contact: W. J. Morgan, Vice-President of Finance
       Market: OTC
       Symbol: ANDW
The Andrew Corporation manufactures microwave antenna systems and related equipment, usually on a turnkey basis, for major telecommunications and telephone companies worldwide, with foreign firms contributing half its revenues. The corporation has a good position and record.

Cable TV Industries
5933 Bowcroft Street
Los Angeles, CA 90016
Telephone: (213) 204-4440
Contact: E. M. Acker, Chief Executive Officer
Market: OTC
Symbol: CATV

This firm is a distributor, and to a minimal extent a manufacturer, of CATV construction hardware, cable, tools, and
reception equipment.

C-COR Electronics
60 Decibel Road
State College, PA 16801
Telephone: (814) 238-2461
Contact: Sally Thiel
Market: OTC
Symbol: CCBL

A leading manufacturer of cable-television amplifiers and
minting money on them, C-COR is dependent on Warner-
Annex (which has accounted for a large percentage of its sales
in recent years) and other major multiple-systems operators
(MSOs) as customers.

Comcast Corporation
One Belmont Avenue
Bala Cynwyd, PA 19004
Telephone: (215) 667-4200
Contact: J. A. Brodsky, Treasurer
Market: OTC
Symbol: CMCSA

Comcast operates cable-television and pay-for-what-you-
watch systems in six Eastern states, serving 210,000 basic and
170,000 pay subscribers.

Cox Broadcasting Corporation
1601 West Peachtree Street, NE
Atlanta, GA 30309
Telephone: (404) 897-7000

Contact: R. T. Tucker or Linda Stewart
Market: NYSE
Symbol: COX

Fourth from the top in cable television, Cox Communications is strong. It operates radio and television stations in eight states for all three of the big networks.

Jones Intercable, Inc.

5275 DTC Parkway
Englewood, CO 80111
Telephone: (303) 740-9700
Contact: R. J. Lewis, President
Market: OTC
Symbol: JOIN and JOINA

Jones Intercable owns and operates cable-television systems as well as marketing participatory shares in CATV systems to the public.

LIN Broadcasting

1370 Avenue of the Americas
New York, NY 10019
Telephone: (212) 765-1902
Contact: M. Berkowitz
Market: OTC
Symbol: LINB

Most of LIN's earnings are from Texas broadcasts. The company operates radio and television stations there, along with radio-paging and mobile-radio systems. It has also applied for cellular-mobile-radio licenses. The good news is fresh top management.

MacLean-Hunter, Ltd.

481 University Avenue
Toronto, Ontario M5W 1A7
Canada
Telephone: (416) 595-1811
Contact: P. F. James, Treasurer
Market: OTC
Symbol: MHPX

Mainly a periodicals publisher, MacLean-Hunter is nevertheless in second place in the Canadian cable industry and a force in the United States cable market as well. The company is also involved in the radio-paging industry.

Microdyne Corporation
P.O. Box 7213, 491 Oak Road
Ocala, FL 32672
Telephone: (904) 687-4633
Contact: Alan Greenlaw
    Market: OTC
    Symbol: MCDY

An equipment manufacturer strong in telemetry receivers, used primarily in commercial satellite systems, Microdyne was to merge with Alpha Industries, of microwave repute, adding antenna strength to components. But reception became poor.

Miller Technology and Communications Corporation
4837 East McDowell Road
Phoenix, AZ 85008
Telephone: (602) 254-1129
Contact: Richard Krahl, Senior Vice-President
    Market: OTC
    Symbol: MECC

This services company operates Arizona Tech, providing training in electronics, computer programming, and broadcasting. Recession and government funding cuts may pose a problem.

Multimedia, Inc.
P.O. Box 1688, 305 South Main Street
Greenville, SC 29602
Telephone: (803) 298-4373
Contact: Donald Barhyte, Vice-Chairman
    Market: OTC
    Symbol: MMED

Multimedia publishes newspapers, broadcasts television and radio programs, and runs sixty cable-television systems encompassing four states and 150,000 basic subscribers.

Oak Industries
100 South Main Street
Crystal Lake, IL 60014

Telephone: (815) 459-5000
Contact: R. J. Hartney
  Market: NYSE
  Symbol: OAK

The lead that this equipment producer had in cable-television converters slipped. The company manufactures a hodge-podge of electronics components and provides subscription television to 595,000 subscribers in five states.

Pico Products

1001 Vine Street
Liverpool, NY 13088
Telephone: (315) 451-0680
Contact: Ralph Yahn, Treasurer
  Market: ASE
  Symbol: PPI

A very small and speculative manufacturer of cable-television security products, Pico Products used to be known as the Product Identification Company.

Radiation Systems

1501 Moran Road
Sterling, VA 22170
Telephone: (703) 450-5680
Contact: Michael Steinman
  Market: OTC
  Symbol: RADS

Radiation Systems makes proprietary antenna systems for military, satellite, and air-traffic-control applications.

Reeves Communications

605 Third Avenue
New York, NY 10158
Telephone: (212) 573-8600
Contact: R. E. Trives, Senior Vice-President and Treasurer
  Market: OTC
  Symbol: RVCC

This company produces and distributes television programs and movies for consumer and corporate markets. It's also a mail-order books-and-such publisher. Half its revenues are foreign, and American Broadcasting recently accounted for another fifth. Reeves moves fast, but it's hard to predict.

Rogers Cablesystems

Commercial Union Tower
Toronto, Ontario M5K 1JS
Canada
Telephone: (416) 864-2373
Contact: W. A. Scarrow, Treasurer
         Market: OTC
         Symbol: RCINZ

Rogers Cablesystems bought UA-Columbia's cable systems in the United States. Profits are presently a problem. The largest cable operator in Canada, it serves a total of 1,900,000 television subscribers.

S.A.L. Cable Communications, Inc.

5 Hub Drive
Melville, NY 11747
Telephone: (516) 694-7110
Contact: L. Johansen
         Market: OTC
         Symbol: SALC

S.A.L. is a distributor of cable-television products moving into manufacturing.

Scientific-Atlanta

3845 Pleasantdale Road
Atlanta, GA 30324
Telephone: (404) 449-2000
Contact: Sidney Topol, President
         Market: NYSE
         Symbol: SFA

An equipment manufacturer with an opportunistic and eclectic product strategy, this company jumped the tracks in 1981 and 1982 when its cable-television channel converter developed profit problems. The question to be answered is, Did the derailment represent simply a delay, or has Scientific-Atlanta run out of steam?

Storer Broadcasting

1177 Kane Concourse
Miami Beach, FL 33154

Telephone: (305) 866-0211
Contact: B. Edell
      Market: NYSE
      Symbol: SBK

Storer is a television broadcaster and cable-television-system operator with 845,000 basic and 880,000 premium subscribers.

TCA Cable TV

3027 Southeast Loop 323
Tyler, TX 75701
Telephone: (214) 595-3701
Contact: R. M. Rogers, President
      Market: OTC
      Symbol: TCAT

Twenty cable-television systems serving 110,000 subscribers in smaller communities of the Mississippi Delta area are operated by this company.

Tele-Communications, Inc.

54 Denver Technology Center
Denver, CO 80210
Telephone: (303) 771-8200
Contact: Donne Fisher, Chief Financial Officer
      Market: OTC
      Symbol: TCOMA

"Teecom" has cable systems in need of upgrading, but large, serving 1,100,000 basic and 470,000 pay-television subscribers in forty states.

Texscan Corporation

2446 North Shadeland Avenue
Indianapolis, IN 46219
Telephone: (317) 357-8781
Contact: Steven McGill, Treasurer, telephone
      (602) 252-5021
      Market: ASE
      Symbol: TXS

Texscan manufactures cable-television test, distribution, and converting equipment. That last item is the problem, because converters are tough to make at a profit.

Time Inc.

Time and Life Building, Rockefeller Center
New York, NY 10020
Telephone: (212) 586-1212
Contact: J. W. Fowlkes
Market: NYSE
Symbol: TL

Time is tops in cable television with its American Television and Communications (ATV) and Home Box Office (HBO). The company's magazine revenues are slipping, and its forest products present a profit problem, but considering the growth in ATV and HBO, who cares? Time also does database publishing.

Times Mirror

Times Mirror Square
Los Angeles, CA 90053
Telephone: (213) 972-3700
Contact: E. M. Higashi
Market: NYSE
Symbol: TMC

Seventh from the top in cable-television-subscriber ranking in this country, Times Mirror also provides data-base information services. Those and the cable-television profits represent one-fourth of its total revenues.

TOCOM, Inc.

P.O. Box 47066, 3301 Royalty Row
Irving, TX 75247
Telephone: (214) 438-7691
Contact: C. R. Gilkerson, Vice-President and Treasurer
Market: OTC
Symbol: TOCM

TOCOM, a replay of Texscan with interactive two-way-cable-systems equipment, has irregular and not very spectacular profits. Selkirk Holdings of Canada owns nearly 40 percent of the company.

Turner Broadcasting System, Inc.

1050 Techwood Drive, NW
Atlanta, GA 30318

Telephone: (404) 898-8700
Contact: Robert Wissler, Executive Vice-President
      Market: OTC
      Symbol: TBSIC

Turner's cable news network serves 4,300,000 subscribers. The firm's main revenues derive from its WTBS-TV broadcasts. It also owns the better part of three Atlanta-based professional sports teams.

United Cable Television

4700 South Syracuse Parkway
Denver, CO 80237
Telephone: (303) 779-5999
Contact: J. Bruning, Vice-President of Finance
      Market: NYSE
      Symbol: UCT

Operator of thirty-seven cable-television systems serving 410,000 basic and 295,000 pay subscribers, United Cable, formerly LVO Cable, just acquired 80 percent interest in Home Entertainment Network, Inc.

Viacom International, Inc.

1211 Avenue of the Americas
New York, NY 10036
Telephone: (212) 575-5175
Contact: A. G. Cooper, Vice-President and Treasurer
      Market: NYSE
      Symbol: VIA

Viacom, a program-syndication-business spinoff from CBS several years ago, has 550,000 basic and 360,000 pay subscribers to its cable television. It also runs radio and television broadcast stations.

LEADING ANALYSTS

Peter Falco
Merrill Lynch, Inc.
One Liberty Plaza
New York, NY 10080
Telephone: (212) 637-1336

Joe Fuchs
Kidder, Peabody and Company
10 Hanover Square
New York, NY 10005
Telephone: (212) 747-2796

Anthony Hoffman
A. G. Becker
55 Water Street
New York, NY 10041
Telephone: (212) 747-4000
   This analyst offers integrated cable-television coverage.

Lee Isgur
Paine Webber Mitchell Hutchins, Inc.
140 Broadway
New York, NY 10005
Telephone: (212) 437-6243
   Lee Isgur's focus is primarily entertainment.

Dennis Leibowitz
Donaldson, Lufkin and Jenrette
140 Broadway
New York, NY 10005
Telephone: (212) 902-2794
   Dennis Leibowitz is a good stock picker.

PERTINENT PUBLICATIONS

Advertising Age
Crain Communications, Inc.
740 North Rush Street
Chicago, IL 60611
Telephone: (312) 649-5200
   Subscription: $40 per year for weekly newspaper
Advertising Age, a general-interest industry publication,
features a second-section magazine pullout which covers a
different marketing subject each week and is often of use to
the high-tech investor.

Broadcasting
Broadcasting Publications, Inc.
1735 De Sales Street, NW

Washington, DC 20036
Telephone: (202) 638-1022
    Subscription: $55 per year for weekly periodical,
                controlled circulation
Business news is beamed toward management in radio and
television broadcasting, cable television, and other electronic
media. Coverage includes regulation, finance, technology, operations, programming, trade shows, and so on.

Cable TV Investor
Paul Kagan Associates, Inc.
26386 Carmel Rancho Lane
Carmel, CA 93923
Telephone: (408) 624-1536
    Subscription: $525 per year for semimonthly newsletter
Cable TV Investor is one of the two newsletters I'd rank
highest from among the twelve Paul Kagan Associates puts
out. The other is the *Pay TV Newsletter*.

Cablevision
Tisch Communications, Inc.
2500 Curtis Street
Denver, CO 80205
Telephone: (303) 573-1433
    Subscription: $54 per year for weekly periodical
Of all the publications in the field, this is the best one to read
if you're reading only one. It takes about two hours a week.

IDP Report
Knowledge Industry Publications, Inc.
701 Westchester Avenue
White Plains, NY 10604
Telephone: (914) 328-9157
    Subscription: $225 per year for biweekly newsletter
Video developments relating to data-base publishing, like
Videotex, for instance, are the primary focus of the *IDP Re-
port*. Digests and a calendar of meetings are also included in
this newsletter.

Pay TV Newsletter
(For address and telephone, see *Cable TV Investor*, above)
    Subscription: $495 per year for semimonthly newsletter

Here's the other top-ranking newsletter from Paul Kagan Associates.

Television Fact Book
Television Digest, Inc.
1836 Jefferson Place, NW
Washington, DC 20036
Telephone: (202) 872-9200
   Subscription: $173 for two-volume annual survey
The *Television Fact Book* comes as a set, one volume on services, the more valuable of the two for investors, and one on stations, more technically oriented. Both give statistics and lists for the broadcasting and cable industries, equipment, services, brokers, regulations, and so on.

Variety
Variety, Inc.
154 West 46th Street
New York, NY 10036
Telephone: (212) 582-2700
   Subscription: $60 per year for weekly newspaper
Cable television, home video, the top-selling video games, television, radio, records, film, theater—you name it, it's listed in *Variety*.

MAJOR MEETINGS

National Cable Television Association (NCTA)
1724 Massachusetts Avenue, NW
Washington, DC 20036
Telephone: (202) 775-3606
The National Cable Television Association meets yearly, each May, in Las Vegas.

XVI

Office Automation: More Than Just Word Processing

First heralded in the early seventies, the "office of the future" simply hasn't made its popular debut yet. As of this writing, only sixty of the thousand largest industrial companies in the United States have automated their offices to a degree that could be considered state of the art. Even the highly publicized word processor has replaced no more than one out of ten typewriters in the five hundred top industrial companies, admits John Cunningham, president of Wang Laboratories.

Why is the electronic metamorphosis so slow in coming? Much of the technology requisite to office automation (OA) is available. It would seem inevitable that self-operating machinery should sweep across the economy's office segment as surely as it raked the country's factories in earlier decades. Of the $1.3 trillion paid out in wages and benefits during 1980, 60 percent went to office workers, including managerial and professional employees. A study by the management consulting firm of Booz, Allen, and Hamilton has shown that managers and professionals could improve the time/work performance records of their staffs by 15 percent via the utilization of automated office equipment—for a productivity gain of $300 billion annually before the year 1990.

Savings, even to that degree, however, cannot mitigate the fact that many people, including a large percentage of the senior management establishment, are uncomfortable with technology, not to mention high technology. Add to this discomfort the dehumanizing Orwellian possibilities automated offices suggest, and the natural human antipathy to change becomes alarmingly amplified. This book does not examine the psychological and moral impacts of technology. Nevertheless, it might be interesting to note, not altogether as an aside, some of the under-reported facets of word-processing technology.

For instance, did you know that it is possible to monitor every keystroke a word-processor operator makes? To tally the day's corrected errors? To keep, in other words, a constant and highly accurate production surveillance over the staff of an electronically automated office?

The surveillance possibilities go far beyond that simple accounting for errors in the case of electronic mail, the other consummate staple of the automated office. Given its facilities, a manager can check, electronically, that the employees under his supervision actually read their mail—and when they do so.

That is a concept always to be kept in the back of the investor's mind—but not too far back. For while the chances of a full-fledged uprising against electronics are slim, there is always the remote possibility that employees as a class will short-circuit the electronics office by pursuing privacy legislation that would, in effect, impede the technology's progress to the point where it might no longer be cost-effective. Some European trade-union contracts, for instance, already prohibit a worker from being assigned for more than half a day to a video terminal.

Quite apart from the thwarting effects of technophobia, the automated office is plagued by the specter of outright failure. One of its most promising adjuncts, teleconferencing, the simultaneous communication among several people in different locations, has turned out to be pretty much of a bust. Whether it's the loss of expense-account lunches and status travel or the human factor of real interaction, for some reason the teleconference, like the moribund picture phone, is simply not pulling in the customers as it was expected to do.

The Booz, Allen, and Hamilton study results notwithstanding, the cost savings of the automated office may well turn out to be a dream in any event. The market-research firm of SRI International surveyed some four thousand offices in an attempt to determine which of their procedures could effectively be automated. The results of the study were quite startling. There were savings in special situations such as legal-department procedures. Otherwise, even if the offices concerned were equipped with word-processing equipment, there were few instances of direct cost savings. Indirect benefits might have been another matter. Those are hard to quantify, however. A word processor may speed up the sending out of a bid, for instance, but how do you measure any savings under such circumstances?

Office automation nevertheless moves on. Copying machines, the leading edge in high technology in their own right only twenty years ago, have been upstaged by personal computers and the incoming video generation of devices. The relatively slow pace of change in office environments to date is about to accelerate rapidly despite prior resistance. For productivity in the office sector must be improved somehow if it is to balance out increasing salary and tax costs. The average age of the work force in this country is increasing. There are simply fewer younger employees available for entry-level salary positions. So employers must rely largely on increasing the productivity of the staffs they have in order to keep profits climbing, and about the only way they see left today to boost that productivity is to offer their employees better tools for their main task, which more and more centers on the handling of information. Hence the attractiveness of word processors and related automation units.

As customer demand for office automation increases, the marketing key will probably be workstations. Workstations are what we used to call desks, except that these come complete with electronic instrumentation, usually including a word processor but also quite often incorporating electronic drafting devices and other design tools. Most have electronic-mail capabilities as well.

The reason workstations are so pivotal in automation marketing is that once employees settle into them, the stations develop a compulsive appeal to their users. As Joe Ramellini, manager of office systems at CBS, put it for *Fortune* magazine, "If users like the equipment, they'll chain themselves to it rather than let you remove it." In the same article, a psychologist called in by Xerox to evaluate what would happen if its workstations were removed phrased his conclusions more elementally. "My God! I haven't seen dependence like this outside a methadone clinic."

If the workers don't want to switch workstations, then any upgrading, any add-ons, any expansion equipment orders will perforce devolve upon the original suppliers. Burroughs, IBM, Honeywell, and Wang have all taken this approach to marketing, trying first to get a typewriter or word processor in the office, and then providing an endless progression of up-grades.

But this broad-scale plan to conquer the office is a relatively new sales technique. For a while the giants slept. It's true that a number of word-processing producers that were leading the field in the late 1970s were bought up by larger companies with the financial strength to promote and expand upon them aggressively. Daconics was acquired by Xerox, Lexitron by Raytheon, Linolex by Minnesota Mining and Manufacturing, Redactron by Burroughs, Vydec by Exxon, and Wordstream by Management Assistance, Inc. But the acquiring companies either couldn't see the market for their money or simply couldn't deal with the management style of the smaller firms. In any event, nothing much came of these mergers. In fact, al-most half of these early word-processing ventures are no more.

The vacuum created by their demise was soon filled. A whole new generation of companies devoted single-mindedly to word processors took their place. The most popular of these word-processors-only companies, from a buyer's standpoint, were probably CPT and NBI, both of which, along with the older Lanier, defined the product gap and the marketing niches, and then proceeded to leapfrog even the big tradi-tional competitors with their fresh, focused marketing ap-proach. For IBM, Wang, and Xerox made it more or less clear that they were going to force the doors of *Fortune*'s top thou-sand companies, leaving everything else, being more costly to reach, to anyone who cared to grab it.

Particularly successful among the companies that took up the gauntlet are Syntrex and Convergent Technologies, the first firms to produce office workstations which put it all— word processing, filing, and data processing—together in one unit. They wrapped their packages in corporately affordable prices and took them to the secondary market of medium and small offices, with excellent sales results.

Eventually the large buyers will come to represent a satu-rated market. If IBM and its ilk should then decide to go after the secondary market, they may well find the premises al-ready occupied by the word processors and workstations of the upstarts—and customers loyal enough not to switch. This is what gives the small manufacturers of such equipment today a chance for really explosive growth.

The niche-filling approach is endemic—and quite successful—in the office-automation industry. Most of the nook-and-cranny companies are small and private. But at least some of them can be expected to go public as their capital demands increase. Certain ones will be bought out by larger companies before that stage arrives, of course. However, given the dismal track record of such buy-outs recently, the investor should not lack for opportunities to purchase stock in specialty office-automation companies in the eighties.

Among the more remarkable new ventures in electronic office equipment are the intelligent machines on which Cognex and Proximity Devices are both working. The experimental systems of these two enterprises are intended to be capable of reading, "understanding," and—so help us—acting upon information fed to them, much in the manner of humans. Cognex's DataMan is already hard at work for Kodak, checking the serial numbers on chemical packages. It does the job by actually "reading" the figures rather than by utilizing the customary fax technology, wherein comparisons are made between the images stored in the computer and those appearing in the outside world.

Then there's the accessory approach taken by Datamarc. Its original subsidiary, Daisytek, was set up as a distributor of daisy-wheel printers. Datamarc itself decided that while everyone might be talking about the paperless office, paper would still be around, no matter how much automation occurred. So it's developing equipment to speed up paper handling. The company's first product in its new line is an automatic envelope feeder designed to complement the five most popular word-processing printers on the market. It is also making a form feeder to insert paper into the printer. As Joe Ballew, Datamarc's founder, succinctly summarized the reasoning behind the move, "Technology has given the office typewriter-quality printers that run automatically. Employers don't want to pay an operator just to feed the paper into the printer."

Printer technology as a whole is lagging in the office-automation race. The fact of the matter is that once you start dealing with mechanical problems, solutions are more difficult to come by. Fast printers for large computers have always suffered from poor print quality, even at their best. Word-processing printers offering letter-quality reproduction, on the other hand, are slow—relative to other computer standards, a span of forty seconds taken to type out a page is slow, whatever it might be by human standards.

Seeing the need for high quality and speed combined, a number of companies are developing machines to fill this market niche. Their devices use laser beams, ion guns, or magnetic heads to write the characters. The technology is not startlingly new. Laser printers, for instance, have been around since 1978, although a two-pages-per-second—yes, that's per second—printer like Xerox's 9700, representative of the type, characteristically commands a price not much under $500,000. What is new is the price drop that is increasingly imminent as more and more manufacturers go after the quality-plus-high-speed end of the market. Canon and General Obtronics are both turning out ten-pages-per-minute gallium arsenide laser printers for the quality market less concerned with speed. At $10,000 to $50,000 per unit, these machines represent a real price breakthrough. So computer-printer manufacturers such as Dataproducts and Printronix may yet offer the investor opportunities for profitable participation in the office-automation trend.

Other identifiable investment segments include the private branch exchange (PBX) and keyset systems and the local-area-network products, among them high-speed links for use between computers in an office environment and various tele-communications devices used in electronic mail. Private branch exchange systems are likely to develop into the central nervous system of the electronic office, tying together all the information-processing devices, or data appliances. Computers, video terminals, copiers, printers, word processors, telephones and disk files will all be linked and connected with the outside world through sophisticated PBX units. Computer Consoles, Datapoint, Intecom, Mitel, Northern Telecom, Rolm, and TIE/Communications are all working on PBX technology. Chances are no single supplier will dominate the industry, but there will be market leaders, and they should become very profitable.

As to networking, one of the reasons suppliers like word processors is that they are the Trojan horses of electronic mail. Once a word processor is on an individual's desk, it's very easy to interconnect it with another, and another, and with yet others geographically quite distant. Far-flung organizations, national and even international, can be effectively knit together, the microprocessor and electronic telecommunications together providing fast and inexpensive exchange of information—two good business arguments for electronic mail.

The technology of electronic mail itself has many facets. Modems (which convert data to and from telephone-transmissible form), data concentrators, and data switches are its most important basic products. Among the companies working on developing and refining these and related devices while simultaneously trying to provide more bang for the buck are Gandalf Technologies, Infotron Systems, Micom Systems, Network Systems, and Paradyne.

The many facets of office automation will all be influenced by the prevailing winds of change. First, the equipment of the futuristic office will have more electronic features, which at the same time will cost less than they have heretofore. Secondly, the breakup of AT&T is a joker in the deck that will fold some companies and give others a full house. Thirdly, the field will be a marketeer's market by the mid-1980s. The technology of automation will be generally available, and the salesmanship of the several companies, their ability to promote a product essentially the same as everyone else's, will spell the difference between success and failure. The tenuous edge in sales will in turn limit a company's life in the high P/E stratosphere. As the real differences between products lessen, only the perceived difference, the illusion, will remain as the true selling point—and illusions don't last more than a couple of years, even in the fantasy world of high technology.

INDUSTRY INVESTMENT DIRECTIONS

There are many subindustries contributing to office automation, as we have seen. Some of them are of more interest to

Projected Market Growth of Word-Processing Equipment

(U.S. Producers Only)

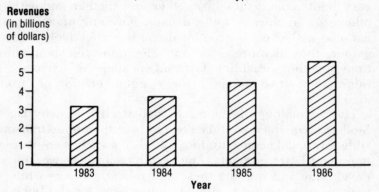

Estimated compound annual growth rate: 22 percent

Note: These figures exclude electronic typewriters.

Projected Market Growth of Serial and Line Printers

(U.S. Producers Only)

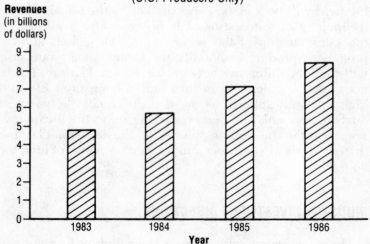

Estimated compound annual growth rate: 24 percent

Projected Market Growth of
Private Branch Exchange and Keyset Systems
(U.S. Producers Only)

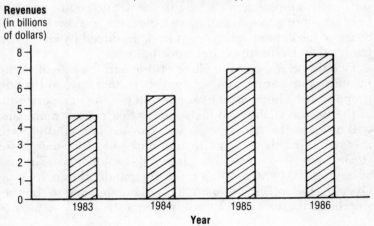

Estimated compound annual growth rate: 21 percent

the investor than others because their potential for growth is greater.

Overall market trends are difficult to define except in the broadest sense. But the workstation of the near future seems likely to include a microcomputer, perched on the user's desk for easy access and probably capable of both independent tasks and activities coordinated within a network of peripheral equipment such as storage devices, printers and copiers, and telecommunications devices to handle both data and voice traffic.

There will be general-purpose business versions of the workstation, addressing large markets, and there will be specialized equipment aimed at those smaller markets which have adequate size and growth potential to attract new companies and new products. In order to gain broad customer acceptance, the business-beamed workstations will have to come down in price to a level competitive with that of the most ubiquitous desktop appliance, the telephone. That's a fairly large order. Companies dealing in the more specialized markets, meanwhile, offer the investor some of the best money-multiplying opportunities available.

Possibly the greatest investment opportunity of all in the office-automation industry may be provided by the companies producing the switching devices likely to evolve during the further development of PBX equipment. Such equipment will become more generalized, more expensive, and probably, because of the capital outlays required, produced by larger companies than those supplying workstations.

Two things are certain: Competition and the rate of change in office-automation products will both increase, to dizzying proportions. The constant variation in the buyer's perception of the best available products means that market dominance will be rare. Also, stock prices will rise and fall rapidly. So the investor is likely to have to buy and sell office-automation stocks more frequently than in less dynamic areas. The days of buying IBM and holding it for the grandchildren are gone. Overall, the office-automation market appears to be best suited to investors with a trading mentality.

KEY COMPANIES

Computer Consoles, Inc.
97 Humboldt Street
Rochester, NY 14609
Telephone: (716) 482-5000
Contact: Herman Affel, President
Market: ASE
Symbol: CCS

Computer Consoles manufactures telecommunications equipment such as fault-tolerant computer (PBX) systems for telephone companies. Its strength has been in its directory-assistance line. The company is diversifying its market.

Convergent Technologies
2500 Augustine Drive
Santa Clara, CA 95051
Telephone: (408) 727-8830
Contact: Alan Michels, President
Market: OTC
Symbol: CVGT

A dual-workstation desktop computer with mainframe characteristics is Convergent Technologies' main product, a unit it delivers to original-equipment manufacturers such as Burroughs, C 3, and NCR for resale.

CPT Corporation
8100 Mitchell Road
P.O. Box 295
Eden Prairie, MN 55440
Telephone: (612) 937-8000
Contact: Greg Chaplin
Market: OTC
Symbol: CPTC

Second in growth as a word-processor manufacturer, CPT prospered by selling via small-town office-machine dealers. Recent management turmoil has raised concern over the company's transition to a tougher era.

Datapoint Corporation
7900 Callaghan Road
San Antonio, TX 78284
Telephone: (512) 699-7000
Contact: Thomas Moldenhauer
Market: NYSE
Symbol: DPT

Office desktop computers, a digital private branch exchange system, fast growth, and persuasive concepts all came unglued in 1982 when sales controls became lax. Rebuilding is in progress.

Dataproducts Corporation
6200 Canoga Avenue
Woodland Hills, CA 91365
Telephone: (213) 887-8000
Contact: Frank McQuaid, Senior Vice-President
Market: ASE
Symbol: DPC

A leader among the independent makers of high-speed line printers for use with computers, this peripheral-equipment manufacturer is moving up in matrix printers, used in cheaper, less demanding applications.

Gandalf Technologies, Inc.
33 John Street
Manotick, Ontario KOA 2NO
Canada
Telephone: (613) 692-2577
Contact: Des Cunningham, Chief Executive Officer
   Market: OTC
   Symbol: GANDF
Gandalf Technologies is a top manufacturer of short-haul data-communications modems for local-area networks, devices less expensive than those designed for long-distance communications.

Infotron Systems Corporation
Cherry Hill Industrial Center
Cherry Hill, NJ 08003
Telephone: (609) 424-9400
Contact: G. L. Rhoades, Executive Vice-President
   Market: OTC
   Symbol: INFN
The foremost maker of multiplexers for mixed-equipment local-area networks, Infotron has the Bell System for a customer, and Ma supplies over a fourth of the company's revenues. Infotron bit off more technology than it could chew in 1981. It's busy catching up.

Inter-Tel, Inc.
3232 West Virginia Avenue
Phoenix, AZ 85009
Telephone: (602) 269-5091
Contact: R. Long, Treasurer
   Market: OTC
   Symbol: INTL
Inter-Tel is a fast-growing distributor of keyset telephones, which serve as alternatives to private branch exchanges in smaller systems. Its customers are commercial users. The company recently had a problem similar to Infotron's, only worse.

Lanier Business Products
1700 Chantilly Drive, NE
Atlanta, GA 30324

Telephone: (404) 329-8000
Contact: W. R. Campbell, Vice-President
      Market: NYSE
      Symbol: LBP

Besides its own word-processing machines, Lanier distributes dictation equipment manufactured by Minnesota Mining and Manufacturing and by AES Data, a Canadian company in which it has part ownership. It's a leader in lower-priced-equipment sales, but vulnerable to competition.

Micom Systems, Inc.

20151 Nordhoff Street
Chatsworth, CA 91311
Telephone: (213) 998-8844
Contact: Jo Anne Martz
      Market: OTC
      Symbol: MICS

Micom Systems manufactures statistical multiplexers and port selectors for data links connecting minicomputers. The selling is done by outside distributors. The company is a comer.

Mitel Corporation

350 Leggett Drive
Kanata, Ontario K2K 1X3
Canada
Telephone: (613) 592-2122
Contact: D. R. Gibbs, Vice-President of Finance
      Market: NYSE
      Symbol: MLT

A fast-stepping Canadian contender for the private branch telephone exchange systems market, Mitel is strong in the low-to-medium-priced range of products. It may be attempting too much, but if Mitel accomplishes even half of what it has set out to do, the prospects are great. Accounting is liberal because of differences in the standards used in Canada and the United States.

NBI, Inc.

P.O. Box 9001, 1695 38th Street
Boulder, CO 80301

Telephone: (303) 444-5710
Contact: Jesse Simmons, Treasurer
  Market: NYSE
  Symbol: NBI
NBI is the fastest grower in the word-processing field, offering a clustered system to complement the stand-alone variety. Easy-to-use software with many user options has been a plus.

Network Systems Corporation
7600 Boone Avenue North
Minneapolis, MN 55428
Telephone: (612) 425-2202
Contact: R. A. Fisher
  Market: OTC
  Symbol: NSCO
Network Systems makes peripheral equipment capable of linking the computers and peripherals of different manufacturers together to allow a high-speed local interchange of data. The company is working on a device to achieve the same results for remote data links. It benefits from the perceived uniqueness of its products.

Northern Telecom, Ltd.
33 City Centre Drive
Mississauga, Ontario L5B 2N5
Canada
Telephone: (416) 275-0960
Contact: Richard Wertheim
  Market: NYSE
  Symbol: NT
The leading Canadian manufacturer of private branch exchange and much other telephone and telecommunications equipment, Northern Telecom could be called the Western Electric of Canada. The firm's strength lies in the higher-priced range of PBX systems.

Paradyne Corporation
8550 Ulmerton Road
Largo, FL 33540
Telephone: (813) 530-2244

Contact: George Pressly, Senior Vice President
   Market: NYSE
   Symbol: PDN

Paradyne manufactures high-speed modems for IBM computer networks, plus network-management equipment. The latter has been a bit slow to take off.

Printronix, Inc.

P.O. Box 19559, 17500 Cartwright Road
Irvine, CA 92713
Telephone: (714) 549-7700
Contact: Dixie Dickenson, Assistant Secretary
   Market: OTC
   Symbol: PTNX

Medium-priced matrix line printers, which have enjoyed great success, are Printronix's product.

Rolm Corporation

4900 Old Ironsides Drive
Santa Clara, CA 95050
Telephone: (408) 988-2900
Contact: Robert Dahl, Chief Financial Officer
   Market: NYSE
   Symbol: RM

A manufacturer of private branch telephone switching systems for commercial and industrial customers, Rolm has strength at the low-to-medium-size end of the product spectrum. A battle looms ahead with larger sizes and digital data systems.

Sykes Datatronics, Inc.

159 East Main Street
Rochester, NY 14604
Telephone: (716) 325-9000
Contact: Monty Bauer, Investor Relations
   Market: OTC
   Symbol: SYKE

Sykes manufactures a line of private branch exchange stations for telephone companies to market to individual and commercial end users for utilization in data processing, computer-aided design, point-of-sale terminals, and so on. Buying on the part of the telephone companies, which had accounted for 80 percent of Sykes's revenues, was irregular during fiscal 1982–83 because of concern over their impending divestiture by AT&T.

Syntrex, Inc.
246 Industrial Way West
Eatontown, NJ 07724
Telephone: (201) 542-1500
Contact: William Alznauer, Treasurer
      Market: OTC
      Symbol: STRX

A late but fast start, with a clever line, in the word-processing arena makes Syntrex a company to watch. It's perhaps too dependent on Olivetti for comfort (that company represented 62 percent of its revenues recently).

TIE/Communications, Inc.
Five Research Drive
Shelton, CT 06484
Telephone: (203) 929-7373
Contact: G. A. Poch, Secretary
      Market: ASE
      Symbol: TIE

Like Inter-Tel, TIE is a fast-growing supplier of keyset telephones to commercial users. Its strategy execution has been impressive.

Wang Laboratories, Inc.
One Industrial Avenue
Lowell, MA 01851
Telephone: (617) 459-5000
Contact: Harry Chou, Vice-Chairman
      Market: ASE
      Symbol: WAN.B and WAN.C

Wang has the largest share of the market in word processing, plus a good position in desktop computers. It also has clever marketers—they had to be to gain on IBM.

LEADING ANALYSTS

Michael DeSantis
Robertson, Colman and Stephens
100 California Street
San Francisco, CA 94111
Telephone: (415) 781-9700
Local-area-network equipment is one of Michael DeSantis's
specialties.

Melody Johnson
Kidder, Peabody and Company, Inc.
10 Hanover Square
New York, NY 10005
Telephone: (212) 747-2790
   Melody Johnson is a word-processing-companies expert.

Sy Kaufman and Bruce Seltzer
Hambrecht and Quist, Inc.
235 Montgomery Street
San Francisco, CA 94104
Telephone: (415) 986-5500
These analysts cover the market for word-processing and
other peripheral computer equipment, along with telephone
private branch exchange systems.

Mary McCaffrey and Charles Reid
Alex Brown and Son
135 East Baltimore Street
Baltimore, MD 21202
Telephone: (301) 727-1700
Companies providing private branch exchange systems for
telephones and those supplying local-area computer-network
equipment are reviewed by this team.

Amy Newmark
Cyrus J. Lawrence, Inc.
115 Broadway
New York, NY 10006
Telephone: (212) 962-2200
   This analyst covers private branch exchange companies.

James Vail
William Blair and Company
135 South LaSalle Street
Chicago, IL 60603
Telephone: (312) 236-1600
James Vail has followed word-processing companies for several years.

Ulric Weil
Morgan Stanley and Company, Inc.
1251 Avenue of the Americas
New York, NY 10020
Telephone: (212) 974-4396
In addition to computers, Ulric Weil follows word-processing and local-area-network-equipment firms.

Ivan Wolff
Donaldson, Lufkin and Jenrette Securities Corporation
140 Broadway
New York, NY 10005
Telephone: (212) 902-2000
Private branch telephone exchange systems and local-area computer-network equipment are Ivan Wolff's field of expertise.

Thomas Wong
F. Eberstadt and Company, Inc.
61 Broadway
New York, NY 10006
Telephone: (212) 480-1393
Thomas Wong covers the word-processing and private-branch-exchange markets.

PERTINENT PUBLICATIONS

Computerworld
CW Communications, Inc.
Box 880, 375 Cochituate Road
Framingham, MA 01701

Telephone: (617) 879-0700, (800) 343-6474 for
   subscriptions
   Subscription: $36 per year for weekly newspaper
Computerworld offers broad coverage of the computer industry, but also detailed news on the office-automation front.

Data Communications
McGraw-Hill, Inc.
1221 Avenue of the Americas
New York, NY 10020
Telephone: (212) 997-1221, (609) 448-8110 for
   subscriptions
   Subscription: $24 per year to nonqualified subscribers
               for monthly periodical, controlled
               circulation $18 per year
This publication supplies coverage of computers, telephony, and the other accoutrements of office automation for
those in the business. An annual technology roundup issue
appears every December.

Datamation
Technical Publishing Company
875 Third Avenue
New York, NY 10022
Telephone: (212) 489-2588
   Subscription: $40 per year for 13 issues
In-depth articles on all phases of data processing, information systems, and office automation are *Datamation*'s
strength. The articles are written for the professional working
in the field, but they are also generally intelligible to the lay
reader.

Office Automation Reporting Service
International Data Corporation
5 Speen Street
Framingham, MA 01701
Telephone: (617) 872-8200
   Subscription: $325 per year for semimonthly newsletter
Written a bit too much from the standpoint of the specialist
in data processing, office management or information systems,
this newsletter often becomes mired in boring details.

Telephone Engineer and Management
Harcourt Brace Jovanovich Publications
757 Third Avenue
New York, NY 10017
Telephone: (212) 232-1400
  Subscription: $34 per year to nonqualified subscribers
        for semimonthly periodical, controlled
        circulation $19 per year (address inquiries
        to 134 South First Street, Geneva, IL
        60134)
This publication is for the telephone-company engineer or
manager, or his counterpart in a large corporation.

Telephony
Telephony Publishing Company
55 East Jackson
Chicago, IL 60604
Telephone: (312) 922-2435
  Subscription: $26 per year for weekly periodical
Telephony gives you more information than you'll ever
want on running a telephone company. The publication is
more regulatory in focus than *Telephone Engineer and Management*.

MAJOR MEETINGS

National Computer Conference (NCC)
American Federation of Information Processing Societies
  (AFIPS)
1815 North Lynn Street
Arlington, VA 22209
Telephone: (703) 558-8617
This behemoth of conventions, all about everything to do
with computers, including their use in office automation, is
held every June in a major city.

PROFESSIONAL ASSOCIATIONS

American Federation of Information Processing Societies,
  Inc.

(For address and telephone, see the National Computer Conference, under *Major Meetings,* above)

Association for Computing Machinery (ACM)
1133 Avenue of the Americas
New York, NY 10036
Telephone: (212) 265-6300
A cosponsor of the National Computer Conference, this association has its own SIGGRAPH show on computer graphics every year as well. Its special-interest group for office automation is SIGOA.

Institute of Electrical and Electronic Engineers (IEEE)
345 East 47th Street
New York, NY 10017
Telephone: (212) 644-7555
The institute sponsors meetings such as WESCON, NEPCON, and so on, useful for office-automation devotees.

XVII

Consumer Products: Filling the Electronic Sandbox

Consumer electronic products may well be the easiest of all the high-technology fields for the investor to track. It's pretty much like following show biz. However, the leading trend in the entertainment industry is a merger of various high technologies, while the end products, for the most part, have "traditional" content. Thus here, as in so many other places in the realm of high-tech investing, no one product can be considered by itself.

To look at the market from a media point of view for a moment, filmed entertainment has been stock in trade for over half a century in this country. Even as a staple industry, however, movieland has gone through three distinct phases. In the first, and longest, lasting from the early twenties to well into the early fifties, the movie theater was the only place to see a film—unless it happened to be a home movie, obviously an entirely different game. The second cycle, sweeping into full financial command within a decade of its early-fifties birth, spanned the development of television, first as a new and different outlet and finally as the primary medium for dramatic productions. By the mid-seventies, the third phase was taking off, a much more complex change involving satellite transponders, which led to pay and cable television, along with video disks and recorders, providing a third distribution force for theatrical releases. Satellite transmission opened a new window of opportunity for home-entertainment programming, even fostering new forms of programming. Suddenly there were many more companies, with more earnings and more assets to protect, joining the battle of the tube.

It's a two-front war, featuring countless small skirmishes on the side. One of the major battlefields involves the hardware. What will dominate the personal entertainment center—

video tape recorders or video disk systems? digital stereo disks or tapes or even solid-state cartridges? pay television or "free" cable? Or, as is more likely, will all these facets eventually be integrated, along with some form of personal-computer access to telephone lines, into one huge electronic sandbox in which the world can play?

The other main battlefield is the software, the programs to drive everybody's personal diversion center. After all, people will want more entertainment than simply possessing the first electronic gizmo on the block.

The production segment of show business, electronically conducted or traditionally conveyed, is unpredictable to the extreme. Audiences are nothing if not fickle. A studio might produce a *Star Wars* or an *E.T.* only to find its next dozen films flopping completely. Sure, there'd be *E.T. II* and *E.T. III*, maybe even *E.T. IV*, but suddenly, when least expected to do so, consumers might turn their backs on sci-fi fantasy altogether and fall in love with Wall Street comedies about Big Bud Bendix, Avenging Allied, and the Martin Marietta Monsters. It could happen.

Whatever the event, the actual programs, the content, will not be truly high-tech. The means by which they are produced will be—which brings us full circle to the hardware again. The hardware is the medium of audience participation.

Hardware is adaptable where public tastes and whims are not. Look at featherbone. According to a recent classic *Wall Street Journal* feature, featherbone was a fine product, made of turkey quills wrapped in cotton binding, used by turn-of-the-century dressmakers to give form to their spectacularly bouffant gowns. Featherbone, as superior hardware, replaced the old whalebone stays technology—and it wasn't a business to sneeze at, by the way. Edward K. Warren, founder of the Warren Featherbone Company, situated in the midst of Michigan's fabled Feather Valley, raked in sufficient loot to charter an ocean liner whenever he so desired to take some eight hundred people on a pilgrimage to Jerusalem. Alas, the featherbone craze died as American fashion was molded into sleeker lines.

And what of the Warren Featherbone Company? It's still well and clucking all the way to the bank. The shift away from featherboning was no overnight about-face. First plastics crept into the marketplace to replace featherbone as featherbone had replaced whalebone. When it did so, the Warren Featherbone Company stayed right on the leading edge of support technology, shifting production to the new wonder material. By the time featherbone went the way of the dodo, the firm was manufacturing various plastic clothing components, including the first plastic baby pants. As Charles E. Whalen, Jr., president of the company and great-grandson of Warren Featherbone's founder, explained, "We took what was our greatest threat—plastics—and made it work for us." The winning consumer electronics producers are going to be birds of the same feather.

The pieces that will eventually fall into place as a single-unit personal entertainment center are currently marketed separately. They may continue to sell in the component fashion of present-day stereo. But if they do so, it will be with the ability to interconnect with each other, something which telephones and video games to date cannot do. Then again, the personal computer, also used for video games, can. It can interface with other components such as a video disk or video cassette recorder too.

The personal computer may, in fact, be the salvation of the electronic-accessories market. Video-cassette sales, while quite respectable, have nevertheless been disappointing, and the video-disk market is almost a disaster area. An extra boost for disk sales, which have always suffered by comparison with the cassette market because disks cannot be erased and rerecorded, may be furnished by a recent breakthrough in Japanese technology. A thin gadolinium cobalt film coating allows disks to be reused just like tape. If it can be commercialized, the process should also allow the disks to be used for home recording, an attractive possibility not realized heretofore.

The older, more established video industry of television itself is changing drastically. First there's the Watchman, Sony's visual successor to the Walkman, that widespread potential destroyer of hearing. Weighing 19 ounces and measuring 8 inches in length, 1¼ inches in thickness, the Watchman has a 2-inch-diagonal screen. It can readily be held in the palm of the hand while one is strolling about. Sinclair Research has a model under a pound in weight and only an inch thick. It sports a 3-inch screen. Already the midgets are shrinking.

Diminishing size is not the only change in store for video. Tridimensionality and stereo sound are both coming to television. The third dimension will probably keep tripping over itself until at least sometime well into the nineties. Stereo, on the other hand, will probably become part of the overall entertainment realm in reasonably short order.

Already both video disks and video cassettes are being issued with stereo sound. Broadcast television is expected to follow suit, at least to a limited degree, by the end of 1983. Japan has had stereo television broadcasts since 1978, so guess who will probably dominate this market—and put your money elsewhere. If you can't resist a play in stereo, Telesonics Systems, so far privately held, may turn out to be an interesting gamble. Together with Zenith and the Electronic Industries Association of Japan, Telesonics is at the forefront of the industry in seeking to develop a standardized system for stereo television broadcasting.

If stereo-sound television is all but a certainty in the near future, and the third video dimension a likelihood only slightly further removed, then digital television is somewhere in between. Digital television probably represents the most fundamental design change to be heralded in video broadcasting since the advent of the color set some thirty years ago. It offers viewers high-resolution color displays like those currently available only on the more expensive personal computers. In essence, it also involves turning the television set into a computer, since it employs the same type of integrated circuits. A vastly improved television should thus become available at a price even lower than that of today's comparative kludges.

Initially, of course, following the traditional trend in consumer electronic products, these supersets will be the top-of-the-line models. But within five years, prices can hardly help but plummet, and such options as automatic ghost cancellation, flicker elimination, freeze frames, and even zoom capabilities to show details of the larger picture—a feature made to order for the video games evolving around the more complex high-resolution graphics—should all be available.

Digital television, then, may well spell trouble for the video-game-machine manufacturers. Who needs a game machine if the television set can do it all? As soon as there are enough digital television units in the family for everyone to have his or her own entertainment center, all bets are off— except those placed on the manufacturers of game cartridges, particularly "portable" ones. Machine-transferable cartridges, usable on a broad variety of personal computers and game apparatus, are not yet available, simply because there are no compatible-equipment standards for them to match. However, firms like Coleco and Imagic do make different cartridges for different machines, unlike such enterprises as Activision and the U.S. Games division of Quaker Oats (a video game in every cereal box, anyone?), whose cartridges are currently designed for the Atari microcomputer only.

The video-game industry is riddled with small private firms whose revenues have an astounding tendency to go from, say, $10,000 to $10 million in something like three years. Companies with such unfamiliar names as Cavalier Computer Corporation, Gebelli Software, On-Line Systems, Sirius Software, and Strategic Simulations aren't likely to need the capital infusion to be gained by going public soon. Then again, some of these enterprises are being financed by venture capitalists, who may eventually suggest that route in order to cash in their chips.

Considering that the compleat personal electronic entertainment center is shortly to represent the kind of cash outlay individuals to date have associated only with buying a new car, one more consumer electronic product is apt to proliferate, namely, the intrusion-detection device, in its manifold modes. Sales of these items, which used to be called burglar alarms, are expected to increase by 45 percent annually—just a shade under the rise in sales predicted for personal computers. Crime may not pay, but at the moment crime prevention is becoming a gold mine. A number of companies, among them privately held Checkpoint Systems and Sensormatic, specialize in retail security devices, and there are other firms such as Universal Security Instruments already heavily involved in residential security systems. Contemplating a population of video zombies sitting inside a personal home entertainment center, one can readily see that residential security systems are truly a wave of the future in consumer products. After all, someone has to keep a check on the real world out there.

**Projected Market Growth
(in U.S. Only)
of Electronic Games, Nonbusiness Software,
and Home Computers**

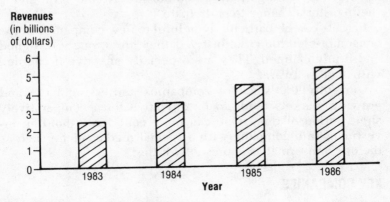

Estimated compound annual growth rate: 28 percent

INDUSTRY INVESTMENT DIRECTIONS

Portable electronics is the current rage. Semiconductor intelligence is revolutionizing consumer electronics. Unfortunately, the changes it has produced have not yet resulted in many new investment opportunities. A large percentage of the domestic public companies dominant today derive the greater portion of their revenues and profits from other endeavors.

Overall, the consumer-electronics market is so large and prices are so relatively low that only highly economical designs and massive unit sales can lead to company profits. This circumstance favors larger companies over smaller ones, a situation unlike that found in most high-tech fields, where successful mice usually run between the plodding elephant's feet.

However, the rapid changes being wrought by semiconductor technology are upsetting this accepted pattern, at least temporarily. Thus we can expect more investment opportunities in the near future. Innovations that can be brought to market quickly, placing a small originating company in a leading position for a while, are the kind of investment opportunity for which you should keep your eyes open. These small specialty producers, even those with very hot items, will soon run up against staggering capital needs if they are fully to supply the huge consumer-electronics market. When they do so, they may well go public in order to raise the cash, giving the investor a chance to participate.

Patents can be particularly helpful to new companies in the consumer-electronics industry if they are strongly designed and firmly claimed. They are especially effective if coupled with good software.

Currently the stock of companies addressing large and growing markets tends to be attractive for a comparatively short period of time. One can more confidently hold an investment in a company with a special market niche such as the one Sensormatics is presently filling.

KEY COMPANIES

Bally Manufacturing Corporation
2640 West Belmont Avenue
Chicago, IL 60613
Telephone: (312) 267-6060
Contact: G. K. Seidenfeld, Jr., Vice-President
       Market: NYSE
       Symbol: BLY
Bally manufactures coin-operated game and gambling machines, a third of them video, and runs casinos, arcades, and amusement parks.

Coleco Industries, Inc.
945 Asylum Avenue
Hartford, CT 06105
Telephone: (203) 278-0280
Contact: A. C. Greenberg, President
       Market: NYSE
       Symbol: CLO
Formerly an above-ground-swimming-pool company, Coleco is now one-third electronic games and rising fast. It may just effect the metamorphosis.

Detection Systems, Inc.
400 Mason Road
Fairport, NY 14450

Telephone: (716) 223-4060
Contact: David Davis, Treasurer
          Market: OTC
          Symbol: DETC

By rights, this is not a consumer company, but it operates in a field dear to the consumer's heart, namely, security. Selling its wares via alarm installers, it supplies commercial and industrial customers with high-tech intruder-detection devices.

General Instrument

1775 Broadway
New York, NY 10019
Telephone: (212) 974-8700
Contact: F. F. Cleminshaw
          Market: NYSE
          Symbol: GRL

"Gorilla," as the brokers call it, has been seen in all the right consumer places. To date, two-thirds of its profits have derived from cable television equipment. But its consumer-bound semiconductors, used in everything from electronic games to "smart" appliances and home communications equipment, are gaining in importance and provide the prospect of real growth.

International Game Technology

520 South Rock Boulevard
Reno, NV 89502
Telephone: (702) 323-5060
Contact: Jon Bengston
          Market: OTC
          Symbol: IGAM

Trouble looms for this manufacturer of coin-operated electronic casino games, since Bally has decided to take its electronic gambling machines to Nevada, International Game Technology's territory.

Irwin Toy, Ltd.

43 Hanna Avenue
Toronto, Ontario M6K 1X6
Canada
Telephone: (416) 533-3521

Contact: Louis Boaretti, Vice-President of Finance
Market: OTC
Symbol: IRWJK (voting) and IRWKF (nonvoting)

Irwin, a Canadian manufacturer and distributor of toys and games, is also the largest north-of-the-border distributor of Atari games and computers. Another feather in its cap is its Activision franchise.

Mattel, Inc.

5150 Rosecrans Avenue
Hawthorne, CA 90250
Telephone: (213) 978-5150
Contact: S. Boise
Market: NYSE
Symbol: MAT

Currently the toy manufacturer with the largest share of the market (10 percent), Mattel seems to be slipping in electronic games, which represent approximately half the company's income.

Sensormatic Electronics

500 Northwest 12th Avenue
Deerfield Beach, FL 33441
Telephone: (305) 427-9700
Contact: L. R. Barbato
Market: OTC
Symbol: SNSR

Beloved by investors for its consistency in growth, Sensormatic's products are the bane of shoplifters frequenting retail stores. Its line consists primarily of various types of tags for merchandise which set off a security alarm if not neutralized before the goods are removed from the store.

Tandy Corporation

1800 One Tandy Center
Fort Worth, TX 76102
Telephone: (817) 390-3730
Contact: Garland Asher, Director of Financial Planning
Market: NYSE
Symbol: TAN

The electronic supermarket of consumer products, operating out of its Radio Shack and computer-store outlets, Tandy sells a variety of electronic devices, a substantial number of which are manufactured in-house. Personal computers probably accounted for 25 to 30 percent of its profits in 1982.

Universal Security Instruments

10324 South Dolfield Road
Owings Mills, MD 21117
Telephone: (301) 363-3000
Contact: Stanley Katz, Chief Financial Officer
      Market: OTC
      Symbol: USEC

Struggling to find a profitable niche, this firm hit upon alarm and telecommunications products and services. It was in the red during fiscal 1981–82.

Vicon Industries, Inc.

125 East Bethpage Road
Plainview, NY 11803
Telephone: (516) 293-2200
Contact: Kenneth Darby, Treasurer
      Market: ASE
      Symbol: VII

Closed-circuit television, cameras, and other security and surveillance systems products have been slow to sell this past year.

Warner Communications, Inc.

75 Rockefeller Plaza
New York, NY 10019
Telephone: (212) 484-8000
Contact: G. W. Holmes, Vice-President
      Market: NYSE
      Symbol: WCI

Movies, books, records, tapes, Atari home video games— you name it, Warner has it.

Williams Electronics, Inc.

3401 North Carolina Avenue
Chicago, IL 60618

Telephone: (312) 267-2240
Contact: N. J. Merell, Executive Vice-President
Market: NYSE
Symbol: WMS

Spun off early in 1981 by Xcor International, Williams Electronics makes coin-operated pinball machines and electronic video games. What it really needs is one big winning arcade game after another to keep machine placements strong.

LEADING ANALYSTS

Joseph Frazzano
Oppenheimer and Company, Inc.
One New York Plaza
New York, NY 10004
Telephone: (212) 825-4307

Barbara and Lee Isgur
Paine Webber Mitchell Hutchins, Inc.
140 Broadway
New York, NY 10005
Telephone: (212) 437-2762 and (212) 437-6243

Barbara Isgur's focus is personal computers, Lee's is entertainment.

Ted Mayer
L. F. Rothschild, Unterberg, Towbin
55 Water Street
New York, NY 10041
Telephone: (212) 425-3147

Michele Preston
C. J. Lawrence, Inc.
115 Broadway
New York, NY 10006
Telephone: (212) 962-2200

Richard Simon
Goldman, Sachs
55 Broad Street
New York, NY 10004
Telephone: (212) 676-7810

Katherine Stults
Morgan Stanley and Company, Inc.
1251 Avenue of the Americas
New York, NY 10020
Telephone: (212) 974-4392

Harold Vogel
Merrill Lynch, Inc.
One Liberty Plaza, 165 Broadway
New York, NY 10080
Telephone: (212) 637-6509

PERTINENT PUBLICATIONS

There are plenty of personal-computer magazines among which to choose (check your newsstand), and new publications following the arcade and home video games are constantly starting up. The periodicals listed here have been around longer, but that in no way gives them a monopoly on consumer interest.

BYTE
Byte Publications, Inc.
70 Main Street
Peterborough, NH 03458
Telephone: (603) 924-9281
    Subscription: $19 per year for monthly periodical
                  (address inquiries to P.O. Box 590,
                  Martinsville, NJ 08836)
Heavy on pages and programs and technology, *BYTE* is nevertheless an industry leader.

Electronic Games
Reese Publishing Company, Inc.
235 Park Avenue South
New York, NY 10003
Telephone: (212) 777-0800
    Subscription: $28 per year for monthly periodical
                  (address inquiries to P.O. Box 1128,
                  Dover, NJ 07801)
Arcade and home video games are the coverage here.

Gaming Business (and *Gaming Industry News*)
BMT Publications, Inc.
254 West 31st Street
New York, NY 10001
Telephone: (212) 594-4120
   Subscription: $65 per year for monthly periodical
With a gambling-casino orientation but room for a fair
amount of news on developments in coin-operated games, this
magazine is expensive for what you get.

Videogaming Illustrated
Ion International, Inc.
32 Oak Ridge Road
Bethel, CT 06801
Telephone: (203) 743-6189
   Subscription: $15 per year for monthly periodical
Here's more arcade and home video games coverage.

MAJOR MEETINGS

COMDEX
Interface Group
166 Speen Street
Framingham, MA 01701
Telephone: (800) 225-4620
COMDEX convenes in Atlantic City every May, in Las
Vegas every November. The Vegas show is older and better
attended.

Consumer Electronics Show
2 Illinois Center, Suite 1607
233 North Michigan Avenue
Chicago, IL 60601
Telephone: (312) 861-1040
The show is on each January in Las Vegas, each June in
Chicago. Admission is free, but you must send in a letter beforehand giving your category of interest (that of a retail
buyer, for example, or a wholesale distributor—you would
probably classify yourself as an analyst, category 12). You
must also indicate your firm and company position, along with
the name and address to which a registration badge should be

sent. Some 100,000 people attend each Consumer Electronics Show, so if you plan to go, you'd best reserve your hotel room early!

In addition to these regularly scheduled conventions, Barbara and Lee Isgur at Paine Webber Mitchell Hutchins and Harold Vogel at Merrill Lynch, Pierce, Fenner and Smith (see *Leading Analysts,* above) sponsor analyst meetings on consumer products for client companies. Other brokers may offer similar seminars. Check with yours.

PROFESSIONAL ASSOCIATIONS

Electronic Industries Association
2001 I Street, NW
Washington, DC 20006
Telephone: (202) 457-4900
The marketing-services department of this association has several publications of note. Ask for descriptions. An annual *Electronic Market Data Book* is too general for anything but overall information. Besides, it costs $55.

XVIII

Medical Technology: The Difficult Mosaic of Miracles

If a single new medical breakthrough is capable of hitting the headlines of every newspaper and the cover of every journalistic periodical in the country as well as most of the six-o'clock news reports for a week running, that breakthrough would probably be a cancer cure. Yet there is much promising research being done in and progress being made toward the cure of a number of specific cancers, little of which headway makes the news. The popular press demands complete and final answers. But it's the partial discoveries, the small pieces falling into place, that fill in the picture and, let's hope, will provide the eventual solution of medical mysteries.

As far as investing in the field of medicine goes, the more exotic research discoveries you will come across while following the industry may never lead directly to your putting money into a particular company. But they will give you that important sense of trends in medical development. At the same time, you will not avoid being fascinated by some of the unique conceptual approaches involved in the advance of the curative arts.

Consider, for instance, the idea of developing magnetic antibodies to draw cancerous cells physically out of an affected area. It sounds bizarre, doesn't it? Yet precisely such a process has been developed by Dr. John Kemshead of the Institute of Child Health in London. Designed specifically to combat a rare but often fatal type of brain cancer called neuroblastoma which attacks only children, the method, currently being tested, may offer some hope for the cure of other cancers as well.

Conventional neuroblastoma treatment involves the administration of low doses of potent antitumor drugs, radiotherapy, and surgery followed by more drugs. The problem with the

284

conventional therapy is that the drugs used also kill normal cells, particularly the bone-marrow cells responsible for the body's immunological response system.

Dr. Kemshead's magnetic method involves, first, the prior development of highly specific monoclonal antibodies hostile to neuroblastoma cells. Then the bone marrow is removed from the patient and the monoclonal antibodies mixed in, there to attach themselves to any cancerous cells. Next microscopic polystyrene beads with a magnetic core covered with a second group of antibodies specially designed to attract the first are combined with the bone marrow. These magnetic antibody-coated microspheres, two microns in diameter, or five times smaller than the average body cell, attach themselves to the antibodies introduced earlier, which have in turn attached themselves to the cancerous cells. Passing the whole mixture through glass columns surrounded by magnets results in a purified and cancer-free bone marrow. The cleansed marrow is returned to the child being treated.

To the uninitiated, it all sounds fantastic. Yet this is but one isolated instance of the kind of research being undertaken in the medical world. Harvard University ophthalmologists have developed a proton beam that can zap an eye tumor. Cryogenic surgery, the hypothermic microwave destruction of malignant cells, and intricate, finely focused laser surgery, as well as electrified braces, are part of the new medical technology.

In the branch known as bioengineering, complex machines are being designed to aid ill bodies. Today's artificial appliances are quite a step up from Peg Leg's oak prosthesis or George Washington's wooden molars, incorporating more modern materials and the technology of electronics. Consider Stanford University's robot wheelchair, completely controlled by the operator's head movements. Designed for quadriplegics, the chair uses a computer chip and ultrasonic sonar to track the operator's nod and headshake commands. University of Utah researchers have designed polyurethane veins and arteries. Artificial lungs, ears, and even eyes are on their drawing boards for the future.

For all their electronic wizardry and awe-inspiring research, many of these advances will not reach fruition in either the hospital or the marketplace at large. They may not work, some of them, when applied in the real world, as opposed to the rarefied milieu of research. Even if they do work, how the public or patients or investors view a specific product of medical technology doesn't matter. What counts, in the last analysis, is how the doctors view it. The medical profession today operates largely within a cozy envelope of peer perceptions and from behind the barricades of malpractice insurance. Usefulness is the operative concept, not drama or breakthroughs. With very few exceptions, doctors will not, and indeed cannot, operate efficiently with the leading-edge technologies in their field. In things medical, it's easy enough for the investor to become enthralled with an exciting new product, but unless the medical profession sees it as a procedure or device both useful and safe, the market money simply won't flow.

Overall, the medical field is so diversified and so complex that it can easily be considered the most fragmented of the high-tech markets covered in this book. Health care in all its forms represents nearly $350 billion in trade annually, or 10 percent of the gross national product, yet individual markets for the investor's consideration sometimes measure up as mere slivers of that total, constituting monetary universes of only $50 million to $100 million apiece. Most of these mini-markets are niches created by new techniques. As such, they blossom quickly. Once they gain the acceptance of the medical profession, however, everybody elbows a way in. Health-care specialty markets thus tend to mature and become saturated in a relatively short span, say five years.

The exceptions to this quick rise toward market maturity are those areas so general and broadly based that a particular company cannot dominate them—hospital management, clinical laboratory services, and patient monitoring are the examples that come quickly to mind. Also the substitution of one service for another in these areas is apt to be more a matter of a particular physician's preferences than of economics, which helps to obscure the investment choices even further. Then too, the expansiveness of these broader fields is constrained by a regulatory environment and an almost perennial skilled-labor shortage.

Yet medical technology, for all its market limitations, offers a particularly fertile field for venture capital. Start-up operations can be expected to carve out market share quickly. A good company with an innovative medical specialty is likely to develop the kind of earnings that market dominance affords in a relatively short time frame as compared with the contenders in other, more competitive technological arenas.

The hothouse environment nurturing these companies to rapid fruition lessens the concern the investor need have about first-rate management, a consideration paramount in so many other fields. Obviously you don't want bad management. But merely good sound handling of company affairs is often enough, provided the product is reliable and accepted. By the time the firm grows to a size where outstanding management is called for, its market has probably matured to the point where you and your investment should have already taken leave.

There are several private companies that should be of interest to small investors, among them Merrimack Laboratories, Sequoia Turner, and Sutter Biomedical. When any of these firms sends out invitations via a public stock offering, if you're following medical technology you should pay careful attention.

The specialty companies supplying the medical-technologies field can be roughly classified into four major areas of product concentration, namely, prostheses, diagnostic tools, monitoring devices, and surgical implements. Within these categories, of course, variety abounds.

Prosthetics, the surgical replacing of missing or damaged bodily parts with manmade substitutes, has had a long and varied history. Cardiac pacemakers are probably the best known of all prosthetic devices, and great strides have been made recently in their development and improvement. Other artificial adjuncts of the almost bionic man include neural substitutes, transmodal sensory prostheses, artificial blood, and tissue-contouring aids such as synthetic bone, skin, and tendons.

To give an example of the outer reaches of prosthetics technology, the Collagen Company is producing demineralized bone for use in an experimental process called induced osteogenesis, or osteoinduction. For reasons not fully understood, when bone cells that have been demineralized with acid are implanted in living tissue, the surrounding fibroblasts, the cells producing connective tissue, transform themselves into chondroblasts, or bone-producing cells. Osteoinduction has already been used to build a new skull for a six-year-old boy with a rare bone disorder known as craniosynostosis, a deformity of the cranium caused by a failure of the soft bones of the upper skull to fuse properly during infancy. In this instance the boy's own bones were demineralized, but there is a medically still more exciting, though perhaps gruesome-sounding, possibility on the horizon, and that is the conceivable use of demineralized bones from cadavers or even animals.

Medical diagnostics is another specialty drawing heavily on new, if sometimes less spectacular, advances in high technology. Ultrasound instrumentation augments the older and more established, but still changing, X-ray tools. CAT scanners are also gaining in professional user acceptance.

Many smaller devices, while perhaps not so exciting as CAT scanners, nevertheless represent real advances in diagnostic technology. One such development is the slideless microscope recently patented by International Remote Image Systems. Samples to be studied are suspended between two layers of fluid rather than being smeared on the traditional glass slide. Cell information is automatically analyzed by computer and displayed on a video monitor.

In addition to the tools designed for professional medical use, there is also a broad and expanding consumer market for self-diagnostic tests. The home pregnancy-verification kits are among the most publicized and promoted of such tests.

Monitoring devices were originally limited strictly to hospital use because of their expense and complexity. The introduction of microprocessor-based systems and the great shrinkage in both cost and size which inevitably follows in the wake of technological discovery have helped to open the doors of the home-use market for such devices as infant-sudden-death-syndrome monitors. A broad range of checking and regulatory functions are handled by parallel warning systems in other critical areas, particularly in acute, cardiac, and pulmonary care. The miniaturization of monitoring devices has reached the stage where a company like Sciencare can now offer an ambulatory electrocardiograph about the size of a cigarette pack which allows patients to be monitored under normal day-to-day activities and stress.

Surgical implements, meanwhile, are undergoing perhaps their most profound change since the introduction of the scalpel, a tool which is being displaced in some areas by laser technology. Actually lasers are doing more than supplanting the scalpel, for although they are used for the same cutting function, they permit surgery to be performed on tissues not previously accessible to the knife and in ways not previously possible. Eye, throat, and organ work are the primary areas currently being served by laser-operative applications, although Merrimack Laboratories, for instance, makes a surgical laser for removal of nonindigenous growths. The laser literally vaporizes cysts and tumors, and it does so without leaving a wound or scar. Professionally, the device appeals particularly to specialists such as gynecologists, who can utilize it to perform a number of their surgical procedures in the office rather than in the operating room. Popularly, it appeals to all potential patients, since it enables them to walk right out the door after undergoing surgery.

There are three more or less distinct markets for the products of medical technology, the hardware itself often crossing market boundaries. Acute-care hospitals, clinical and diagnostic laboratories, and physician group practices may use any or all of the various categories of equipment.

With the government under budget pressures and the insurance companies restraining spending on health-care facilities in order to curb insurance-rate increases, the current dollar emphasis in all areas is cost containment. Products that lower the price of "health-care services"—the industry euphemism for all those items enumerated on your multipage hospital bill —are thus in high demand. Devices particularly sought after by the medical profession are those that increase productivity, speeding up "throughput" (the medical newspeak term for how quickly whatever procedures the patient requires can be performed). Reducing the qualifications and training time needed by ancillary personnel through the use of increasingly "smart" instruments is another way of controlling labor costs currently in vogue.

A final factor in the growth of medical technology is the concomitant growth in the number of physicians and surgeons. During the past decade their numbers have swelled from 300,000 to 500,000, proportionately a far greater increase than that of the population as a whole. Along with this surge in suppliers of medical services, an attendant trend toward greater specialization in the profession has stimulated the use of high-technology products. The aging population with voter influence in Washington also augurs well for continuing growth in medical high technology.

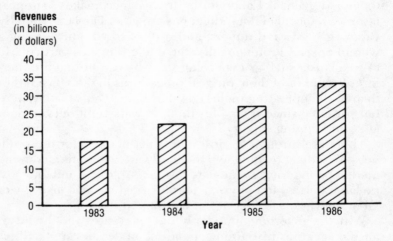

Projected Market Growth of High-Tech Medical Equipment and Services

Estimated compound annual growth rate: 24 percent

Note: These figures include the faster-growing high-tech companies only. The entire high-tech medical industry as a whole, including the slower-growing companies, is roughly twice as large and has an estimated compound annual growth rate of 9 percent.

INDUSTRY INVESTMENT DIRECTIONS

What trips up many amateur investors in health care is the length of time between product development and commercially significant revenues and profits. Unlike ordinary manufacturing, where selling can begin as soon as the vendor has a product, the health-care industry is full of regulatory constraints dictating long periods of testing. First safety must be demonstrated, then effectiveness. As a rough rule of thumb, three years of safety testing and two of efficacy testing are routine.

Medical devices are currently less stringently circumscribed by efficacy standards than are drugs. But any device designed for internal use is also subject to further delays occasioned by testing for side effects. Be sure to check the approval status of any new medical products upon which you are making investment decisions.

Regardless of how glowing a company's description of its products is, the telling factor for their future sales is how well they are accepted among influential users such as leading physicians and hospitals. The opinion of medical leaders on competing products and the decision chain followed in the actual purchase of a product or service are also contributing factors. If the doctors are enthusiastic about, say, CAT scanners, but the hospital boards whose financial approval is required for the acquisition of such large-ticket devices consider them extravagant, chances are that not very many of them will be sold.

The valuation of medical-related companies is nearly always too high in relation to their merits, as compared with investments in other industries. If only one or two companies make a particular product and a lot of investors want a piece of the action, the stock is bound to trade at an inflated price. This doesn't mean you shouldn't invest in medical technology. It simply means you should make sure that what you pay for the stocks does not discount more years of future growth than the often small medical specialty markets have in them.

KEY COMPANIES

ADAC Laboratories
255 San Geronimo Way
Sunnyvale, CA 94086
Telephone: (408) 736-1101
Contact: Charles Cantoni, President
Market: OTC
Symbol: ADAC

ADAC manufactures diagnostic image-processing apparatus and has a new digital line. Its equipment interfaces with gamma and X-ray cameras.

Baxter Travenol Laboratories, Inc.
One Baxter Parkway
Deerfield, IL 60015
Telephone: (312) 948-2000
Contact: J. DeYoung
          Market: NYSE
          Symbol: BAX

A company whose intravenous feeding and kidney-dialysis equipment and supplies provide it with a steady source of revenues, Baxter Travenol is a steady, but slowing, grower.

Biochem International
W 238 N1650 Rockwood Drive
Waukesha, WI 53186
Telephone: (414) 542-3100
Contact: H. L. Lanzet, telephone (212) 867-6160
          Market: OTC
          Symbol: BIOC

Biochem makes systems and supplies for the continuous monitoring of blood chemistry and pressure during and after surgery.

Bio-Rad Laboratories, Inc.
2200 Wright Avenue
Richmond, CA 94804
Telephone: (415) 234-4130
Contact: Norman Schwartz, Treasurer
          Market: ASE
          Symbol: BIO.A and BIO.B

Clinical diagnostic test kits, specialty chemical and biological materials, and separation systems are Bio-Rad's major products. The firm hit an earnings pothole stretching from 1980 to 1982.

Cobe Laboratories, Inc.
1201 Oak Street
Lakewood, CO 80215
Telephone: (303) 232-6800
Contact: Ronald Plusk, Chief Financial Officer
          Market: OTC
          Symbol: COBE

A manufacturer of systems and supplies used in the treatment of kidney disease and in open-heart surgery, Cobe Laboratories has a large share of the United States market in each equipment field. Its revenues are three-quarters hemodialysis-related, one-quarter cardiovascular.

Concept, Inc.
12707 U.S. Route 19 South
Clearwater, FL 33516
Telephone: (813) 536-2791
Contact: W. H. Clark, Vice-President of Finance
        Market: OTC
        Symbol: CCPT

Concept, which makes specialized surgical devices and lights, is placing a big capital bet on C-Flex, a new thermoplastic material it is developing.

Cooper Laboratories
3145 Porter Drive
Palo Alto, CA 94304
Telephone: (415) 856-5000
Contact: R. V. Mahoney, Jr., Treasurer
        Market: NYSE
        Symbol: COO

Only a quarter of Cooper's line is strictly high-tech, but the company has a pretty good growth record. It has taken to spinning out its higher-tech operations.

Cycare Systems, Inc.
P.O. Box 1278, 520 Dubuque Building
Dubuque, IA 52001
Telephone: (319) 556-3131
Contact: R. E. Gray, Treasurer
        Market: OTC
        Symbol: CYCR

This firm supplies remote information-processing services and programs to physician group practices.

Datascope Corporation
580 Winters Avenue
Paramus, NJ 07652
Telephone: (201) 265-8800

Contact: Stuart Levy, Controller
>   Market: OTC
>   Symbol: DSCP

The main product lines here are intra-aortic balloon catheters, defibrillators, and monitors for vital life signs.

Diagnostic Products Corporation

5700 West 96th Street
Los Angeles, CA 90045
Telephone: (213) 776-0180
Contact: Dr. Sigi Ziering, Chief Executive Officer
>   Market: OTC
>   Symbol: DPCZ

Diagnostic makes clinical and hospital laboratory test kits
for body-fluids analysis using radioimmunoassay and enzy-
matic immunoassay techniques.

Electro-Biology, Inc.

300 Fairfield Road
Fairfield, NJ 07006
Telephone: (201) 227-8611
Contact: T. A. Duerden, Chief Executive Officer
>   Market: OTC
>   Symbol: EBII

Electrobiology is the only noninvasive bone-fracture therapy using electromagnetic techniques approved by the Food
and Drug Administration. The therapeutic electromagnetic
equipment is sold to orthopedists by this firm.

Elscint, Ltd.

Advanced Technology Center
P.O. Box 5258
Haifa
Israel
Telephone: (04) 52 516
Contact: W. Hauser, telephone (212) 838-3341
>   Market: OTC
>   Symbol: ELSTF

Elscint manufactures nuclear medical instrumentation,
used principally in visually oriented tumor and disease diagnosis, for hospitals, research laboratories, and individual use.

The export market for its equipment accounts for 80 percent of its sales.

Haemonetics Corporation
400 Wood Road
Braintree, MA 02184
Telephone: (617) 848-7100
Contact: Gordon Kingsley, Chief Executive Officer
      Market: OTC
      Symbol: HAEM

Haemonetics supplies equipment and disposables for blood processing in connection with blood donations, transfusion, and therapy. Hospitals and blood banks, domestic and foreign, are its main customers.

HBO and Company
219 Perimeter Center North
Atlanta, GA 30346
Telephone: (404) 393-6000
Contact: Austin Kearney
      Market: OTC
      Symbol: HBOC

Hospital information-processing turnkey systems are HBO's specialty, with the emphasis on patient data.

Healthdyne, Inc.
2253 Northwest Parkway
Marietta, GA 30067
Telephone: (404) 955-9555
Contact: Yvonne Scoggins, Director of Investor Relations
      Market: OTC
      Symbol: HDYN

Healthdyne supplies home-health-care and hospital equipment, its main line being a device for monitoring babies subject to sudden infant death syndrome. It recently acquired Narco Scientific, a larger company.

Health Information Systems, Inc.
4522 Fort Hamilton Parkway
Brooklyn, NY 11219
Telephone: (212) 435-6300

Contact: Barry Septimus, Chairman
        Market: OTC
        Symbol: HISI

This company is a designer and purveyor of software systems for financial management in the health-care industry.

Home Health Care of America, Inc.

2871 South Pullman Street
Santa Ana, CA 92705
Telephone: (714) 556-7841
Contact: Dick Allen, Chief Financial Officer
        Market: OTC
        Symbol: HHCA

The leader in its specialized field, Home Health Care of America feeds parenteral solutions to patients in their homes.

Intermedics, Inc.

P.O. Box 617
Freeport, TX 77541
Telephone: (800) 231-2330 or (713) 233-8611
Contact: Theodore Swift, Vice-President of Investor
        Relations
        Market: OTC
        Symbol: ITEM

An enterprising challenger of *Medtronic* with its cardiac pacemaker, Intermedics has gained market share quickly. The company's aggressive sales tactics recently have caused controversy.

International Remote Imaging Systems

9232 Deering Avenue
Chatsworth, CA 91311
Telephone: (213) 709-1244
Contact: Fred Deindoefer, President
        Market: OTC
        Symbol: IRIS

A development-stage company with an interesting microscopic image-processing capability in the works, this firm is slanting its first product for clinical laboratory urinalysis.

Kallestad Laboratories, Inc.

2000 Austin National Bank Tower
Austin, TX 78701

Telephone: (512) 477-1111
Contact: S. S. Yates, Senior Vice-President
       Market: ASE
       Symbol: KAL

Kallestad makes hospital test kits for determining hormone, protein, and drug concentrations in patients' blood. Mont-Edison International has announced plans to acquire this company.

Medtronic, Inc.

3055 Old Highway Eight
Minneapolis, MN 55440
Telephone: (612) 574-4000
Contact: D. L. Duclos
       Market: NYSE
       Symbol: MDT

With the largest share of the market in the United States for implantable heart pacemakers, Medtronic has other arrows in its quiver, but they have been less successful to date.

National Medical Care, Inc.

200 Clarendon Street
Boston, MA 02116
Telephone: (617) 262-1200
Contact: A. M. Nogelo
       Market: NYSE
       Symbol: NMD

National Medical Care operates kidney-dialysis centers across the country and manufactures related supplies. A negative whack to its stock price was the 1982 government proposal to reduce the rates of payment to the centers.

Omnimedical

2560 Woodland Drive
Anaheim, CA 92801
Telephone: (714) 527-7071
Contact: Gary Mounts, Chairman
       Market: OTC
       Symbol: OMNI

Financially strapped, Omnimedical has bet the store on the success of its new Quad line of products for diagnostic imaging.

Sci-Med Life Systems, Inc.
13000 County Road 6
Minneapolis, MN 55441
Telephone: (612) 559-9504
Contact: Fred LeGrand, Vice-President of Finance
          Market: OTC
          Symbol: SMLS
"Smalls" makes disposable medical products and is a leader in membrane oxygenator systems for open-heart surgery and respiratory support.

Stryker Corporation
420 Alcott Street
Kalamazoo, MI 49001
Telephone: (616) 381-3811
Contact: Joseph Marks, Chief Financial Officer
Stryker manufactures a broad line of powered surgical instruments, orthopedic implants, patient-handling equipment such as high-tech hospital beds, and other efficient cost-cutting equipment.

Thoratec Laboratories Corporation
2033 Eighth Street
Berkeley, CA 94710
Telephone: (415) 841-1213
Contact: R. J. Harvery, Chief Executive Officer
          Market: OTC
          Symbol: TTEC
Barely profitable, but exciting, describes this firm specializing in cardiovascular and respiratory medical devices.

Trimedyne, Inc.
2452 East Oakton Street
Arlington Heights, IL 60005
Telephone: (312) 952-1200
Contact: David Peterson, Treasurer
          Market: OTC
          Symbol: TMED
A company still in the development stage, Trimedyne is working on fiber-optic laser catheters, an artificial pancreas,

and a batch of other wonders. It has lots of big-name medical talent, but we don't know yet whether it's a business.

U.S. Surgical Corporation
150 Glover Avenue
Norwalk, CT 06850
Telephone: (203) 866-5050
Contact: Marianne Scipione, Vice-President of
          Corporation Communications
          Market: OTC
          Symbol: USSC

U.S. Surgical makes automatic surgical stapling instruments, artificial bone and hip joints, and patient-monitoring equipment.

LEADING ANALYSTS

Richard Emmitt, Joy Gidley, and Scott King
F. Eberstadt and Company, Inc.
61 Broadway
New York, NY 10006
Telephone: (212) 480-0835
  This is the strongest broadly based team in the business.

Gene Gargiulo
Goldman, Sachs and Company
55 Broad Street
New York, NY 10004
Telephone: (212) 676-7190
  Gene Gargiulo is new, but good.

David Goldsmith
Robertson, Colman and Stephens
100 California Street
San Francisco, CA 94111
Telephone: (415) 781-9700

Steve Handley
L. F. Rothschild, Unterberg, Towbin
55 Water Street

New York, NY 10041
Telephone: (212) 425-3300
   Steve Handley covers lots of small companies.

Linda Miller and John Nehra
Alex Brown and Son
135 East Baltimore Street
Baltimore, MD 21202
Telephone: (301) 727-1700
   These two analysts are outstanding.

James Tullis
Morgan Stanley and Company, Inc.
1251 Avenue of the Americas
New York, NY 10020
Telephone: (212) 974-4414

Annette Campbell White
Hambrecht and Quist, Inc.
235 Montgomery Street
San Francisco, CA 94104
Telephone: (415) 986-5500

PERTINENT PUBLICATIONS

Medical technology, unlike many of the other industries
covered in this book, has virtually no publications useful for
tracking the industry as a whole, reflecting both its diversity
and the small scale of all but a few of its operations such as
the drug and pharmaceutical companies.

American Laboratory
International Scientific Communications, Inc.
P.O. Box 827, 808 Kings Highway
Fairfield, CT 06430
Telephone: (203) 576-0500
   Subscription: $48 per year for monthly periodical
American Laboratory is edited for research chemists and
biologists. The articles focus on products, trends, and appli-
cations.

Analytical Chemistry
American Chemical Society
1155 16th Street, NW
Washington, DC 20036
Telephone: (202) 872-4600, (614) 421-7230 for subscriptions
    Subscription: $20 per year to nonmembers for monthly
                periodical (address inquiries to P.O. Box
                3337, Columbus, OH 43210)
The August issue of *Analytical Chemistry,* the Lab Guide,
lists upcoming meetings as well as supplying a directory of
vendors.

Biomedical Business International
Information Resources International, Inc.
P.O. Box 366
Tustin, CA 92680
Telephone: (714) 838-8350
    Subscription: $265 per year for 20 issues
This manager-oriented newsletter is for industry execu-
tives.

The Gray Sheet
Drug Research Reports, Inc.
One National Press Building
Washington, DC 20045
Telephone: (202) 624-7600
    Subscription: $220 per year for weekly newsletter
Medical devices are covered in the "Gray Sheet."

Medical Electronics and Equipment News
Reilly Publishing
532 Busse Highway
Park Ridge, IL 60068
Telephone: (312) 693-3773
    Subscription: $25 per year for bimonthly periodical
Designed to keep instrumentation users and purchasers
abreast of technology, this publication reviews products, systems, and services—what they all are, how they work, important features, who supplies them, and so on—as well as
running a calendar of meetings and conventions.

Medical Electronics/Medical Electronic Products
Measurements and Data Corporation

2994 West Liberty Avenue
Pittsburgh, PA 15216
Telephone: (412) 343-9666
   Subscription: $17 per year for bimonthly periodical
The coverage here is the medical, biomedical, scientific, and engineering uses of electronics in laboratories and hospitals. Product news, legal issues, and safety reports are presented, gleaned from a variety of fields, including analytical testing, the blood-chemistry specialties, chromatography, electrophoresis, pacemaker technology, radioactivity, and ultrasonics.

New England Journal of Medicine
Massachusetts Medical Society
10 Shattuck Street
Boston, MA 02115
Telephone: (617) 734-9800
   Subscription: $48 per year for biweekly periodical
One of the oldest and most widely read publications in the field, the *New England Journal of Medicine* covers new developments in major aspects of medicine, medical practice, science, and so on, with an emphasis on internal medicine. It's written for the physician.

Scrip
PJB Publications, Ltd.
18/20 Hill Rise
Richmond, Surrey TW10/6UA
England
Telephone: (01) 948-3262 (Pat Kinsella)
                             or
c/o Barnum Communications
500 Fifth Avenue
New York, NY 10110
Telephone: (212) 221-7363 (Janet Gann)
   Subscription: $430.50 per year for delivery once a week,
                  $522.90 for delivery twice weekly, of this
                  semiweekly publication.
Worldwide pharmaceutical news is covered by *Scrip*, a British publication.

MAJOR MEETINGS

There are various specialty medical-society and trade-group meetings, virtually one for every niche of the industry, and far too many to attend. It's a good thing to pick one or two to visit, as that's the only way to judge customer (doctor/technician) reaction to products. Here are some of the best among the multitude available. Ask for the meetings department or services group of the sponsoring agency when you inquire.

American Association for Clinical Chemistry Annual
  Convention
1725 R Street, NW, Suite 903
Washington, DC 20006
Telephone: (202) 857-0717
This clinical chemistry convention meets in late July or early August of each year in a major city (New York in 1983).

American College of Cardiology
9111 Old Georgetown Road
Bethesda, MD 20014
Telephone: (301) 897-5400
Physicians and scientists specializing in cardiology and cardiovascular diseases make up the membership of this college, which meets for four days every March in a major city (New Orleans in 1983). Exhibits are free, and you can register at the door. Scientific tutorial sessions cost $175 and require advance registration. The college, in addition to sponsoring the annual convention, publishes the monthly *American Journal of Cardiology* and the quarterly *Cardiology Newsletter*.

Radiological Society of North America
1415 West 22nd Street
Oak Brook, IL 60521
Telephone: (312) 920-2670
The society of radiologists and physicians and scientists in related fields convenes annually for five days in November at Chicago's McCormick Place. A $25 registration fee covers both exhibits and scientific sessions. The society's specialty publication is *Radiology,* a monthly journal.

In addition to these professional assemblies, many brokers sponsor meetings for analysts at client institutions. Check with yours. Three such regularly scheduled conferences follow.

Alex Brown and Son
(For address and telephone, see Linda Miller and John
    Nehra, under *Leading Analysts,* page 300)
Alex Brown's annual meeting on medical developments is held each May in Baltimore.

Hambrecht and Quist, Inc.
(For address and telephone, see Annette Campbell White,
    under *Leading Analysts,* page 300)
Hambrecht and Quist sponsors a medical-technology review in San Francisco each January.

Morgan Stanley
(For address and telephone, see James Tullis, under
    Leading Analysts, page 300)
The Morgan Stanley medical session meets every April or May in New York.

XIX

Military Technology: The Dollars of Doom?

Money may be the lesser evil, but warfare has been around longer. Today the two are well-nigh inseparable, of course. Whether the investor wishes to remove himself, or at least his money, from the horrors of war is a personal moral choice this book cannot make for him. It can be done.

Historically, man had little choice in the matter of war investment or, as far as that's concerned, personal participation. Wars were paid for by taxes, levies usually as unjust as the engagements themselves. The sums involved were always exorbitantly high, at least in proportion to a country's wealth. Even before the advent of the staggeringly expensive high-tech warfare strategies currently in vogue, it was not unusual for a nation to spend 10, 15, or even 20 percent of its gross national product on military affairs. Consider the city-state of Venice in 1588. According to historical records, some six million pounds of coarse gunpowder (as opposed to the more expensive and "high-tech" fine variety) were stored in its magazines—enough to fire each of the four hundred guns in Venice's fortress three hundred times. By conservative estimates, the ammunition represented an expenditure, on powder alone, equivalent to the total annual receipts of the state. This was during peacetime, mind you, and obviously well before the development of technology as we conceive it.

Since World War II, however, what President Eisenhower forebodingly dubbed the military-industrial complex has developed into a multibillion-dollar production machine, many of whose parts are publicly held corporations. So it is no longer necessary for someone wishing to invest in that sure thing called war to be a Krupp or Howard Hughes. It is, however, necessary to tread carefully among the land mines on

Wall Street, because while military spending may be inevitable, profits for military producers are not.

In the eighties, the investor in military technology should probably focus for the most part on defense electronics. Expenditures in this direction will be a rising percentage of the Department of Defense (DOD) budget, both in the area of procurement and in research, development, test, and evaluation (RDT&E) programs, these being the budget categories affecting investments most directly.

During periods of budget-watching—and the decade of the eighties readily qualifies as one—the emphasis in expenditures tends to shift toward procurement at the expense of RDT&E. Current spending on procurement is two and a half times what it is for RDT&E. But this is neither an average nor a typical situation, being due to the research and development (R&D) costs of such superprojects as the MX missile. As these expenses wind down and funding pressures increase, the ratio will change. The year 1986 is expected to see procurement expenditures at three and a half times those for RDT&E.

Such a ratio does not mean that the Defense Department will continue to buy the same old weaponry all the time. It does mean that the emphasis will be on modification and extension of existing programs. Thus companies presently well positioned with regard to contracts are likely to remain so—if they don't mess up their programs and products. Those with proprietary devices, particularly electronic ones, should have the highest profit margins.

Within defense electronics itself, the main areas of production, ranked by expected growth from the fastest to the slowest, are electronic warfare (EW) equipment, communications and navigational instrumentation, radar, and data-processing apparatus. But while electronic warfare is the fastest-growing segment of defense electronics, it is not yet the largest. Ranked by current size, the order becomes communications and navigational instrumentation, data-processing apparatus, electronic-warfare equipment, and radar.

Electronic warfare, however, besides being positioned as a rapidly growing market, offers the investor three other very specific advantages. First of all, its programs tend to have a recurring stream of revenue regardless of whether the "platforms" are still in production. "Platform" is militarese for what the weapons are carried on. For example, a specific fighter plane may no longer be coming off the production line, but the electronic-warfare components on that plane are still subject to periodic updates and improvements, which means EW parts production just keeps rolling along. Overall, electronic-warfare systems usually need to be upgraded significantly every four or five years in order effectively to overcome newly developed enemy threats. Replacement due to usage plus a heavy level of support activity, including training simulators and test equipment, further contribute to production.

A second boost to electronic-warfare companies' earnings is provided by the fact that successful EW programs undertaken for the government are eligible for 85 to 90 percent progress payments. Contractors who qualify by virtue of small size or other special circumstances are entitled to 95 percent reimbursement. In essence, then, the companies concerned have almost all their development expenditures paid for before they deliver the product, which means a most enviable cash flow. Together with the above-average after-tax profitability these companies enjoy—5 to 8 percent of revenues for cost-plus development work and 10 to 20 percent for successful production programs—the progress payments generate a steady stream of funds for company growth and contribute to a very high return on invested capital.

A last electronic-warfare consideration working in favor of the investor is that many EW participants are subdivisions of larger corporations. Their earnings contributions are quite small compared with total corporate revenues. This factor helps to effect potentially explosive stock-price growth in those few companies that are available as pure plays in electronic warfare. Investors itch to get their hands on the shares of such companies—when the time is right. What you have to do is to get your hands on them before everyone else does, and then ride with the crowd, something you'll learn how to do in Part III of this book.

There are a few risks for contractors inherent in the electronic-warfare field, naturally. Failure to win the contract for a key "building-block" program ranks very high among these hazards, since losing one of these initial contracts on which further development work is predicated effectively locks a company out from further bidding.

Even the winner of a development contract entering the subsequent initial production phase of a program may encounter unforeseen problems capable of short-circuiting the whole deal, despite the fact that once a program has been in production for a number of years, profitability tends to be stable and consistent. One potential start-up problem concerns the availability of qualified personnel. Engineering talent is at a premium these days, and the current shortage is expected to continue for several years. A company expanding rapidly because of a large new contract may thus find it very difficult to hire enough good engineers in short order, a factor that can severely curtail profits, either because of time delays sustained in pulling together a complete team or because of extra salary and perquisites proffered to hire staff away hurriedly from other companies similarly engaged.

Time delays can also be caused by subcontractors failing to deliver on time and by funding not being released as scheduled. When you're working under a fixed-price contract, to have plant and staff idling in wait is to eat up a lot of potential profit very quickly.

The actual weapons of electronic warfare are not so easy to categorize as the profit angles and the pitfalls of the field. They're not ray guns. That much at least can be said with certainty, although only for now. Other than that, the investor must be content with the fact that electronic warfare is a broad category indeed, with no universally accepted definition of its boundaries. However, EW generally includes the activities of communications and communications disruptions (which are opposite sides of the same coin), passive-intelligence-related electronic procedures, and self-protective operations.

You are already acquainted with the technologies of communications. Communications disruption is exactly what that term would imply, namely, devices which prevent enemy communications, whether from aircraft to home base, ship to shore, or base to base, from being completed. Keep the opposition from communicating and you keep it from fighting effectively. Of course, the enemy has the same idea and is busy developing similar disruptive devices, which leads in turn to "hardening" technology, the attempt to make friendly communications links immune to disruption.

Passive-intelligence electronic techniques, involving the interception and analysis of enemy radio, radar, and other electromagnetic transmissions, are considered part of electronic warfare. Active intelligence operations such as the use of radar to detect enemy movements, on the other hand, are not regarded as lying within the domain of EW.

Self-protection, the last major category of electronic warfare, entails preventing the enemy from successfully employing electromagnetic signals such as those of radar and sonar to locate or detect friendly forces. The best known of the self-protective techniques is radar jamming.

Airborne electronic defense currently represents the largest market in EW self-protection. Since World War II, radar has been the most effective means by which enemy air-defense installations could locate and track unfriendly aircraft. So in order to protect planes from radar detection, one must know a lot about radar.

The different types of radar in use today are staggering to contemplate. To the simple pulse of the early sixties have been added Doppler, continuous-wave, monopulse, millimeter, beam-switching, and look-down/shoot-down radar, to name just a few of the esoteric techniques. And each new development in radar technology must be countered by new and constantly changing electronic-warfare techniques.

At first the self-protective electronic-warfare apparatus for an aircraft consisted solely of a warning receiver enabling a pilot to know when he had been intercepted by enemy radar so he could take evasive action. Then jammers were developed to overwhelm, or at least confuse, radar signals.

Jamming technology is every bit as complex and involuted as the radar it counteracts. Suffice it to note here that early jamming equipment was "hard-wired." That is to say, the signals it would intercept and jam were limited by the physical design of the equipment to a few anticipated radar pulses, those expected to be used by the enemy. If intelligence was wrong, or if the opposing forces had developed radar signals of a type that had escaped investigation by intelligence, the pilot was in trouble.

Hard wiring had two other drawbacks. First of all, every time a system required resetting to cover a newly emerged radar threat, it had to be physically altered, an expensive and, more important, a time-consuming process—in an area where time was crucial. Second, the pilot, who had enough other things to do, was forced to activate the jamming apparatus manually.

All this changed with the chip. Memory and microcomputers together could analyze received radar signals and then initiate jamming of the appropriate type.

Radar countermeasures today consist primarily of noise jammers, which overpower the enemy receiver by transmitting signals so strong that they drown out the aircraft's radar reflection. It's like putting out a lot of static during a phone conversation—you still hear noise, but not the sounds you want to hear.

This form of high-powered transmission requires a lot of energy, and because fighter planes are not large enough to carry the prerequisite broad-band jamming equipment plus the tools of their own trade, "escort jamming" developed. But the use of special dedicated noise-jamming aircraft, primarily the air force's EF-111 and the navy's EA-6B, once more involves a trade-off, since the Raytheon ALQ-99 jammers used on these planes are so powerful that they can be spotted by quite unsophisticated electronic detection equipment merely picking up the electromagnetic radiation emanating from them. Thus escort jammers must "stand off," or remain at the edge of the battle scene, safely out of range of enemy fire. From that peripheral position they blast their jamming into the disputed territory.

Further refinements in jamming techniques include co-op and deception jamming, which are essentially worrying distractions to the enemy radar, and "expendables," decoys such as bits of metallic material called chaff scattered like synthetic snow to confuse the opposition's detectors. Overall, there's probably as much to jamming operations as there is to radar itself.

The future in airborne self-protection technology seems to lie with miniaturization. Any diminution in the size of jamming equipment will relieve the already overstrained weight and size limitations imposed on such devices by the aircraft. More built-in flexibility and potential for upgrading, to counter the successive sophistication of radar, also need to be incorporated in the arsenal of electronic warfare.

Perhaps the ultimate weapon in electronic warfare is the use of enemy radar itself to effect its own destruction, an intercepting technique fairly dubbed "lethal countermeasures" (LCM). In the LCM system principally employed by the air force today, for instance, a guided missile picks up the signals emitted by enemy radar and uses them as a homing beacon to steer itself.

Whatever the system, the Department of Defense will have initials for it. To cover them all would be to compile a dictionary. However, to lead you at least partway through the wonderland of military acronyms, the following is a decoding of the DOD classification of electronic-warfare operations. It is entitled the Joint Electronics Type Designation System (that's right—you're getting good at this—it's referred to as JETDS).

Prefix letters

    AN   DOD inventory

First letter—designates where the EW equipment is installed

    A   piloted aircraft
    D   pilotless carrier
    G   ground use
    P   portable
    Q   sonar (underwater)
    S   shipboard
    U   general utility
    W   water (surface and underwater combined)

Second letter—describes the type of apparatus

    C   carrier signal
    G   telegraph or teletype
    K   telemetering
    L   countermeasures
    P   radar
    R   radio
    S   special
    T   telephone (wire)
    Y   data processing

Third letter—identifies the purpose of the device

    A   auxiliary assemblies
    C   communications
    M   maintenance and testing
    Q   special purpose
    R   receiving
    T   transmitting

Suffix letters (in parentheses)

    V   variable component
    XN   prototype

The numbers following the DOD classification letters give the equipment model number, generally increasing over time.

The JETDS code is only the beginning of government classification. But its deciphering at least allows you, when you come across something like Raytheon's ALQ-99 jammer, to discern that the apparatus is a special-purpose countermeasures device for use in piloted aircraft. That still doesn't tell you very much, which may be portentous of the real message of modern military electronic technology—confusion to everyone, but especially to the enemy.

INDUSTRY INVESTMENT DIRECTIONS

For investment purposes, military-technology companies can be divided into two categories: systems houses, which actually build the equipment, and which are thus closely identified with particular Defense Department programs; and components, or subassembly, suppliers, which sell to the systems houses. Components companies, if well run, are the more profitable of the two groups, because they usually have proprietary technology and state-of-the-art products of interest to the military buyer. However, the components suppliers are rarely involved solely in the military market. Their leading-edge electronic products are employed by other users such as the telecommunications industry. (You will find many of the components suppliers listed in the chapter on fiber optics, lasers, and microwaves.)

Another reason why it is difficult to isolate the leading military-components manufacturers as a separate investment area is that a growing number of systems houses now also manufacture components. Increasingly, the subassembly route is viewed by the systems houses as a way of reducing their excessive dependence on the currently dwindling aggregate of major systems programs.

Good management in both company categories, systems and subassembly alike, consists in establishing a balanced mix of program involvement. This strategy involves bidding for low-risk as well as high-risk contracts, making sure to have products in various stages of development (prototype, full production, spares) at all times. By such diversification, a firm

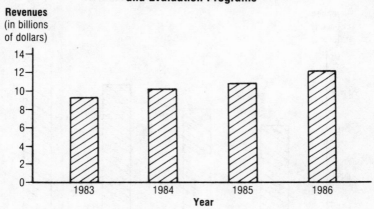

**Projected Market Growth of
Military Research, Development, Test,
and Evaluation Programs**

Estimated compound annual growth rate: 10 percent

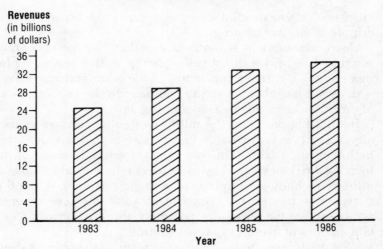

**Projected Market Growth of
Military Procurement Expenditures**

Estimated compound annual growth rate: 10 percent

Projected Market Growth
(in U.S Only)
of Electronic-Warfare Equipment

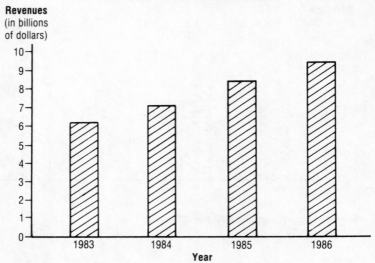

Revenues
(in billions
of dollars)

Year

Estimated compound annual growth rate: 10 percent.

Note: Figures for the international market would add approximately 25 percent to these projections.

ensures that unexpected changes in one program area do not cripple its overall earnings.

Good management also makes sure that the type of contract sought—fixed price, fixed price plus incentive fee, cost plus incentive fee, cost sharing, or any of the other variants offered —does not unduly expose the company to the consequences of errors and changes in a single program.

It would appear that the military-oriented companies usually sell at a lower price-to-earnings ratio than do other high-tech industries. This discrepancy arises because of the increased risk perceived by investors in the virtual reliance of military-technology suppliers on a single customer. While this perspective is arguable, since many different governmental agencies sign the suppliers' contracts, there is in truth a certain amount of overall top-level control.

What with recessionary economic results raising fears about other sectors of the economy, investors have seen government military spending as a plus. And so it is—until such point as the economy starts recovering. At that juncture, the price-to-earnings premium of the shares may erode as investors begin to switch to hotter buys, for military-technology stocks do not benefit from economic recovery. The bottom line then for military suppliers might well be overall underperformance, relatively speaking. So be forewarned. You'd best be nimble if you're going to invest in military technology.

KEY COMPANIES

Andersen Group
1280 Blue Hills Avenue
Bloomfield, CT 06002
Telephone: (203) 242-0761
Contact: F. E. Baker, President
        Market: OTC
        Symbol: ANDR
The Andersen Group manufactures components for a variety of military plus civilian electronics-industry customers, but seems to have no real focus.

Argo Systems
884 Hermosa Court
Sunnyvale, CA 94086
Telephone: (408) 737-2000
Contact: Gary Kimmel, Chief Financial Officer
        Market: OTC
        Symbol: ARGI
Argo leads in electronic countermeasures (ECM) against radar and automated intercept equipment used on a wide variety of air, sea, and ground military platforms.

Atlantic Research Corporation
5390 Cherokee Avenue
Alexandria, VA 22314
Telephone: (703) 642-4000
Contact: Coleman Raphael, Chief Executive Officer
        Market: OTC
        Symbol: ATRC

Atlantic Research used to be a manufacturer solely of rocket motors, but has made a successful move into data communications test equipment, which is now contributing about a fourth of the company's revenues.

Base Ten Systems
Number One Electronics Drive
Trenton, NJ 80619
Telephone: (609) 586-7010
Contact: William Erickson, Secretary
          Market: OTC
          Symbol: BASEB
Base Ten manufactures the weapons control system for the European Tornado military aircraft, an alarm reporting system and data acquisition systems.

C 3, Inc.
11425 Isaac Newton Square South
Reston, VA 22090
Telephone: (703) 471-6000
Contact: John Ballenger, Chief Executive Officer
          Market: NYSE
          Symbol: CEE
A systems integrator for the United States government, C 3 specializes in software for different computer-equipment combinations.

Diagnostic Retrieval Systems
16 Thornton Road
Oakland, NJ 07436
Telephone: (201) 337-3800
Contact: Mark Newman, Chief Financial Officer
          Market: OTC
          Symbol: DRSI
The United States Navy is the main customer for Diagnostic Retrieval's systems used in antisubmarine warfare.

Electromagnetic Sciences, Inc.
125 Technology Park/Atlanta
Norcross, GA 30092

Telephone: (404) 448-5770
Contact: J. E. Pippin, President
          Market: OTC
          Symbol: ELMG

About half of this firm's revenues derive from the government, which it supplies with microwave components and equipment for data communications, radar, electronic countermeasures, and so on.

Electrospace Systems, Inc.

P.O. Box 1359, 1601 North Plano Road
Richardson, TX 75081
Telephone: (214) 231-9303
Contact: Robert Carrel, Executive Vice-President and
          Secretary
          Market: OTC
          Symbol: ELEC

Military electronics and related technologies account for 90 percent of Electrospace's profits. Systems-contract bidding skills are the company forte.

E-Systems

6250 LBJ Freeway
Dallas, TX 75266
Telephone: (214) 661-1000
Contact: Virgil Pettigrew, Vice-President of Finance
          Market: NYSE
          Symbol: ESY

About 86 percent military electronics, the company is a leading systems contractor.

Loral Corporation

600 Third Avenue
New York, NY 10016
Telephone: (212) 697-1105
Contact: Bernard Schwartz, Chief Executive Officer
          Market: NYSE
          Symbol: LOR

Another electronics contractor, this one about 87 percent military, Loral acquired Frequency Sources in 1980, adding microwave components to its systems business.

Sanders Associates
Daniel Webster Highway South
Nashua, NH 03061
Telephone: (603) 855-4321
Contact: J. A. Ruggiero, Treasurer
    Market: NYSE
    Symbol: SAA
Military electronics supply roughly half the Sanders revenues, graphics-systems components the other half.

Technology for Communications International
1625 Stierlin Road
Mountain View, CA 94043
Telephone: (415) 961-9180
Contact: J. W. Ballard, Chief Executive Officer
    Market: OTC
    Symbol: TCII
The expertise here is in radio and high-frequency antenna systems, sold to both the United States and foreign governments.

Tech-Sym Corporation
6430 Richmond Avenue, Suite 460
Houston, TX 77057
Telephone: (713) 785-7790
Contact: W. W. Gamel, Chief Executive Officer
    Market: ASE
    Symbol: TSY
A little over half of Tech-Sym's revenues and profits derive from military electronics, the fastest-growing part of the company. Microwave components and radar systems are the main products.

Tracor, Inc.
6500 Tracor Lane
Austin, TX 78721
Telephone: (512) 926-2800
Contact: J. A. Newley
    Market: NYSE
    Symbol: TRR

Only one-third military electronics, Tracor nevertheless tends to react like one of the group. The rest of the company is a miscellany of government services and electrical products.

UTL Corporation
4500 West Mockingbird Lane
Dallas, TX 75209
Telephone: (214) 350-7601
Contact: John Benson, Vice-President of Finance
        Market: OTC
        Symbol: UTLC
UTL has C^3 (communications, command, and control) expertise, which it deploys in tactical systems for the United States Army. It has been on a steep up ramp in profits for the last couple of years.

Watkins-Johnson Company
3333 Hillview Avenue
Palo Alto, CA 94304
Telephone: (415) 493-4141
Contact: O. T. Paul
        Market: NYSE
        Symbol: WJ
One-half systems, one-half components, Watkins-Johnson is a relatively pure play, but eccentric management has produced an erratic record.

LEADING ANALYSTS

Phillip Brannon
Merrill Lynch, Inc.
One Liberty Plaza, 165 Broadway
New York, NY 10080
Telephone: (212) 637-4982

Wolf DeMisch
Morgan Stanley and Company
1251 Avenue of the Americas
New York, NY 10020
Telephone: (212) 974-4412

Sandy Greene
Hambrecht and Quist, Inc.
235 Montgomery Street
San Francisco, CA 94104
Telephone: (415) 986-5500

Chuck Hill
Kidder, Peabody and Company
100 Federal Street
Boston, MA 02110
Telephone: (617) 357-6762

Herb Kleiman
Prescott, Ball and Turben
1331 Euclid Avenue
Cleveland, OH 44115
Telephone: (216) 574-7411

Gary Reich
Wertheim and Company
200 Park Avenue
New York, NY 10017
Telephone: (212) 578-0200

Cai Von Rumohr
Cowen and Company
28 State Street
Boston, MA 02109
Telephone: (617) 523-3221

PERTINENT PUBLICATIONS

Aviation Week and Space Technology
McGraw-Hill, Inc.
P.O. Box 432
Hightstown, NJ 08520
Telephone: (212) 997-2123 for customer services
  Subscription: $50 per year to nonqualifying subscribers
              for weekly periodical
The aerospace bible, and a must for the field, this publica-
tion covers it all—the airlines, space, defense, and so on. Its
weakest link is its coverage of the small companies.

Defense Electronics
EW Communications, Inc.
P.O. Box 50249, 1170 East Meadow Drive
Palo Alto, CA 94303
Telephone: (415) 494-2800
   Subscription: $24 per year for monthly periodical
EW Communications also publishes the *International Countermeasures Handbook, Microwave Systems News,* and related periodicals.

MAJOR MEETINGS

EASCON
The Institute of Electrical and Electronics Engineers, Inc.
345 East 47th Street
New York, NY 10017
Telephone: (212) 664-7555
Held each September, the Electronics and Aerospace Systems Conference, cosponsored by the Aerospace and Electronic Society (AES) and the Washington, DC, section of the Institute of Electrical and Electronics Engineers (IEEE), covers technological developments in various fields pertinent to the armed forces.

International Defense Electronics Expo
Cahners Exposition Group
222 West Adams Street
Chicago, IL 60606
Telephone: (312) 263-4866
This is the big one, held every year at the Hanover Fairgrounds in West Germany, concurrently with the Hanover International Aerospace Exhibition put on, usually in June, at Langerhagen Airport.

PROFESSIONAL ASSOCIATIONS

Association of Old Crows
2300 Ninth Street, S, Suite 300
Arlington, VA 22204
Telephone: (703) 920-1600

How to Make the Most Profitable High-Tech Investment

XX

These Times Demand Timing—
and More

In 1968, Standard and Poor's year-end stock guide listed forty-five companies with names prefixed by Compu-, Data-, Electro-, Scien-, and Techno-. The first great boom in technology stocks was in full flower. The concept was hot, and names were the name of the game.

By the time the 1970 edition came out, twelve of the companies had been dropped from the guide entirely—merged out of existence, bankrupt, or in such straits as to be not worth listing. Of the remainder, twenty-three had declined more than 50 percent in market value, eight had declined considerably if not quite so precipitately, and two stellar performers had actually gained a bit.

A lot of paper profits went through the shredder for people who didn't sell in time during the two-year interim. Which way your investments went would have depended largely on that old bugaboo, market timing. It's a central consideration still, in the great new wave of high-tech investing for the eighties.

Your first concern is not to buy too soon—not too soon in the development of a new industry, not too soon in the development of a new company within that industry, and not too soon in the overall business or market cycle. An industry's or a particular company's development and that of the overall market may constitute two totally different cycles, one heading up (or down) before the other. An important part of your task as a winning high-tech investor is to synchronize the two.

One of the early signs that a specific industry is opening up into a profitable investment area is the emergence of several companies with equivalent, although technically different, products. Even as famous a company as Xerox spent many of its early years languishing, making little profit for its investors.

Not until other photocopiers validated the concept and gave customers a choice of products did the market develop and Xerox take off.

Here we are assuming that you are not a venture capitalist looking for someplace to tuck away a million dollars, but rather an average investor with risk capital in the neighborhood of, say, $5,000 to $50,000 to invest. In this case you can't afford striving to get in on the ground floor of a company's growth, which in any event may turn out to be the subbasement. Let those who can afford it—who are prepared to lose their entire investment or wait ten years for their return— cope with the risks of being first.

That doesn't mean you should relegate yourself to amateur status. Don't join those small investors who, seeing an exciting article on some new technological development in the popular press or the Sunday supplements, say, "Gee whiz, that looks fantastic," and run out lemminglike to buy stock in the fabled companies described.

Neither should you invest on the basis of academic research. There are thousands of marvelous ideas being developed by research teams in higher education. Only a few of these schemes will develop into commercially viable products. The time it takes for them to do so, assuming you somehow manage to pick the survivors, is apt to be far too great.

Stay with an area of visible growth, one where several companies are seen—according to the trade press, not the popular press—homing in on the same market. When lots of dollars are being pumped into an industry, they keep the technology vigorous and growing. To turn a profit from the products being developed in such a robust field then becomes a matter of elementary good business strategy and capturing market share. It's at this stage in the career of an industry, when the technical obstacles have been overcome and the only barriers remaining are managerial and economic—hurdles such as price, volume, and production determinants—that you want your investment money to enter the picture.

Each of the fourteen industries with separate chapters in this book has met this test. Not all of their individual segments have matured adequately, however. For example, gallium-arsenide technology is not presently a viable investment area, simply because the firms involved are not yet public. Cellular mobile radio offers investment potential, but not for another year or so. The same can be said for genetic engineering, with the exception of a few instances of current investment readiness. Robotics awaits the pleasure of the economic cycle. Until industry once more begins to invest in equipment, robotics companies will at best remain in a holding pattern. Meanwhile, firms peripherally involved with robotics offer the better investment potential.

How can you tell when a particular company is ready for a buy? That point is a bit tougher to define than is the readiness of an industry as a whole. The difficulty increases, furthermore, as you narrow your focus.

Partially the answer depends on the growth of the industry base itself. The more rapid its growth, the sooner you can reap a profit from it. Then too, the faster the growth of an individual company within a fast-growing industry, the sooner you may reasonably expect to invest safely.

In order to merit your investment, a company in an emerging technology either should have been growing at a clip of 30 percent per year for the last three to five years or should be in an industry that is less than purely high-tech, where slower growth is acceptable. As a general rule, however, a public company that has not reached $10 million in annual revenues is a poor bet. You're looking for companies that are small, but not that small. A firm that is really hot will not go public while sales are so low. By waiting a year or two, growing steadily meanwhile, it will be able to raise a lot more capital without giving up as great a share of the firm to outsiders.

The exception to this rule is companies whose growth is truly meteoric. When revenues double, triple, or multiply by an even greater factor per year, a company's front capital requirement, the amount needed simply to keep growing and meeting demand, may become so high that the firm virtually must seek either a corporate buy-out or an instant public infusion of cash.

Three caveats need stating here. They may seem obvious, but they should always be kept in mind. Too many investors shrug them off as being self-evident—and then fail to heed them.

1. High profits alone may not be significant. If a company's profits are high but its growth is slow, the market may be

saturated. Saturated markets almost always spell future trouble.

2. Irregular profits are easy to explain away by finding a likely cause each time there is a setback and then thinking the problem has been solved. But recurring irregular profits besetting a company usually indicate that the managers don't have the business under control.

3. Even high-tech companies eventually reach a level where profits begin to grow more slowly. High technology isn't high technology forever. Product maturity sets in. When that happens, you as an investor must set out for other companies.

Firms that have done well before bear watching, however, in case there's a turnaround, a situation in which a firm's growth trajectory is regained after a period of decline, indicating that profits have begun to recover on a steadily increasing basis. The mythical phoenix does rise from the ashes of high-tech companies occasionally. Look at ISC Systems Corporation, a manufacturer of automated teller equipment. From 1980 to 1981 its share price (adjusted for stock splits) rose from 6½ to 24. Then the company began developing commercial-bank markets for its teller machines. Expenses bulged, while orders for its original savings-bank teller equipment slowed in the recession. The share price sagged to 11 in mid-1982 as earnings fell sharply. But in the third and fourth quarters of 1982, ISC rose to 19, nearly doubling in price, as commercial-bank orders started coming in.

Turnaround buys are more difficult to handle because of the psychological problem of admitting to sometimes being wrong about them. Another month or two before recovery comes often stretches into another year or two or three. Meanwhile your capital could have been better deployed elsewhere. You should be able to answer yes to all six of the following questions before investing in a turnaround situation. Otherwise you're buying too soon. Going by these stiff criteria, you might miss a couple of good turnaround opportunities, but all those you do invest in should stand you in good stead. And you'll miss a lot of ulcers besides the occasional winner passed by.

1. Is the company's industry as a whole in good or improving shape?

2. Have the company's previous problems been rectified by management? (If you have any nagging doubts about this, don't answer yes.)

3. Has management mapped out a clear and credible recovery strategy for the company?

4. Have improved results been evident for at least three-quarters of a year?

5. As an indication that disenchanted stockholders have all finally left the ship and selling pressure has abated, has the company's stock price begun to recover?

6. Overall, does the industry in which the company is positioned have high-P/E stocks as compared to the Dow Jones industrials? A high price-to-earnings ratio is necessary to allow a substantial catch-up move in the company's share price based on the firm's turnaround.

Waiting for the right moment to buy a stock sometimes seems a bit like waiting for Godot. But don't buy a stock you've discovered that's otherwise just right except for its high price. You may feel you're missing out on a good opportunity. You may be tempted to pay the going price for a stock that doesn't seem about to become any cheaper. But such buying is almost always buying too late. Over time, only one out of every ten of these seemingly irresistible stocks will validate its price by growing into it. Since you are not an institutional investor with megabucks to invest in hundreds of companies, you had best stay where the odds are in your favor.

When you find the perfect stock, but you also find that a lot of investors have discovered the company before you, then the wisest course is to let them ride their profits and look for yours elsewhere. Probably you'll not miss much in terms of percentage gains, for stocks that seem to be always just out of buying range usually fall when least expected to do so. Sometimes it's a year or two before they head down in price, but meanwhile they don't usually go up much either.

Consider for a moment a company like Scientific-Atlanta. In 1981, its stock was bobbing around between 18 and 34 a share. After a six-year run-up from next to nowhere, it seemed as if it would never go any lower again, and being in the television-satellite-antenna business, the company was a tempting investment. So even though the company was selling for thirty to forty times earnings, by the beginning of 1982 you might have decided the stock was worth buying—only to watch it plummet below 11 in price as costs soared and orders sank in belated reaction to internal and external problems.

A lot of people, savvy and otherwise, began dumping their shares of Scientific-Atlanta. Some people were selling because, unable to resist any longer, they had bought shares when the stock was trading in the thirties, and as they watched it go into the twenties and then below, the agony became too much for them. They sold at a loss. Other investors, having bought shares a year or two earlier at a more realistic price, saw the decline coming, because they were following the company closely and they noted such accumulating hazards as the simultaneous development of a sophisticated product, weak management controls, and the predictable negative impact of recession on the firm's major customer industry, cable television. Some of these investors may have sold a month or two or even more before the decline began in earnest. The point is that they sold and made a profit.

Selling right is as difficult a technique to master as buying right, if not a more difficult one. To improve your odds, watch for the following five signs as you follow your stock.

1. The failure of good news to send a company's stock price up is always a warning sign. It's true that if the news is disseminated slowly enough to the stock-buying public, by means of minor announcements rather than by splashy write-ups in the business press, a stock may not move dramatically if and when the story subsequently suddenly grows. But there should be a steady upward trend in the share price during the interval.

The type of good news that should move a stock consists of higher earnings estimates projected for the company by analysts, recommendations of the company to clients by brokers who paid little attention to the firm before, announcements by the company of increases in order backlogs or earnings greater than those called for by previous projections, large new orders, and similar developments that can be expected to further the company's growth dramatically. When a lot of investors are just beginning to follow the career of the company, such announcements are bound to drive share prices up.

If prices fail to respond to favorable news, it usually means that early investors have decided the good news can't last and are taking their profits while they can. In such an event, the last one out is left holding the bag—the empty bag.

2. If the stock of a company in which you hold shares begins to act worse than its siblings in the industry group do, then it's time for concern, and possibly for selling your shares. Faltering price action is an early-warning signal, particularly in companies that are industry leaders or those that constitute the weakest members of an industry group. The latter are usually the first to suffer a deterioration in business.

3. On the other side of the investment coin, if your holdings are acting all right but share prices of other companies in the industry are heading south, start investigating. If the problem is industrywide, or if it is related to broad economic causes that can be expected to affect the industry as a whole, your shares will not remain immune. Sell before the plague spreads.

4. "Grow or die" is the motto of high technology. When a company's growth slows, it's usually for a good reason—and the reason is usually a good one to get out of your investment. You need to keep your eye open for signs that market saturation is setting in or that competition is gnawing away at your company's market share. Watch out, too, for the departure of key personnel as reported in the trade press or in *Electronic Business*. If they're starting up a new firm, it may be that your money should follow them.

5. If the customers of a company of which you are a stockholder or the clientele of the industry as a whole are having a tough time, the results of their adversity will show up on your company's shipping dock in the not-too-distant future. As you read your industry sources, keep an eye out for related-industry news. The time to sell is before shrinking profits reach your investment.

The most easily observed and carefully tracked examples of this periodic phenomenon—which is cyclic, moving stocks both ways—are to be found in the electronics and computer industries, although parallels exist in all the rest of the high-tech groups. When interest rates are falling and consumer sentiment is optimistic, a chain of events beginning with increasing sales starts to work its way back through high-tech

companies that use semiconductors in a very regular and predictable fashion. When interest rates rise and consumer sentiment slips into gloom, on the other hand, a converse
sequence of events is initiated, this time involving declining
sales and stock prices.

A somewhat simplified breakdown of the relative time sequence involved in this phenomenon is as follows:

Industry Segment	Number of months until business picks up/declines after economy bottoms out/peaks	Number of months until stock prices increase/decline after economy bottoms out/peaks
Semiconductors	3	0
Microcomputers and consumer electronics	6	3
Instrumentation	9	6
Minicomputers and peripheral equipment	9–12	6
Mainframe computers	12	9
Semiconductor manufacturing equipment	15	12

Note that as the unit costs of a product increase (a minicomputer costs more than a microcomputer does, and semiconductor manufacturing plants cost the most of all), so does the
time lag. This general rule of "larger comes later" can be
broadly applied to the responses of all the high-tech industry
segments to national and international cycles.

Note also that we have gradually moved from strictly company or even industry concerns to the broader implications of
the business market. The two are meshed—but not synchro-
nized. It is thus very possible to strip one's investment gears
if one is not careful.

Overall, the business/stock market cycle—for it is cyclic—
can be classified for investment purposes into three different
sets of circumstances. First there's the once-in-a-generation
bull move, when the stock market, or at least segments of it,
erupts explosively, doubling or tripling share prices. Such a
move is easy to see in retrospect but difficult to spot coming,

because everyone is so frightened when the news about the end of the American way of life as we know it breaks that no one is thinking of investing. Yet headlines beginning to read consistently like a litany from the obituary of American industry—"Record Bankruptcies Threaten," "Japanese Have U.S. High Tech on the Run," "Pension Funds Put All New Money in U.S. Bonds"—usually portend the arrival of a bull market. The definitive sign is cover stories by major national media on the death of high-tech and small-company investing. Reinforcing the omen is a noticeable dearth of stories from your friends and neighbors about their latest investing coups. This is the time to invest.

Terrible times for investing during the business/stock market cycle are those in which the reverse is true. The periods 1967 to 1969, 1972 to 1973, and 1981 are representative. When media articles on superprofits in the stock market are raining down like ticker tape in the parades of yore, when pension funds are endowing themselves with common stock as the road to the future, when everybody is talking about the money they've made—this is no time to invest, and probably time to divest yourself of any winners you hold.

If you can't resist placing a market bet when everyone is touting stocks, do your preliminary research twice. Then be doubly prepared to sell if share prices aren't going your way. Set a definite price for getting out of your investment, and stay with it. This is absolutely not the time to say, "It can't go down much further; I'll just hold on a little longer."

For 75 percent of the business/stock market cycle the available investment opportunities are neither terrible nor great. They're something in between. These times exhibit some, but not all, of the following favorable investment characteristics:

1. Price-to-earnings ratios tend to be low relative to their norm, and the return on investing in some of the companies you have been following may compare favorably with what you could expect to earn from such alternative investments as money funds, Dow Jones blue-chip stocks, gold, or real estate.

High-tech stocks offer higher potential returns than most comparable investment vehicles. At the same time, they involve higher business risks. The investor must always remember the no-free-lunch principle. But one way of offsetting business risk is by taking less market risk. When price-to-earnings ratios are low, the investor's market risk is lower.

2. Interest rates are apt to be low or declining, a factor to the advantage of high-tech companies. Fast-growing firms nearly all need outside money. If money in general is inexpensive relative to their return on assets, this circumstance is more easily translated into higher profits. Higher profits normally mean rising share prices.

3. Market averages generally drop substantially during the year previous to a neutral period. Typical market declines average eighteen months in duration and result in a 25 percent pull-back in prices. This is a very broad rule. Individual market retreats may vary from these averages by as much as 50 percent. However, once the average adjustment has been reached, price risk, or market risk, is much lower, even though there may still be substantial business risk.

The later impact of a decline in both interest rates and market averages may be significant from a high-tech investor's point of view. A good example is what happened in mid-1982. When the Federal Reserve's inflation-fighting tight-money policy prevailing from late 1979 to the middle of 1982 began to choke off business activity, it clobbered industry worldwide. Fear rose that the drawn reins would check particularly the growth of high technology. Thus prices of shares in high-tech companies dropped by 30 to 70 percent in the period from mid-1981 to July 1982, and pundits prognosticated the demise of both America's technological expertise and its leading edge in technological development. Yet, true to form, the August 1982 monster rally that followed in the wake of declining interest rates was led by the very high-tech companies whose certain doom had been foretold.

Not all the high-tech stocks were in the forefront of the bull herd charging up Dow Jones Hill. The old Wall Street chestnut about a rising tide lifting all boats is certainly still true in principle, but somehow certain stocks always seem to rise more quickly than others. When the market falls, of course, these same stocks often plummet.

The degree to which a given stock will outperform the market, upward or downward, can be predicted to some extent by a measurement called beta. A stock's beta is the ratio of its percentage price change over the last six to twelve months to that of Standard and Poor's 500 Stock Index over the same period. While you can calculate the beta rating of a given stock yourself, it's simpler to use the figures published by analysts and investment services in their company coverage.

Suppose you are following Acorn Advanced Systems, a growing little company specializing in tissue culture. An analyst's report states that the firm's stock beta is 1.5. This means that, on the average, the Acorn share price will tend to advance one and a half times as fast as the stock market as a whole. All things being equal, if the market goes up 10 percent, Acorn Advanced Systems shares will probably rise about 15 percent in value. If the market declines 10 percent, they will probably decline 15 percent.

By definition, the average beta is 1. That is, the stock of a company with a beta of 1 performs, at least on paper, just like Standard and Poor's 500. Most companies fall into a beta range of 0.85 to 1.15. Conservative stocks such as electric utilities and food companies, stocks in relatively slowly changing, stable industry segments representing a defensive investment posture, usually have the lowest beta of all, ranging from 0.5 to 1. Small computer software companies and similar firms at the more volatile end of the high-tech spectrum may have betas as high as 3 or even higher.

Beta measurement is no sure indicator of relative stock performance. But it's another factor to take into consideration when you are making your investment choices. If you sincerely wish to participate in the high-tech revolution but feel you might have trouble sleeping at night with even a portion of your money invested in a company whose shares could decline three times faster than the stock market as a whole were the world suddenly to take an economic tumble, stay away from companies with high betas. If, on the other hand, you view an investment opportunity potentially three times greater than the average as irresistible despite its market dangers, you know where to look for it.

Buying stocks purely on their betas doesn't work, as many a now broke go-go operator from the sixties will tell you. For one thing, betas change over time. But they can be a valuable adjunct to your other research, although they are no substitute for it.

Apart from supplying a measure of a given stock's volatility, the beta factor is useful in monitoring the overall direction of the market. When the relative movement—either up or down —of high-beta stocks begins to slow, the market itself is usually reaching a turning point. If the market has been strong and the high-beta stocks, those in your portfolio or such stocks in general, start to act sluggish, prepare to bail out. The same principle, in reverse, holds true for downswings. If the market as a whole has been declining and the high-beta stocks hesitate in their precipitous drop, be prepared for the buying opportunities of a market upturn.

Another trend emerges when one looks at the "price of growth" by comparing the P/E to growth rate ratio of high-technology stocks with those of the more traditional industrials. In order to evaluate their true growth, however, one must first discount inflation. The ratio of a company's P/E to its growth rate taking inflation into account is expressed as:

$$\frac{P/E}{\text{growth rate minus inflation rate,}} = \text{adjusted "price of growth"}$$
$$\text{in percent} \qquad \text{ratio}$$

Returning to our Acorn example for a moment, if the company has a current apparent growth rate of 30 percent and inflation is running at 10 percent, then its real growth rate is only 20 percent. So if its stock is selling at a P/E of, say, 16, it's being traded at 0.8 times the company's growth rate. This is the price of its growth.

$$\frac{16}{30 \text{ percent - } 10 \text{ percent}} = 0.8$$

By comparison, a typical Standard and Poor's 500 mature growth company such as Stodgy Corporation might have a nominal current growth rate of 12 percent, but an after-inflation growth rate of only 2 percent. If it is selling at a P/E of 12, then one might be led to conclude that it is selling at its growth rate. However, the adjustment for inflation, reducing the growth rate to a sixth of its size on paper, puts a far different perspective on the matter, for one would discern that the company is actually selling at six times its growth rate. There's a crucial difference.

How does such a paradoxical buying situation come about? The explanation lies in the fact that a firm like Acorn is new and unproven. Investors are less sure of its prospects, and thus will not pay a high proportional price for its stock. A company like Stodgy Corporation, on the other hand, with a long record of consistent, if diminishing, growth, will attract a following—investors love consistency.

Historically, the inflation-adjusted price of growth ratio rate for technology stocks has ranged between 0.5 and 2.5. Stocks whose price of growth ratio is lower than the median of this range, that is, under 1.5, are thus historically cheap and may represent a buying opportunity—again, all things being equal, for obviously you can't discount the various companies' potential, changes in management, new product possibilities, and all the other factors we've discussed.

Considering the many industry-market as well as stock-market variables, then, how does one avoid making mistakes? Truthfully, one doesn't. Winning in high-tech investing means being right more often than one is wrong. It certainly doesn't mean being right all the time.

What you need at this point is insurance to cover your losses on a stock that takes a nosedive because of factors you were unable to foresee or might have forgotten to take into account. That insurance is summed up in the old cliché not to put all your eggs in one basket. Never bet on one seemingly sure stock. Always manage a small personal portfolio.

If you have $5,000 to invest and the choice you think best for you is a stock selling at 50 a share, don't buy a hundred shares simply because it's a round lot. There's nothing at all wrong with buying fifty shares and putting your remaining $2,500 into a second stock or two. On the other hand, if you have $100,000 to invest, don't do so in fifty different stocks simply to ensure that you've included a real winner somewhere. No one can follow that many stocks successfully. Besides, by overdiversifying, you'll negate a lot of your research efforts, because the positive impact of even three or four superwinners will be relatively minor in relation to your overall portfolio.

A small portfolio of $5,000 to $20,000 should include a minimum of three stocks. Five would be better. (See Appendix A

for a representative small portfolio.) A medium-sized portfolio
of $20,000 to $100,000 should have eight to sixteen different
investments. A larger portfolio might extend its coverage to
twenty stocks. Beyond that number there's little to be gained,
and your portfolio-monitoring burden increases to the point
where your time is spent counterproductively.

Portfolio diversification at its best involves owning shares
not only in different companies but in different industry segments as well. We recommend following at least two, and
possibly three, of the industries in Part Two. Don't pick a field
in which you're not really interested, however, in an attempt
to develop an industry balance.

For further diversity, buy some stocks that tend to be affected more by one particular economic sector, such as the
consumer market or the government, plus some more affected
by other influences, such as capital-goods demand. This tactic
will spread your investment exposure over different parts of
the business cycle. Try to put in a bit of geographic variety
too, so that adverse events in one metropolitan area or one
state won't destroy your holdings.

One important portfolio factor not to be overlooked is time.
Too many people plant their first vegetable garden beginning
with a row of lettuce. All the heads mature at once. There's
feast, then waste, then famine. Much the same holds true for
investors. Make your investments gradually over a period of
time. This will give you the leisure to study industries and
choose companies very carefully. It will also help you to compensate for the inevitable timing errors that every investor
makes.

Purchase some stocks which your research indicates should
do well over the next six to nine months. Add to these some
others that may take a year or more to reach fruition. As a final
touch, invest in some companies that no one seems to care
much about because, while the potential is there, the real
growth probably won't come for two or three years. Buying
for the quick gain and for the long term means investing in
what have been dubbed "eat well" stocks and "sleep well"
stocks. You want both.

Whatever the number and different types of stocks you buy,
set for each of them a target price at which to sell the shares.
There may be reasons to change that target price—a compa-

ny's prospects for growth might increase dramatically because of new product development, for instance—but in determining a target selling price you provide a yardstick by which to measure a stock's performance against your expectations. The failure of a stock to meet expectations may in itself be a reason for selling.

To establish a target price, first estimate a company's earnings for the next twelve months. In doing so, try to average out as many opinions as you can glean—from analysts, from the company itself, from suppliers, and so forth—and weigh your own biases against them. Then define the appropriate price-to-earnings ratio for the stock. Your target selling price will be the per-share earnings estimate times your best estimate of the stock's future P/E. For example, let's say your best estimate of Electrogenoptics' per-share earnings for the year to come is $2. Electrogenoptics has been selling at a P/E of between 20 and 25 for the past two years. But lately the earnings curve has increased in steepness, and you feel the public is becoming more and more aware of the company. Considering this increased demand for the stock, a P/E of 30 would not seem unreasonable. So you set a target price of $60 for the stock (30 × 2 = 60).

Once you've chosen your portfolio, keep a constant eye on your holdings and their relation to both industry and overall economic factors. But view each company's shares with an investor's jaundiced eye. If you had the cash to buy those stocks *today*, would you *add* them to your portfolio? Assuming you're like most amateur investors—and too many professionals—the answer to that question may sometimes be unprintable. When it is, why hold on to the offending shares? Even the best-planned garden won't thrive unless you pull the weakest seedlings in order to let the better plants mature. Keep a constant lookout for weeds and runty seedlings in your portfolio. Pull them when you spot them, and your harvest should be bountiful.

XXI

Letting Others Pick the Right Stocks for You—Underwriters and Mutual Funds

Everyone these days tends to look for shortcuts, and investors are no exception. By now you may well be asking yourself if there isn't an easier way to make money than this. The answer is yes and no. There are shortcuts, and they can be profitable. They are never as profitable as putting in the work yourself. There's really no such thing as a free lunch, at least not a legal one, even on Wall Street. The closest you can come to acquiring something for nothing is by following the company underwriters.

Underwriting, in which brokerage firms and investment bankers raise capital for corporations by selling their new stock or bonds to the investing public and institutions, used to be part of the old-school-tie network. Gentlemanly, sedate firms brought hopeful shares to market in a relatively leisurely fashion, and ran one of those black-bordered tombstone ads in the financial section of the newspapers to announce the success of their offering. The tombstone ads are with us still, but many of the proud names in their bottom halves today were unheard of a few years ago.

In the proliferation of high-technology companies, a lot of the old-line Street firms were left behind at their club. Numerous upstarts took their place on the corners of commerce. Now there are almost as many underwriters as there are high-tech companies themselves. Vendors inevitably go where there is a market.

In a competitive and potentially very profitable situation like this, some underwriters are bound to acquire a better reputation than others, and since a company first going public wants to enhance its position as much as possible, it will go with the hot, but also respected, underwriter—provided that the underwriter will take it. An underwriting firm has its good name, and its long-term profits, to protect, so it may be very selective. On the other hand, some hungrier underwriters will peddle anything that can issue a stock certificate.

A couple of years ago, Meridian Productions went public. It had no operating history and no capital, and its assets consisted of some film footage of Muhammad Ali plus some ideas for television movies. It wasn't exactly the kind of investment most people were looking for. Nevertheless, there were plenty of takers for Meridian stock when the underwriting firm of John Muir and Company brought out the shares at 30¢ apiece. The shares even jumped to 40¢ (think percentages— that's a 33⅓ percent gain) before settling down to a price of 6¢ as of this writing.

Unfortunately, Muir had too much of its capital, and that of its customers, tied up in stocks like Meridian. When these stocks sagged, Muir and its customers were unable to meet margin calls. The subsequent forced liquidation of their holdings put further downward pressure on the share prices of Meridian and its ilk. Muir simply didn't have enough money to absorb the losses from all the lemons it had been selling. John Muir and Company was very hot in 1980. John Muir and Company is no more.

The top-drawer underwriters would never have touched Meridian Productions. So one way to minimize the risk of disaster in buying new issues is to ascertain that the major underwriter of the stock has a reputation worth putting on the line. By choosing an underwriter with a good track record, in effect you let the firm screen out thousands of new companies and pick what it regards as probable winners for you. Also most of the good high-tech underwriters concentrate on particular industry areas and are thus perhaps better versed in the affairs of the specialty fields than any single investor could hope to be.

Underwriters save the investor a lot of work, but they don't come free. Because an underwriting firm takes a percentage of the money garnered by a public offering, it tries to obtain the highest price possible for the stock it is selling. It charges what the traffic will bear.

The following firms, which tend to have a preponderance

of high-tech underwritings, currently handle some of the better new issues to hit the market. They are listed together with their specialties.

Alex Brown and Son
135 East Baltimore Street
Baltimore, MD 21202
Telephone: (301) 727-1700
   Primary fields: Computer software, medical
               technology, telecommunications

Hambrecht and Quist, Inc.
235 Montgomery Street
San Francisco, CA 94104
Telephone: (415) 986-5500
   Primary fields: Information technology, electronics,
               medical technology, telecommunications

Robertson, Colman and Stephens
100 California Street
San Francisco, CA 94111
Telephone: (415) 781-9700
   Primary fields: Information technology, electronics,
               telecommunications

L. F. Rothschild, Unterberg, Towbin
55 Water Street
New York, NY 10041
Telephone: (212) 425-3300
   Primary fields: Information technology, electronics,
               telecommunications

In addition to the major national underwriting companies, there are a number of regional firms active in the high-tech area that make a serious effort to follow various technologies, particularly nearby companies active in those industries. If you live close to one of these firms, trading through it could be to your benefit, since much of your research could be concentrated within limited geographical bounds, saving you both time and expense while still providing an opportunity for you to remain abreast of industry developments. Regional brokers of particular interest to the high-tech investor include:

Adams, Harkness & Hill
55 Court St.
Boston, MA 02108
(617) 227-5500

F. Eberstadt & Co., Ltd.
61 Broadway
New York, NY 10006
(212) 480-0800

Amdec Securities
515 South Figueroa St.
Los Angeles, CA 90071
(213) 489-2260

Montgomery Securities
235 Montgomery Street
San Francisco, CA 94104
Telephone: (415) 989-2050

Cable Howse & Ragen
4170 Fifth Avenue Plaza
Seattle, WA 98104
(206) 343-5000

Piper Jaffray and Hopwood
733 Marquette Avenue
Minneapolis, MN 55402
Telephone: (612) 252-6909

Dain Bosworth, Inc.
100 Dain Tower
Minneapolis, MN 55402
Telephone: (612) 371-2711

Robinson, Humphrey/AMEX
Atlanta Financial Center
3333 Peachtree Road, NE
Atlanta, GA 30326
Telephone: (404) 266-6000

Investing regionally offers an added bonus in that the stocks of local firms often remain undervalued in relation to the national market until they are picked up by researchers of a major Wall Street firm. Investing intelligently in such companies before they are discovered by the general investing public will boost your profits. The drawback to an investment of this type is that for slower-growing firms, those with a growth rate under 25 percent, considerable time—years, in many cases—may elapse before the discovery occurs.

One problem with using an underwriter to screen your investment prospects for you is that a lot of other people have the same idea, on a regular cyclical basis, in fact. When speculation in the stock market really accelerates, there's always a flood of new issues. Many of these stock offerings are for cash-starved marginal companies that normally would not be able to persuade the public to buy their shares. By dealing with quality underwriters, you can largely eliminate these companies. But you must also face the fact that you may not be able to buy all the shares you'd like in the better companies these underwriters offer. Their regular big-buying customers quite naturally have first crack at any potentially stellar performers.

Another way of acquiring quality high-tech stocks is to wait for the dust to settle after the initial public offering and then make your purchase. Quite often, when the market becomes hot, a company's newly issued shares will skyrocket in price —and then sag as early investors decide to take their quick profits and run. When you see this happening, if the overall prospects for the company remain as bright as ever, an opportunity may have arrived for you to invest and ride a second wave of profits.

Whenever you decide to buy your shares, be it at the initial offering or after the hysteria has settled down a bit, read the company's prospectus beforehand as carefully as you would if you were doing all the basic research yourself. Brokerage firms change—John Muir was once a very sedate and respectable firm. Even if you rely on an underwriter to select the right stocks for you, you still need to double-check that the firm is really doing the job. As you read the prospectus, watch for the following warning signs of an imprudent undertaking.

1. A lack of current revenues is a sure sign that your money belongs elsewhere. Development-stage companies are for venture capitalists with a minimum of $100,000 they can afford to lose, or at best recoup, perhaps profitably, in three or four years.

2. An all-in-the-family firm doesn't need your help. When the president's wife is treasurer and his brother-in-law is executive vice-president, the personnel are obviously too talented for your money. If they're all that good, why are they trying to get your little old dollar?

3. Me-too products are not for you too. The world does not need another personal-computer company or another word-processing firm. It *may* need a *better* one, but here is one place where you can't depend on the underwriter to handle the screening for you. You'll have to do some careful investigating to be sure a company entering such a crowded field deserves your money.

4. Criminal records count. Yes, people who have had "legal problems" do quite often start new companies. Their legal problems may be totally unrelated to business and in fact might not affect the firm at all. But you'd better be certain that they won't. Some company builders are on their third or fourth fortunes—off other people's money.

As you can see, an underwriter's screening of investment possibilities does not eliminate the need for work on your part. Relying on underwriters is a strategy that can reduce your personal research time but never replace it. It is our hope that you will find investment research interesting enough to pursue primarily on your own as you become more and more involved with two or three high-tech industries. That, after all, is the best way to invest profitably.

If you are starting with a small amount of investment capital, say $1,000, you might want to make use of a mutual fund to increase your savings base while you begin to research your own ideal investments. Mutual funds that concentrate on high-tech companies are beginning to come to the fore. Among these, the so-called load funds charge an initial sales commission, usually around 8 percent, part of which goes to the broker who sells the fund, the rest going into the advertising and promoting of the fund. The sales charge comes out of your initial investment before it begins earning money. No-load funds have no sales commission—and thus no salesmen. You call or write the fund to obtain the prospectus and the information you need, and you have to figure out what to ask. A no-load fund, like any discount sale, is cheaper than its loaded counterpart. That does not necessarily imply that it is better. But in the long run, since the best peformance is *not* related to load or no-load features, you're probably better off picking a no-load fund, making your choice on the basis of its past record, and saving. Even in the case of a no-load fund, however, there will be a management fee to cut into your profits.

Because of diversification, the risks in a mutual fund are lower than in a portfolio of two or three volatile stocks. But so are the potential rewards. Still, if you are on a very limited budget of either time or money, a mutual fund is a way to get started in high-tech investing.

The three best performers over the past five years among mutual funds with an emphasis on high technology are:

Nautilus Fund, Inc.
24 Federal Street
Boston, MA 02110
Telephone: (617) 482-8260

Nautilus is a closed-end fund, traded just like a regular stock with a limited number of shares. Its dealings occur over the counter under the symbol NTLS.

Explorer Fund
1300 Morris Rd.
The Chesterbrook Complex
Wayne, PA 19087
Telephone: (800) 523-7025, or (800) 362-0530 in PA
   Explorer is no-load.

Nova Fund, Inc.
303 Wyman Street
Waltham, MA 02154
Telephone: (617) 890-4415
   This fund is also a no-load one.

The three newest high-tech mutual funds, two of them heavily invested in medical technology, are:

Fidelity Select Portfolios
82 Devonshire Street
Boston, MA 02109
Telephone: (800) 225-6190, in Massachusetts (617)
   726-0650
Here you pick your concentration area and buy the applicable portfolio. The fund is a load fund.

Medical Technology Fund
c/o Pro Services, Inc.
1107 Bethlehem Pike
Flourtown, PA 19031
Telephone: (800) 523-0864, in Pennsylvania (215) 836-1300
   Medical Technology is a no-load fund.

Putnam Health Sciences Trust
One Post Office Square
Boston, MA 02109
Telephone: (617) 292-1100
   This medically oriented fund is a load fund.

If you take the mutual-fund route, here are some of its guideposts.

1. Very few of the mutual funds concentrating their holdings in high-tech stocks are truly specialized yet. It is only in

the last few years that a genuine emphasis on high technology has become viable. Prior to the formation of the Nautilus Fund, the heaviest concentration on truly high-tech industries to be found in any fund was 60 percent or so. National Aviation was high-tech for its day, but its lack of success as a closed-end fund scared people off from the fund approach to technology investing for years. It's true that Fidelity Select allows you to choose your areas of investment interest to a certain extent, but few other funds are going to remain consistently invested in any given industries, because they are concerned with short-term performance. Particular areas might be out of fashion for several years, after all. That could kill fund sales.

2. Portfolio managers change—often without notice. If you are impressed with a fund's historic performance, call and find out who the fund personnel think produced the outstanding record. Jot down the names of the analysts and managers to whom the fund's performance is attributed. Then if those people leave, be forewarned. Organizations sponsor funds, but people produce records.

3. Measure a fund's performance over a full market cycle— trough to trough or peak to peak. It's easy enough for a fund to look good or bad for a couple of years when its areas of investment are doing respectively well or poorly. But let the full business cycle run its course, and you'll have a better indication of how good the fund really is.

4. Don't sell out of a fund at the bottom of its performance. Most inexperienced investors buy into a mutual fund after hearing about its fine accomplishments, and then are disappointed when its subsequent achievements seem less exciting. What else did they expect? They bought at the top. Disillusioned, they give up just as the fund reaches a cyclic low point, or, worse yet, they wait until they break even at their investment cost and then sell—only to watch the fund swing high aloft afterward. That's what is known as oscillation in the trend line at work. Wait out the full performance cycle of a fund before you bail out.

5. Don't buy any funds until you have obtained copies of their latest annual and quarterly reports listing what they own. They will send you a prospectus, which you should read as well, but prospectuses are revised only once a year, so they tend to be out of date. Study the reports, and you will find that

some funds invest in much smaller companies than others do, some carry more cash reserves, some have other differences in their investment approach. A comparison of funds is most effective if you study several of them simultaneously. Their variations are more clearly seen in conjunction. Investment services such as the *Current Performance and Dividend Record* published by Weisenberger Investment Companies Service (available in most major libraries or from the publisher at 210 South Street, Boston, MA 02111) will also have lots of helpful statistical information on the funds.

XXII

Looking at the Stock Market Laterally

Emotion has—or should have—no role in investing. Mood swings lead inevitably to a portfolio of ever-decreasing value. Yet people too often buy just as the stock market begins to decline and sell only weeks before it makes a major upward charge. Then, watching their former losers regain their value and go on to surpass the price originally paid for them, they decide to buy once more. They bounce painfully from greed to fear and then again to greed—shedding dollars all the way.

To be a successful investor, particularly a successful investor in high technology, you must avoid the mood swings that affect the market. Stock-market analysts are fond of saying, "We get behind the numbers and find out what's *really* going on." What they mean is simply that market results are reported according to accounting rules. You need to understand the game in order to look behind the numbers. You need to probe deeply enough to find the causes of increasing or decreasing earnings, revenues, and orders and to appreciate the implications of those causes for your investments.

In 1982, a stock called Flight Safety International took a sudden dive, losing over half its value within a few short days, when its management announced an unexpected decline in earnings. The announcement was no surprise to astute investors, however. They had already sold their shares at a good profit months before the stock plunged.

Flight Safety International used a sophisticated method for training pilots of corporate aircraft fleets. Its business, as indicated by the numbers on its balance sheet, was solid, with profits marching right along during 1981 and early into 1982. Then came the drop. Why? And why did some investors know about the plunge far enough in advance to have sold their shares before it arrived?

In the corporate world at large, profits and balance sheets were shrinking throughout 1981. Countless executives were looking for ways to cut costs quickly without too much bloodshed. Most of them did not sell all their corporate aircraft, but they certainly didn't add expensive new planes to their fleets. Among other reasons, the stockholders wouldn't have liked it.

So corporate aircraft sales ground to a halt. No new aircraft, no new pilots; no new pilots, no new profits for Flight Safety International. In retrospect the unexpected announcement turns out to have been very predictable.

Avoiding fiascoes like the Flight Safety International one calls for developing one's intuitive skills. Good investors, entrepreneurs, and artists all have a similar skill in that they take parts of the common, everyday world and mix them up into new and unexpected combinations until they find something different and exciting. This is the creative viewpoint described by Edward de Bono in his book *Lateral Thinking* (Harper Colophon Books, 1970). If you are unfamiliar with this volume, you should read it. Meanwhile, simply remember that successful investors put old ideas together in new ways. In no investment area is this more important—and more feasible—than in the fast-changing world of high technology.

Winning in the market, however, requires more than creative thinking, lateral or otherwise. It requires looking at the market as if it were a gambler's game. You must avoid losing streaks, which would eat up all your chips and cash you out before your winning streak has a chance to hit, allowing you to pyramid your successes. Hence our emphasis on spreading your risks, developing investment discipline, and resisting the sway of emotion. You don't always try for a royal flush. You win through lots of little successful decisions made about the hard facts dealt out by the market.

As in war, winning in the stock market requires a coherent strategy. It must be one based solidly on your own strengths and weaknesses if it is to work for you. Somebody else's strategy won't do.

First, think about your past investment failures and successes. What were they? What caused them? How did you react? Analyze your own investment pluses and minuses. They are the armor and the Achilles' heel you must take with you into the market fray.

Next, look hard at high technology. You must be able to find fields that truly interest you if you are to invest your savings in them. You will have to study and review these fields regularly. Immerse yourself as far as your interest takes you, filing details away in your mind. But keep physical files on industries and companies of interest as well. You can't remember it all.

Then look at the newsworthy events and the things around you in terms of how they might affect the economy in general and your potential investments in particular. High technology is global, and requires a global perspective.

Think, for instance, about such things as where you and your family and friends will be five years from now. What will you be doing? Is almost everyone you know playing with home computers? Will they keep on spending a lot of time with computers, do you suppose? Would you? Or do you find the idea of a personal computer as appealing as an Edsel?

Then again, what about those people who *made* money on Edsels? Could there be a parallel in your future?

Or what about dining out? Would you, or maybe your kids, find restaurants more appealing if there were something to do there besides just eat? Maybe the entertainment-center fast-food outlets with their robotic shows are really on target.

Does it sometimes seem as if the subject of pregnancy crops up in almost every conversation? Does that bode well for the disposable-diaper industry, or for the more high-tech companies making crib monitors to alert parents to potential crises in sudden-infant-death-syndrome cases, or for the manufacture of the new home pregnancy- and gender-testing kits?

An investor can benefit by daydreaming about the future while keeping the investment potential of those reveries always in the background. Past and present can help you choose where to put your savings for the best return. But the fact is that neither history nor the present pays the investment dollars. Only the future does.

An Actual High-Tech Portfolio

As we were in the midst of writing this book, a mutual friend asked to see the manuscript. He had decided to invest some of his money in high-tech stocks and didn't want to wait until the volume was published to read it.

We consented on two conditions. The first was that he keep a record of his holdings so we could track the investment results for this appendix. The second was that he must sell the entire portfolio in time for us to publish the results.

Most investment books include hypothetical portfolios. You know the kind. They're introduced with such assertions as "If you had followed our advice and bought IBM and Xerox back in 1957, you'd be rich now." The hypothetical portfolios of market letters fall into the same category. They show what might have happened *if*. They don't take such factors as commissions into account, and they assume the investor bought at the best price and sold at the best price. Unfortunately, the real world doesn't match the hypothetical one.

The problem with our friend's investing his money at the specific time when he made his request was that the August 1982 monster rally had already sent the Dow Jones averages up like skyrockets, and since he would have only three months in which to hold his portfolio, he might well turn out to be buying at a market top. That wouldn't make for a particularly profitable investment—or exciting reading either, for that matter. On the other hand, it certainly was a real-world situation. Here's what happened.

After reading our manuscript, this particular investor decided his interest lay mainly in the areas of telecommunications, computers, and medical electronics. With the roughly $15,000 he had to invest, he purchased a hundred shares each of ADAC Laboratories, at 25¾; C 3, Inc., at 17; Communications Satellite (Comsat), at 67⅞; Computer Associates International, at 24¾; and Healthdyne, Inc., at 20.

The stocks' prices bobbed along for about a month. Then it was announced that C 3 had been barred from all further government contracts because of questionable billing practices. Since almost all of C 3's work had been for the government, the company's stock promptly fell out of bed. Talk about the real world!

Our friend—he still claimed to be one—sold C 3 at 8, taking a loss of over 50 percent on that particular investment. For the record, he

353

would have held on to his C 3 shares, feeling from his reading that
the government ban would be rescinded, had he not thought that the
stock's recovery would probably take considerably longer than the
two-month period left him.

The next mishap wasn't a real disaster, but it resulted in his selling
the Healthdyne shares. The company announced that it would buy
out Narco Scientific, Inc., a company four and a half times its own
size. As you know from reading this book, such amalgamation may
leave a firm's management with a too-big-for-its-breeches problem.
A highly successful small company often becomes an only mediocre
big company, at least in respect to its earnings-per-share growth rate,
if it becomes too large too fast. The Healthdyne shares were sold at
21⅞—not a real loss, but, after the very real commissions, not much
of a profit either.

Taking the proceeds from the liquidation of these two holdings,
the investor now purchased a hundred shares of TIE/Communica-
tions, Inc., at a share price of 28. The AT&T divestiture was coming
up. Telephone and telecommunications equipment was undergoing
a sales explosion. TIE looked like a good way to participate in the
growth. The stock promptly fell several points.

Meanwhile, however, the other holdings were rising slowly but
steadily. ADAC Laboratories split two for one. Computer Associates
International broke through 30, and Comsat looked as if it would
break through 90.

Then Comsat announced a large secondary offering. The company
would be selling a lot of new stock in order to raise capital. After
reading this book, shareholders should normally have taken this as a
warning signal. The reason our investor did not sell was that there
wasn't much time left before he had to liquidate his entire portfolio
anyhow, according to our agreement. That cost him a few points. He
should have followed his instincts even if there wasn't enough time
to reinvest in another stock. Still, again that's the real world.

And how did his portfolio, with all its trials and tribulations, prosper? It rose 24.94 percent in one quarter, from September 14, 1982,
when he bought his original shares, to December 14, when he sold
all the portfolio stocks. That works out to an increase of over 100
percent on an annualized basis. The Dow Jones Industrial Average
during the same period rose from 923.01 to 1009.38, for a quarterly
gain of only 9.36 percent. The broader-based Standard and Poor's
400 Industrials average went from 138.03 to 153.85, for a gain of
11.46 percent. In other words, his portfolio, after paying those very
real commissions that exist in the investment world, outearned both
of these leading market indicators by over 100 percent.

Obviously there are no guarantees that your reading of this book
will assure the same results. However, the portfolio included here

not only indicates what is possible, but, more important, shows what has actually been achieved by one new-to-high-technology investor.

The broker's confirmations of our friend's trades are reproduced below so that you can follow his portfolio's activity on a blow-by-blow, dollar-by-dollar basis. His commission costs are on the low side for a full-service brokerage firm, because he has an old, established account and thus receives favorable terms. On the basis of what a discount broker would charge, however, the commission costs are quite high. The lack of a commission charge on the sale of his C 3 shares is due to the fact that the brokerage firm makes a market in the stock and purchased them at the going price for its own account. Obviously the firm felt, as our reluctantly selling investor did, that C 3's problems would be resolved.

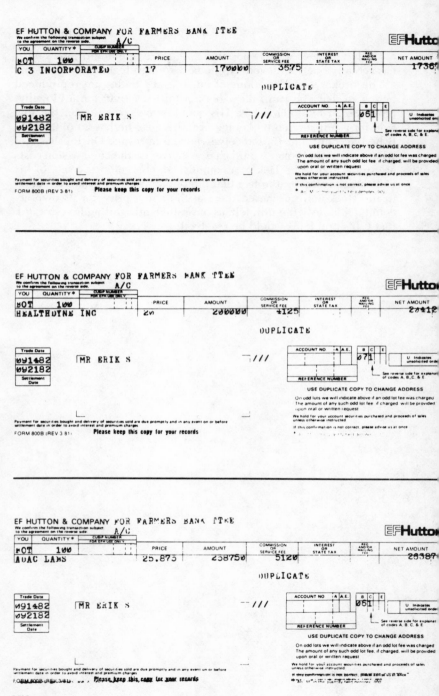

EF HUTTON & COMPANY FOR FARMERS BANK TTEE

We confirm the following transaction subject
to the agreement on the reverse side.   A/C

YOU	QUANTITY *	CUSIP NUMBER FOR EFH USE ONLY	PRICE	AMOUNT	COMMISSION OR SERVICE FEE	INTEREST OR STATE TAX	REG AND OR MAILING FEE	NET AMOUNT
BOT	100		17	170000	35.75			1736
C 3 INCORPORATED								

DUPLICATE

Trade Date
091482
092182
Settlement Date

MR ERIK S

///

ACCOUNT NO	A	A.E.	B	C	E
			0	51	
REFERENCE NUMBER					

U Indicates unsolicited order

See reverse side for explanation of codes A, B, C, & E

USE DUPLICATE COPY TO CHANGE ADDRESS

On odd lots we will indicate above if an odd lot fee was charged
The amount of any such odd lot fee, if charged, will be provided
upon oral or written request

We hold for your account securities purchased and proceeds of sales
unless otherwise instructed.

If this confirmation is not correct, please advise us at once

Payment for securities bought and delivery of securities sold are due promptly and in any event on or before
settlement date in order to avoid interest and premium charges

FORM 800B (REV 3-81)   **Please keep this copy for your records**

EF HUTTON & COMPANY FOR FARMERS BANK TTEE

We confirm the following transaction subject
to the agreement on the reverse side.   A/C

YOU	QUANTITY *	CUSIP NUMBER FOR EFH USE ONLY	PRICE	AMOUNT	COMMISSION OR SERVICE FEE	INTEREST OR STATE TAX	REG AND OR MAILING FEE	NET AMOUNT
BOT	100		20	200000	4125			20412
HEALTHDYNE INC								

DUPLICATE

Trade Date
091482
092182
Settlement Date

MR ERIK S

///

ACCOUNT NO	A	A.E.	B	C	E
			0	71	
REFERENCE NUMBER					

U Indicates unsolicited order

See reverse side for explanation of codes A, B, C, & E

USE DUPLICATE COPY TO CHANGE ADDRESS

On odd lots we will indicate above if an odd lot fee was charged
The amount of any such odd lot fee, if charged, will be provided
upon oral or written request

We hold for your account securities purchased and proceeds of sales
unless otherwise instructed.

If this confirmation is not correct, please advise us at once

Payment for securities bought and delivery of securities sold are due promptly and in any event on or before
settlement date in order to avoid interest and premium charges

FORM 800B (REV 3-81)   **Please keep this copy for your records**

EF HUTTON & COMPANY FOR FARMERS BANK TTEE

We confirm the following transaction subject
to the agreement on the reverse side.   A/C

YOU	QUANTITY *	CUSIP NUMBER FOR EFH USE ONLY	PRICE	AMOUNT	COMMISSION OR SERVICE FEE	INTEREST OR STATE TAX	REG AND OR MAILING FEE	NET AMOUNT
BOT	100		25.875	258750	5120			26387
ADAC LABS								

DUPLICATE

Trade Date
091482
092182
Settlement Date

MR ERIK S

///

ACCOUNT NO	A	A.E.	B	C	E
			0	51	
REFERENCE NUMBER					

U Indicates unsolicited order

See reverse side for explanation of codes A, B, C, & E

USE DUPLICATE COPY TO CHANGE ADDRESS

On odd lots we will indicate above if an odd lot fee was charged
The amount of any such odd lot fee, if charged, will be provided
upon oral or written request

We hold for your account securities purchased and proceeds of sales
unless otherwise instructed.

If this confirmation is not correct, please advise us at once

Payment for securities bought and delivery of securities sold are due promptly and in any event on or before
settlement date in order to avoid interest and premium charges

FORM 800B (REV 3-81)   **Please keep this copy for your records**

356

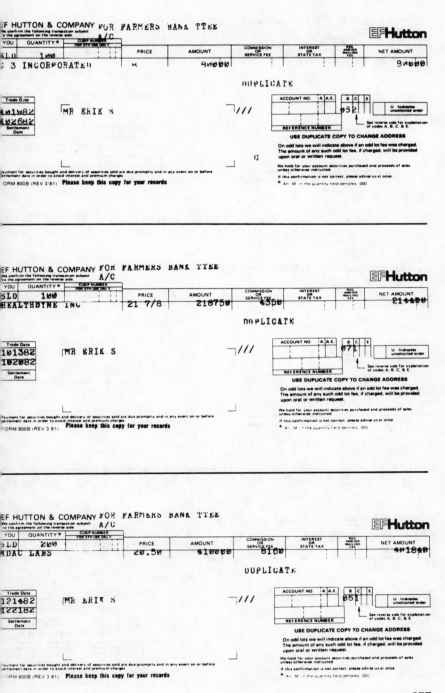

EF HUTTON & COMPANY FOR FARMERS BANK TTEE
We confirm the following transaction subject   A/C
to the agreement on the reverse side.

EFHutton

YOU	QUANTITY *	CUSIP NUMBER FOR EFH USE ONLY	PRICE	AMOUNT	COMMISSION OR SERVICE FEE	INTEREST OR STATE TAX	REG AND/OR MAILING FEE	NET AMOUNT
SLD	1000		H	8000				8000

3 INCORPORATED

DUPLICATE

Trade Date		
101982	MR ERIK S	¬///
102682		
Settlement Date		

ACCOUNT NO.	A	A.E.	B	C	E	U - Indicates unsolicited order
			052			
REFERENCE NUMBER						See reverse side for explanation of codes A, B, C, & E.

USE DUPLICATE COPY TO CHANGE ADDRESS

On odd lots we will indicate above if an odd lot fee was charged. The amount of any such odd lot fee, if charged, will be provided upon oral or written request.

We hold for your account securities purchased and proceeds of sales unless otherwise instructed.

If this confirmation is not correct, please advise us at once

* An M in the quantity field denotes 000

C

Payment for securities bought and delivery of securities sold are due promptly and in any event on or before settlement date in order to avoid interest and premium charges.

FORM 800B (REV 3-81) **Please keep this copy for your records**

EF HUTTON & COMPANY FOR FARMERS BANK TTEE
We confirm the following transaction subject   A/C
to the agreement on the reverse side.

EFHutton

YOU	QUANTITY *	CUSIP NUMBER FOR EFH USE ONLY	PRICE	AMOUNT	COMMISSION OR SERVICE FEE	INTEREST OR STATE TAX	REG AND/OR MAILING FEE	NET AMOUNT
SLD	100		21 7/8	218750	4350			214400

HEALTHDYNE INC

DUPLICATE

Trade Date		
101382	MR ERIK S	¬///
102082		
Settlement Date		

ACCOUNT NO.	A	A.E.	B	C	E	U - Indicates unsolicited order
			071			
REFERENCE NUMBER						See reverse side for explanation of codes A, B, C, & E.

USE DUPLICATE COPY TO CHANGE ADDRESS

On odd lots we will indicate above if an odd lot fee was charged. The amount of any such odd lot fee, if charged, will be provided upon oral or written request.

We hold for your account securities purchased and proceeds of sales unless otherwise instructed

If this confirmation is not correct, please advise us at once

* An M in the quantity field denotes 000

Payment for securities bought and delivery of securities sold are due promptly and in any event on or before settlement date in order to avoid interest and premium charges.

FORM 800B (REV 3 81) **Please keep this copy for your records**

EF HUTTON & COMPANY FOR FARMERS BANK TTEE
We confirm the following transaction subject   A/C
to the agreement on the reverse side.

EFHutton

YOU	QUANTITY *	CUSIP NUMBER FOR EFH USE ONLY	PRICE	AMOUNT	COMMISSION OR SERVICE FEE	INTEREST OR STATE TAX	REG AND/OR MAILING FEE	NET AMOUNT
SLD	200		20.50	410000	8160			401840

ADAC LABS

DUPLICATE

Trade Date		
121482	MR ERIK S	¬///
122182		
Settlement Date		

ACCOUNT NO.	A	A.E.	B	C	E	U - Indicates unsolicited order
			051			
REFERENCE NUMBER						See reverse side for explanation of codes A, B, C, & E.

USE DUPLICATE COPY TO CHANGE ADDRESS

On odd lots we will indicate above if an odd lot fee was charged. The amount of any such odd lot fee, if charged, will be provided upon oral or written request.

We hold for your account securities purchased and proceeds of sales unless otherwise instructed.

If this confirmation is not correct, please advise us at once

* An M in the quantity field denotes 000

Payment for securities bought and delivery of securities sold are due promptly and in any event on or before settlement date in order to avoid interest and premium charges.

FORM 800B (REV 3 81) **Please keep this copy for your records**

357

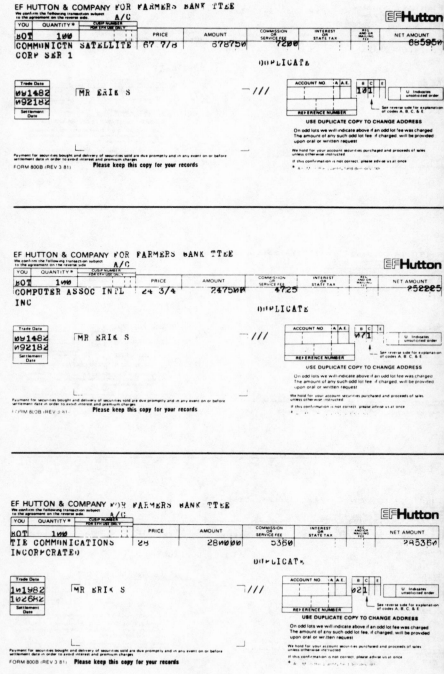

EF HUTTON & COMPANY FOR FARMERS BANK TTEE

We confirm the following transaction subject
to the agreement on the reverse side.   A/C

EF Hutton

YOU	QUANTITY *	CUSIP NUMBER FOR EFH USE ONLY	PRICE	AMOUNT	COMMISSION OR SERVICE FEE	INTEREST OR STATE TAX	REG. AND OR MAILING FEE	NET AMOUNT
BOT	100		67 7/8	678750	7200			685950

COMMUNICTN SATELLITE
CORP SER 1

DUPLICATE

Trade Date
091482
092182
Settlement Date

MR ERIK S

—///

| ACCOUNT NO | A.E. | B | C | E |
| | | 101 | | |

U Indicates unsolicited order

REFERENCE NUMBER

See reverse side for explanation of codes A, B, C & E

USE DUPLICATE COPY TO CHANGE ADDRESS

On odd lots we will indicate above if an odd lot fee was charged
The amount of any such odd lot fee, if charged, will be provided
upon oral or written request

We hold for your account securities purchased and proceeds of sales
unless otherwise instructed

If this confirmation is not correct, please advise us at once

Payment for securities bought and delivery of securities sold are due promptly and in any event on or before
settlement date in order to avoid interest and premium charges

FORM 800B (REV 3 81)   **Please keep this copy for your records**

EF HUTTON & COMPANY FOR FARMERS BANK TTEE

We confirm the following transaction subject
to the agreement on the reverse side.   A/C

EF Hutton

YOU	QUANTITY *	CUSIP NUMBER FOR EFH USE ONLY	PRICE	AMOUNT	COMMISSION OR SERVICE FEE	INTEREST OR STATE TAX	REG. AND OR MAILING FEE	NET AMOUNT
BOT	100		24 3/4	247500	4725			252225

COMPUTER ASSOC INTL
INC

DUPLICATE

Trade Date
091482
092182
Settlement Date

MR ERIK S

—///

| ACCOUNT NO | A.E. | B | C | E |
| | | 071 | | |

U Indicates unsolicited order

REFERENCE NUMBER

See reverse side for explanation of codes A, B, C & E

USE DUPLICATE COPY TO CHANGE ADDRESS

On odd lots we will indicate above if an odd lot fee was charged
The amount of any such odd lot fee, if charged, will be provided
upon oral or written request

We hold for your account securities purchased and proceeds of sales
unless otherwise instructed

If this confirmation is not correct, please advise us at once

Payment for securities bought and delivery of securities sold are due promptly and in any event on or before
settlement date in order to avoid interest and premium charges

FORM 800B (REV 3 81)   **Please keep this copy for your records**

EF HUTTON & COMPANY FOR FARMERS BANK TTEE

We confirm the following transaction subject
to the agreement on the reverse side.   A/C

EF Hutton

YOU	QUANTITY *	CUSIP NUMBER FOR EFH USE ONLY	PRICE	AMOUNT	COMMISSION OR SERVICE FEE	INTEREST OR STATE TAX	REG. AND OR MAILING FEE	NET AMOUNT
BOT	100		28	280000	5360			285360

TIE COMMUNICATIONS
INCORPORATED

DUPLICATE

Trade Date
101982
102682
Settlement Date

MR ERIK S

—///

| ACCOUNT NO | A.E. | B | C | E |
| | | 021 | | |

U Indicates unsolicited order

REFERENCE NUMBER

See reverse side for explanation of codes A, B, C & E

USE DUPLICATE COPY TO CHANGE ADDRESS

On odd lots we will indicate above if an odd lot fee was charged
The amount of any such odd lot fee, if charged, will be provided
upon oral or written request

We hold for your account securities purchased and proceeds of sales
unless otherwise instructed

If this confirmation is not correct, please advise us at once

Payment for securities bought and delivery of securities sold are due promptly and in any event on or before
settlement date in order to avoid interest and premium charges

FORM 800B (REV 3 81)   **Please keep this copy for your records**

358

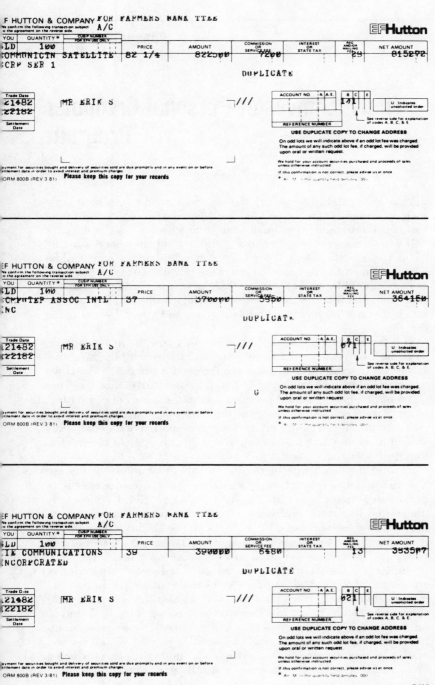

F HUTTON & COMPANY FOR FARMERS BANK TTEE A/C

EFHutton

We confirm the following transaction subject to the agreement on the reverse side

YOU	QUANTITY*	CUSIP NUMBER FOR EFH USE ONLY		PRICE	AMOUNT	COMMISSION OR SERVICE FEE	INTEREST OR STATE TAX	REG. AND/OR MAILING FEE	NET AMOUNT
LD	100			82 1/4	822500	7200		25	815272
COMMUNICTN SATELLITE									
CRP SER 1									

DUPLICATE

Trade Date	21482
	22182
Settlement Date	

MR ERIK S

⌐///

ACCOUNT NO	A.A.E.	B	C	E	
		171			U indicates unsolicited order
REFERENCE NUMBER					See reverse side for explanation of codes A, B, C, & E

USE DUPLICATE COPY TO CHANGE ADDRESS

On odd lots we will indicate above if an odd lot fee was charged. The amount of any such odd lot fee, if charged, will be provided upon oral or written request.

We hold for your account securities purchased and proceeds of sales unless otherwise instructed

If this confirmation is not correct, please advise us at once

* An 'M' in the quantity held denotes 000

Payment for securities bought and delivery of securities sold are due promptly and in any event on or before settlement date in order to avoid interest and premium charges. **Please keep this copy for your records**

ORM 800B (REV 3 81)

F HUTTON & COMPANY FOR FARMERS BANK TTEE A/C

EFHutton

We confirm the following transaction subject to the agreement on the reverse side

YOU	QUANTITY*	CUSIP NUMBER FOR EFH USE ONLY		PRICE	AMOUNT	COMMISSION OR SERVICE FEE	INTEREST OR STATE TAX	REG. AND/OR MAILING FEE	NET AMOUNT
LD	100			37	370000	5550			364150
COMPUTER ASSOC INTL									
INC									

DUPLICATE

Trade Date	21482
	22182
Settlement Date	

MR ERIK S

⌐///

ACCOUNT NO	A.A.E.	B	C	E	
		071			U indicates unsolicited order
REFERENCE NUMBER					See reverse side for explanation of codes A, B, C, & E

G

USE DUPLICATE COPY TO CHANGE ADDRESS

On odd lots we will indicate above if an odd lot fee was charged. The amount of any such odd lot fee, if charged, will be provided upon oral or written request.

We hold for your account securities purchased and proceeds of sales unless otherwise instructed

If this confirmation is not correct, please advise us at once

* An 'M' in the quantity held denotes 000

Payment for securities bought and delivery of securities sold are due promptly and in any event on or before settlement date in order to avoid interest and premium charges. **Please keep this copy for your records**

ORM 800B (REV 3 81)

EF HUTTON & COMPANY FOR FARMERS BANK TTEE A/C

EFHutton

We confirm the following transaction subject to the agreement on the reverse side

YOU	QUANTITY*	CUSIP NUMBER FOR EFH USE ONLY		PRICE	AMOUNT	COMMISSION OR SERVICE FEE	INTEREST OR STATE TAX	REG. AND/OR MAILING FEE	NET AMOUNT
LD	100			39	390000	6480		13	353507
TE COMMUNICATIONS									
INCORPORATED									

DUPLICATE

Trade Date	21482
	22182
Settlement Date	

MR ERIK S

⌐///

ACCOUNT NO	A.A.E.	B	C	E	
		021			U indicates unsolicited order
REFERENCE NUMBER					See reverse side for explanation of codes A, B, C, & E

USE DUPLICATE COPY TO CHANGE ADDRESS

On odd lots we will indicate above if an odd lot fee was charged. The amount of any such odd lot fee, if charged, will be provided upon oral or written request.

We hold for your account securities purchased and proceeds of sales unless otherwise instructed

If this confirmation is not correct, please advise us at once

* An 'M' in the quantity held denotes 000

Payment for securities bought and delivery of securities sold are due promptly and in any event on or before settlement date in order to avoid interest and premium charges. **Please keep this copy for your records**

ORM 800B (REV 3 81)

359

The Techinvestor Personal Computer Program

You can significantly reduce the time you need to evaluate high-tech investment information by using a personal computer—a fitting tool considering the investment focus of this book.

If you do not yet own a personal computer but have been thinking of buying one, its potential use in investment planning may well be a final argument in its favor. Under these circumstances its purchase is tax deductible as well. If you still have reservations about the machines, you might want to borrow one for a while and see how the three of you—the computer, our program, and yourself—get along together.

This is a book on investing, not on learning how to run a computer, so by necessity we must assume some familiarity with the machine. However, by reading the recommended sections in the manuals we mention below and following our step-by-step instructions, even a computer neophyte should be able to learn the basics of computing, to enter our Techinvestor program into the computer, and have it up and running in ten hours or so. Someone familiar with computers should need only five hours or so to start his investment future plotting itself along at a smart clip.

Despite the multitude of personal computers around, many are able to run only a limited range of software, and space does not here permit an attempt to set up a portable program, that is, one easily transferred from one machine to another. Thus we have chosen to make Techinvestor compatible with the Apple II Plus, currently the most popular of the personal computers. The program should run with equal success on the Apple II Plus's successor, the Apple IIe.

Similar reasons of popularity and broad-based ownership underlay our choice of VisiCalc as our base software. VisiCalc performs automated spreadsheet calculations, in effect turning your computer screen into an electronic blackboard whose columns (A, B, C, and so on) and lines (1, 2, 3, and so forth), laid out like those of the accounting sheets used in bookkeeping, can be filled in, erased, and revised endlessly and effortlessly. It's a magic accounting sheet on which a broad range of calculations are automatically performed on any numbers you enter into a given coordinate, or cell (A1, for example, or B3). Change one entry (such as the figures for B3) and the computer will automatically recalculate the changes for any and all of the other entries affected.

Our Techinvestor program sets up the columns and lines provided by VisiCalc in preparation for the entry of the specialized data you will be collecting after reading this book. It also provides the formulas needed by the computer to calculate the pertinent interactions between the various items of information you supply. For instance, if the number of outstanding shares for a given company changes, the price-to-earnings ratio, the estimated price-to-earnings ratios for future years, the earnings per share, compound annual growth rate, and so on will all be altered right before your eyes.

The twelve-year-old kid next door who has been programming since before Pac-Man could probably modify the Techinvestor program to run on other equipment. Unless you're a computer whiz, though, you will need this hardware to operate the program: an Apple II Plus or Apple IIe computer with a minimum of 48K of memory, a RAM card providing an additional 16K of memory if you plan to track more than ten companies at a time (and have an Apple II Plus), a compatible disk drive, a monitor (or a black-and-white television set), an Apple Silentype printer or its equivalent, a box of disks, and interface cards for your disk and printer.

The VisiCalc must be version 3.3 or later. Software is often updated following its original release, and versions labeled with lower numbers, signifying earlier releases, may not work properly.

The first thing to do if you've never played with a computer before is to read the instruction manual on how to set up and run the equipment. You need to learn the basic key functions and how to format, or initialize, the blank, all-purpose memory disks—in other words, how to prepare them so that the VisiCalc software can write on them. These preliminary steps are not difficult to follow.

To familiarize yourself with the hardware we have suggested here, you will need to read, in addition to the short *Apple Family System* manual, the setup instruction chapters of the disk and printer manuals. For the software, you should read the Introduction plus Lessons One and Two of the VisiCalc manual—while sitting at the console of your computer so your fingers can follow the instructions. Sometime later you will probably want to plow through this manual in its entirety, because VisiCalc can perform, besides the procedures needed for Techinvestor, a vast number of other practical operations which you may wish to explore further as your investment horizons expand and fascination with your personal computer's capabilities sets in.

Once your equipment, borrowed or bought, is running, you are ready to tackle Techinvestor itself. You will be dealing with the thirty-five variables and characteristics listed below. The numbers to the left of the entries designate the lines on which the variables will appear on the screen. You will be entering data represented by the labels presented below in the first column shown on the monitor. The description following each entry listing explains the information you will enter into the computer once you have the format for that information set up and tested.

Data Entry Section of Techinvestor

The data entry section of Techinvestor handles the input for the various companies to be evaluated. The actual data you will be entering on these thirteen lines—much of which can be gathered for you by your computer, using The Source, Compuserve, and the Dow Jones data bank—will provide the basic information for the calculations to be performed by the remainder of the program. Alternative sources are statistical services like S&P, Moody's, Value Line; company reports, analyst writeups; and newspapers like *Barrons'* and Media General.

1 SYMBOL

The symbol line provides for the entry of the three-, four-, or five-letter standard designators used by stock quotation machines (for example, GSCC is the stock symbol for the company Graphic Scanning).

2 FY

The fiscal-year figure you will be entering for each firm will be the number of the month in which the company's fiscal year ends. If for accounting purposes a firm's fiscal year terminates at the end of June, you will enter the number 6. If it parallels the calendar year, ending in December, you will enter the number 12.

3 EPS 79
4 EPS 80
5 EPS 81

In our sample run of the Techinvestor program, the years 1979, 1980, and 1981, the most recent year for which full statistics were available, were used in order to provide real data. You can update the program, changing the entry numbers to EPS 81, EPS 82, and EPS 83, or whichever years are the pertinent ones for the stock-performance results you wish to analyze in the future. As you enter the data for each new year, you will of course use the figures corresponding to the years you list.

6 EPS 82E
7 EPS 83E

The earnings-per-share estimates for each firm, as projected by your most trusted analyst, the companies concerned, yourself, or, better yet, a consensus, will be entered in these columns for the two years to come.

8 TGT P

This is the target price per share of a stock, your best estimate of the price at which it should sell sometime in the next nine to eighteen months, assuming everything in fact conforms to your present analysis. Here is one place where the computer really saves time, for it is best to run this variable through three times: once using the price per share you would estimate if everything were to go just right —the market remaining strong, the company's new products coming out on time, and so on—the second time using your estimate if everything were to go wrong, and the third time estimating a number in the middle ground. The middle-ground figure is what you will be relying on most, but the other two numbers will give you a feel for the variability of future outcomes.

To incorporate this feel into something more concrete, weight the probabilities of your estimates. In all likelihood, the middle ground has a little better than a fifty-fifty chance of occurring, so it could be assigned a probability of 0.6. The chances of either of the extremes materializing are about even, so, splitting the difference, each would have a probability of 0.2. The total of all the probabilities must equal 1. (After all, something must happen—0.2 + 0.2 + 0.6 = 1.0). Now take each of your target factors and multiply them by their probabilities. For example, let's say you're following a company called Godzilla Medical. Suppose your best estimate is that if everything were to come up roses, the stock would sell at 50; if Murphy's law (anything that can go wrong will go wrong) were to manifest itself, the stock would probably sell for 20; and assuming things simply proceeded normally, the shares could be expected to climb to 36. Your target price in this case would be 35.6.

$$
\begin{array}{rcl}
0.2 \times 50 &=& 10 \\
0.2 \times 20 &=& 4 \\
\underline{0.6 \times 36} &=& \underline{21.6} \\
1.0 && 35.6
\end{array}
$$

The relationship between your best estimate of a stock's future price and its current price is crucial. The higher your target price is when compared with the current trading price, the greater your profit opportunity. As a broad investment rule, the target price should exceed the current price by 30 percent or better.

⊓ CUR P

The figure to be used here is a stock's current price as listed in the newspaper stock tables.

10 SHS80 {MM}
11 SHS81 {MM}

The number of outstanding common shares in millions to the nearest tenth (for instance, 3,560,000 becomes 3.6) is entered for the two consecutive most recent years. If you update your EPS years (lines 3–7), make sure you have the correct number of shares for those years. For the S&P 400 (the data in column B, headed "Spin") Industrials, we use 1.0, as the actual total market shares are not needed.

12 AST80 {MM}
13 AST81 {MM}

A company's total assets for any given year should be expressed in millions of dollars just as you have done with lines 10 and 11, above. Here again if you will be updating the annual figures make sure these match lines 4, 5 and 10, 11. You can find these figures at the bottom of the balance sheet in the company's annual report. Again for the S&P 400, we use the book value of the index, (matching our approach in items 10, 11) rather than the actual total.

Calculation Section of Techinvestor

The following sixteen program lines will perform the actual stock calculations for you. They represent the program's output. Included are calculations to determine the price-to-earnings ratios (P/Es) of each company you are following, based on your earnings estimates; the historic compound annual growth rate of the earnings per share (EPS CAGR); the company's market capitalization (MKT CAP), based on current stock price; and its return on assets (ROA) for the most recent year and the previous year. Comparative calculations determine the percent difference between your target price for the stock and its current price (PCTCHTGTP) as well as the stock's price-to-earnings ratio and earnings-per-share annual growth rate relative to those of Standard and Poor's 400.

14 Y1EPS

This entry identifies for the computer the first year of the time span for which you wish to determine the compound annual growth rate of a company's earnings per share If a company has a loss year (for example, 1979) then start with the following year. Our program will calculate two- or three- year growth rates, as applicable, as well as four-year (1979–1983).

15 EPSGR

The actual calculation of the compound annual growth rate in percent for the period you have defined (from YIEPS to the year used in line 7) is made by the computer using the following formula:

$$\left[\left(\frac{FV}{PV} \right)^{\left(\frac{1}{n} \right)} - 1 \right] \times 100$$

$$\text{where FV} = \text{Future Value}$$
$$\text{PV} = \text{Present Value}$$
$$n = \text{number of years}$$

For example, if your ending ('83e) year EPS is $4 and the start year ('81) is $1, then n is 2 ('83 − '81) and 4 ÷ 1 equals 4. The formula takes the square root (½ power), gets 2, subtracts 1, leaving 1, and multiplies by 100, for a 100 percent growth rate as the solution.

Remember, as you are going through the agony of entering Techinvestor into your computer, that among all the other calculations it will be performing for you, it will run through this formula time and time again in a very small fraction of a second.

16 RELEPSGR

This row will generate a 4, 3, or 2 year compound annual growth rate relative to the Standard and Poor's 400 CAGR by dividing a firm's CAGR by the CAGR for Standard and Poor's 400.

17 ROA EPS

Line 17 of the program feeds the return-on-assets information entered to subsequent lines of the program as needed for their calculations. In our examples, we used 1982 estimated EPS here.

18 ROA:CUR

A company's return on assets is calculated using the generalized formula below:

$$\frac{\text{earnings per share for the year selected in line 17}}{\left(\begin{array}{c}\text{year-end assets} \\ \text{for preceding year}\end{array}\right) \div \left(\begin{array}{c}\text{number of shares outstanding} \\ \text{for preceding year}\end{array}\right)} \times 100$$

19 ROA:PRE

This line calculates the company's return on assets for the year before that calculated in line 18.

20 AVG ROA

As the label implies, the figure arrived at here is the average of the return on assets calculated in lines 18 and 19.

21 REL ROA

Selecting the appropriate year for Standard and Poor's 400 return on assets, Techinvestor divides the company's return-on-assets value by the Standard and Poor's equivalent.

22 P/E81

This line divides a stock's current price by the latest reported annual earnings per share. The year we used is 1981. For subsequent calculations simply change the number 81 to 82, 83, and so on. The corresponding data for the appropriate year must be supplied, of course, before the program is run.

23 P/E82E
24 P/E83E

Here the stock's current price is divided by the following and subsequent years' estimated earnings per share—in the case of our example, the 1982 and 1983 estimates.

25 RELP/E81
26 RELP/E82
27 RELP/E83

These lines establish a company's relative P/E by dividing the stock's P/E for a given year by the Standard and Poor's P/E for the same year.

28 MKT CAP

Calculates market capitalization in millions of dollars by multiplying a company's current stock price by the number of shares outstanding, in our example, the number of shares in 1981.

29 PCTCHTGTP

Techinvestor line 29 calculates the difference between the target stock price of a company and the stock's current price. The difference is expressed as a percentage.

Limit-Setting Section of Techinvestor

The final six lines of Techinvestor contain formulas for evaluating a company's earnings-per-share growth, return on assets, price-to-earnings ratio, percent change in relation to current price, and market capitalization. They allow you to enter the criteria you feel a stock must meet in order to be considered a viable investment opportunity for your personal portfolio and then to have the computer calculate whether a given stock does in fact meet those criteria.

If you are interested only in companies that may sell at, say, 30 percent above their current price, for instance, you will enter that limit on line 33. A stock meeting or exceeding your criteria in this respect, then (a stock you would consider buying because it has a potential gain of 30 percent or more), will be flagged with an asterisk in that particular cell.

A stock meeting or exceeding your criteria for all the factors in column B, lines 30, 31, 33, and 34 will have a whole series of asterisks. If a company is below the upper limits set by lines 32 and 35, the same asterisk will appear. These two lines raise their buy flags (asterisks) at the lower rather than upper limits because you are looking for a relatively low P/E and market capitalization as favorable investment signs. The more asterisks there are in a company column, the more likely that stock is to fulfill your investment requirements.

30 EPSGRLOLI

Techinvestor line 30 defines the minimum earnings-per-share compound annual growth rate you will accept before investing in a company.

31 ROA LOLI

The minimum return on assets you will accept is entered on this line.

32 P/E HILI

This entry defines the maximum price-to-earnings ratio acceptable.

33 PCTCHLOLI

The minimum difference you will accept between a company's target stock price and its current price is stated in percent on this line.

34 MKTKLOLI

The minimum market capitalization you will accept is set here.

35 MKTKHILI

On this line is entered the maximum market capitalization acceptable to you.

The above listing is an overview of the program you will be using in your stock analysis. Now you have to feed it to the computer.

First load the VisiCalc program and initialize several blank disks, following the instructions in the first section of the VisiCalc manual. Whenever you have entered more program lines than you would care to enter all over again were you accidentally to lose your data, save the work you've done so far by transferring it to one of these storage diskettes, again following the VisiCalc manual instructions if you are unfamiliar with the process.

Formulas and Format

Before you begin entering Techinvestor, type **/CY**. This clears the screen, just as erasing a blackboard gives you a clean slate. Next type in **/GC8Ⓡ/GF$Ⓡ/GRMⓇ/GOCⓇ/TBⓇ**. The symbol Ⓡ stands for the return key. Being a standardized symbol in the VisiCalc manual, it is the convention we will use here.

What you have just done by typing your first line into the computer is the following:

/GC8

You have told the computer to limit to eight the visible characters in a cell. More characters can actually be put into a cell, and you will see them displayed on the edit line when you do put them in. But if they were all displayed, that would greatly reduce the number of columns that could appear on the screen at a time.

A cell is the intersection of a column and a line, akin to the little block on an accountant's ledger sheet in which you enter a figure. Column A, line 1 is a cell, as is C12, and so on.

/GF$

You have instructed the computer to limit all numerical displays to two decimal places. VisiCalc will still perform its calculations using up to nine decimal places.

/GRM /GOC /TB

You have further established the methods and the order of the calculations to be performed. Check the VisiCalc manual for the particulars if you're interested.

Proceed to type in the entries for the A cells, starting with A1 at the top lefthand corner of the VisiCalc screen. Type SYMBOL into cell A1. Then press the arrow key to bring the cursor down to A2 and type FY. You do not have to press ® in order to make the new entry. Moving the cursor will make the entry automatically.

Once you have completed the entries for the A cells, type >B1® to move the cursor over to column B. Continue entering data until you reach cell B29, then type >C30® and continue to cell C35.

Note that when you enter an item beginning with /F, you will see the symbols up on the edit line as usual. However, once you move the cursor on to the next cell, the /F entry will disappear. Don't panic. Entries like this are formatting commands instructing the computer what to do with information put into the cell. As yet there is no real data in the cell, however. Hence the blank.

Cell Coordinates	Entry to Be Typed
A1	SYMBOL
A2	FY
A3	EPS 79
A4	EPS 80
A5	EPS 81
A6	EPS 82E
A7	EPS 83E
A8	TGT P
A9	CUR P
A10	SHS80{MM}
A11	SHS81{MM}
A12	AST80{MM}

Cell Coordinates	Entry to Be Typed
A13	AST81{MM}
A14	Y1EPS
A15	EPSGR
A16	RELEPSGR
A17	ROA EPS
A18	ROA:CUR
A19	ROA:PRE
A20	AVG ROA
A21	REL ROA
A22	P/E81
A23	P/E82E
A24	P/E83E
A25	RELP/E81
A26	RELP/E82E
A27	RELP/E83E
A28	MKT CAP
A29	PCTCHTGTP
A30	EPSGRLOLI
A31	ROA LOLI
A32	P/E HILI
A33	PCTCH LOLI
A34	MKTKLOLI
A35	MKTKHILI
B1	/FRSPIN
B29	/FRLIMIT
C30	/F*
C31	/F*
C32	/F*
C33	/F*
C34	/F*
C35	/F*

Once you have completed entering the Techinvestor format into the computer, bring the cursor back to cell A1 and go through your entries line by line to double-check for errors. Then you will be ready to proceed to the entering of the actual formulas the computer will use to perform its calculations.

You will be typing formulas into some cells, like C30, where previously you entered /F*. Don't worry about putting something into a cell apparently already filled. However, do worry about accuracy. Misplace a single character, even a parenthesis, in the formulas which follow, and you'll gum up the whole works.

Note that long formulas like the one to be entered in cell C15 are printed on several lines. This is done solely to make them easier for you to transcribe. They must be typed into the computer as a single continuous entry. Make no space breaks or returns until you have typed in the last character on the last line of the formula.

Also note that when you have entered a formula, you may be greeted with the message "Error." This is once again because no real data has yet been supplied. The computer is using the formula to divide by zero. Just keep going.

Before starting your formula entries, type >C14Ⓡ to bring the cursor up to the right cell, C14. Then type in, very carefully, the formulas, as follows:

Cell Coordinates	Entry to Be Typed
C14	+C3
C15	@IF{C14=C3,{{{C7/C3}∧{1/4}}−1}*100,
	@IF{C14=C4,{{{C7/C4}∧{1/3}}−1}*100
	@IF{C14=C5,{{{C7/C5}∧{1/2}}−1}*100,@NA
C16	@IF{C14=C3,C15/{{{{B7/B3}∧{1/4}}−1}*100}},
	@IF{C14=C4,C15/{{{{B7/B4}∧{1/3}}−1}*100}},
	@IF{C14=C5,C15/{{{{B7/B5}∧{1/2}}−1}*100}}
C17	+C6
C18	100*C17/{C13/C11}
C19	@IF{C17=C6,100*C5/{C12/C10},
	@IF{C17=C5,100*C4/{C12/C10},@NA
C20	{C19+C18}/2
C21	@IF{C17=C6,C18/{100*B6/{B13/B11}},
	@IF{C17=C5,C18/{100*B5/{B13/B11}},@NA
C22	+C9/C5
C23	+C9/C6
C24	+C9/C7
C25	+C22/{B9/B5}
C26	+C23/{B9/B6}
C27	+C24/{B9/B7}
C28	+C9*C11
C29	{{C8−C9}/C9}*100
C30	@IF{C15>=B30,1,0
C31	@IF{C20>=B31,1,0
C32	@IF{C24<=B32,1,0
C33	@IF{C29>=B33,1,0
C34	@IF{C28>B34,1,0
C35	@IF{C28<B35,1,0

Before you take a break after entering all this, put a blank but initialized diskette into the drive. Substituting the current date for our fictitious 12/12/93, type in /SSFORMULAS 12/12/93Ⓡ to store the formulas. Remove the disk and label both sleeve and disk with the same identification. Now if anything goes wrong when you ask for a printout, you'll have a complete backup copy of all those laboriously entered formulas.

To obtain a printout of the Techinvestor format and formulas, you need to know which computer slot your printer card is in. Usually it is in slot 1. If so, type in >C35Ⓡ followed by /SS,S1Ⓡ. If the card is in another slot, say slot 3, use /SS,S3Ⓡ following the >C35Ⓡ. When you're done, compare your printout to that in Figure 1 to be sure you have introduced no errors. Don't be concerned about unexpected extra lines preceded by /W1 or /X. They represent internal checking within the VisiCalc program. Mistakes in your lines can easily be rectified by taking the cursor to the appropriate cell and then simply typing in the entire line for that cell as it should read. The new entry will automatically replace the incorrect one when you again move the cursor. But you must save the corrected version, as in the preceding paragraph!

Figure 1

```
>C35:/F*@IF{C28<B35,1,0
>A35:""MKTKHILI
>C34:/F*@IF{C28>B34,1,0
>A34:""MKTKLOLI
>C33:/F*@IF{C29>=B33,1,0
>A33:""PCTCHLOLI
>C32:/F*@IF{C24<=B32,1,0
>A32:""P/E HILI
>C31:/F*@IF{C20>=B31,1,0
>A31:""ROA LOLI
>C30:/F*@IF{C15>=B30,1,0
>A30:""EPSGRLOLI
>C29:{{C8-C9}/C9}*100
>B29:/FR""LIMIT
>A29:""PCTCHTGTP
>C28:+C9*C11
>A28:""MKT CAP
>C27:+C24/{B9/B7}
>A27:""RELP/E83E
>C26:+C23/{B9/B6}
>A26:""RELP/E82E
>C25:+C22/{B9/B5}
>A25:""RELP/E81
>C24:+C9/C7
>A24:""P/E83E
>C23:+C9/C6
>A23:""P/E82E
>C22:+C9/C5
```

Figure 1, *continued*

```
>A22:""P/E81
>C21:@IF{C17=C6,C18/{100*B6/{B13/B11}},
     @IF{C17=C5,C18/{100*B5/{B13/B11}},@NA
>A21:""REL ROA
>C20:{C19+C18}/2
>A20:""AVG ROA
>C19:@IF{C17=C6,100*C5/{C12/C10},
     @IF{C17=C5,100*C4/{C12/C10},@NA
>A19:""ROA: PRE
>C18:100*C17/{C13/C11}
>A18:""ROA:CUR
>C17:+C6
>A17:""ROA EPS
>C16:@IF{C14=C3,C15/{{{{B7/B3}^{1/4}}-1}*100},
     @IF{C14=C4,C15/{{{{B7/B4}^{1/3}}-1}*100},
     @IF{C14=C5,C15/{{{{B7/B5}^{1/2}}-1}*100
>A16:""RELEPSGR
>C15:@IF{C14=C3,{{{C7/C3}^{1/4}}-1}*100,
     @IF{C14=C4,{{{C7/C4}^{1/3}}-1}*100,
     @IF{C14=C5,{{{C7/C5}^{1/2}}-1}*100,@NA
>A15:""EPSGR
>C14:+C3
>A14:""Y1EPS
>A13:""AST81{MM}
>A12:""AST80{MM}
>A11:""SHS81{MM}
>A10:""SHS80{MM}
>A9:""CUR P
>A8:""TGT P
```

Figure 1, *continued*

```
>A7:""EPS 83E
>A6:""EPS 82E
>A5:""EPS 81
>A4:""EPS 80
>A3:""EPS 79
>A2:""FY
>B1:/FR""SPIN
>A1:""SYMBOL
/W1
/GOC
/GRM
/GF$
/GC8
/X>A1:>A1:/TV
/X!/X>A16:>C35:
```

Provided you have entered your Techinvestor format and formulas correctly the first time around, you are ready for some replicating. That is to say, instead of typing in all the information you have just finished entering for column C all over again for columns D, E, F, and so on, turn the job over to the computer.

For a good background on replication, you can read pages 3–51 to 3–59 of the VisiCalc manual. But if you simply want to go ahead and replicate without going into the nitty-gritty details, type in >C14Ⓡ /R.C35Ⓡ D14.L14Ⓡ. VisiCalc will then begin highlighting cells, one at a time, up on the edit line of the screen. The highlight is a prompt, requiring you to respond by typing R if the cell highlighted is a C cell or N if it is a B cell. For instance, if VisiCalc highlights C22, you should type R. If B9 is highlighted, you will type N. Once you respond by typing either an R or an N, everything in that particular cell will be duplicated on the same line in the next nine adjoining columns, D through L.

Note that if you type in an N for a C or vice versa, you cannot back up to make a correction. To correct such an error, you must type >C followed immediately by the line number, with no intervening space, then Ⓡ/ⓇD, then the line number again, then .L, the line number once more, and, finally, Ⓡ.

Save your duplicated format, replicated error messages and all, by typing /SS10FIRMTEMPLATE. This is your completed high-tech program which, used in conjunction with VisiCalc, will enable your personal computer to make comparative calculations for you on the data you enter for up to ten different companies. Don't forget to label the disk "10FIRMTEMPLATE" before filing it. You will probably be looking for it often once your investment plotting is well underway.

If your Apple is equipped with 64K of memory, you can create a template for up to twenty-eight companies. Where previously you replicated column C in columns D through L, now, after inserting a fresh diskette, you can enter >L1®/R.L35RM1.AD1® and carry the repeat function further. This time, when a B column cell is highlighted, you will type N as before, but the other cell highlighted will be in column L, not C. You still type in R. When you are done, put a new disk in the drive and type in /SS28FIRMTEMPLATE. Again don't forget to label the disk so that you, as well as the computer, can identify it.

A Test Run

To put all this software to work for you, of course, you must enter some real numbers on the stocks to be analyzed. For a test run, you might want to use our sample data in Figure 2.

Start by typing >A36®. This brings you down to cell A36. Then type in /FR/R®B36.L36®. Now you are ready to enter the sample headings from the bottom of Figure 2. First enter COMPANY. Then move the cursor over to B36 and enter S&P 400. Move to C36 and enter APPLE C, and so on.

Type >C1® to get to cell C1. Then type /FR/R®D1.L1®. This will position the stock symbols over their data. Then type in the stock symbols in Figure 2. Next type >B2®, then /FR/ R®C2.L2®. This will print the fiscal years as integers, instead of dollars and cents. Now you are ready to enter the rest of the sample data.

Figure 2

SYMBOL	SPIN	AAPL	AVAK	CCBL	CUL	ESY	HBOC	INGR	MOLX	NEWP	VRB	LINE 1
FY	12	9	12	6	4	12	3	12	6	7	6	2
EPS 79	16.21	0.12	0.26	0.20	0.44	1.47	0.39	0.29	2.28	0.33	0.30	3
EPS 80	16.13	0.24	0.43	0.53	0.73	0.93	0.51	0.50	2.62	0.79	0.45	4
EPS 81	16.70	0.70	0.55	1.12	1.10	1.67	0.74	0.75	3.15	1.24	1.80	5
EPS 82E	14.50	1.00	0.65	1.65	1.40	2.25	1.00	1.15	3.75	1.60	2.30	6
EPS 83E	17.25	1.50	0.85	2.15	1.80	2.80	1.30	1.65	4.00	2.20	2.75	7
TGTP	140.00	18.00	17.00	24.00	32.00	34.00	31.00	33.00	48.00	35.00	36.00	8
CURP	125.17	13.25	13.88	20.00	28.13	33.00	24.50	23.38	44.25	26.00	31.13	9
SHS80{MM}	1.00	48.40	16.30	2.70	2.70	13.80	4.00	9.50	6.50	2.10	2.10	10
SHS81{MM}	1.00	56.20	18.10	3.00	3.10	14.00	7.20	11.50	6.60	5.40	5.40	11
AST80{MM}	108.10	65.40	43.70	3.80	13.70	236.00	25.00	42.80	94.50	36.10	36.10	12
AST81{MM}	117.22	254.80	76.50	10.00	38.60	280.00	41.00	87.00	116.20	59.00	59.00	13
COLUMN A	B	C	D	E	F	G	H	I	J	K	L	
COMPANY	S&P 400	APPLE C	AVANTEK	C-CORE	CULLINA	E-SYSTE	HBO&CO	INTERGR	MOLEX	NEWPRT	VERBATI	

After you are finished with line 2, you can easily enter each stock's data by proceeding down the proper column. To speed up this somewhat tedious process, you can skip any zeros trailing integers to the right of decimal points. VisiCalc will fill them in automatically.

Once all the company data has been entered, type **>B30Ⓡ** and key in the following final data:

Cell Coordinates	Entry to Be Typed
B30	30
B31	20
B32	15
B33	30
B34	60
B35	300

Then hold your breath, type **>C33Ⓡ**, and follow this entry by pressing, appropriately enough, !. After about forty seconds, your screen should provide the calculations for each of the ten companies entered (see Figure 3).

You may notice a couple of error messages lingering on the screen. At this stage they indicate true mistakes. Go back and recheck your formulas. But first save the work you've already done by typing **/SSTECHINVESTORⓇ**, just in case you dump all your data while trying to correct the mistakes.

One of the best ways to debug a program, or remove your errors, is to work from a printout. Obtaining one is a simple step. Merely type in **>A1Ⓡ** followed by **/P1ⓇJ36Ⓡ**. If the printer is not in slot 1, type the right slot number after the "P". When the printer stops, enter **>K1Ⓡ/P1ⓇM36Ⓡ** to print the part that didn't fit on the paper in the first run. Compare the results with those in Figure 3. If there are discrepancies, go through the following debugging list on the screen:

1. Do you have the right data on lines 2 through 13?
2. Check the replications in columns D through L. Did you hit the B key when you should have during replication, that is, in lines 16, 21, 25, 26, 27, 30, 31, 32, 33, 34, and 35?
3. Recheck the formulas in column C.

Patience—lots of it—and careful checking should resolve any difficulties you might encounter. If they don't, as a last resort, check with the local computer whiz kid. Every neighborhood has one these days.

Graphical Analysis with VisiPlot

Once you have conquered using Techinvestor with VisiCalc, you may want to add graphing capabilities to your computer-aided investment repertoire. VisiTrend/Plot (version 1.0 or later) makes possible a pictorial display of the data compiled with Techinvestor.

First load VisiCalc, followed by Techinvestor, to enter your data. This input information will need to be rearranged, however, before VisiPlot can absorb it. It must be put into what is known as Data Interchange Format, or DIF files.

Each line of Techinvestor you wish to use with VisiPlot must be assigned its own DIF file. However, you should DIF only the actual information you intend to plot graphically. For example, suppose we wish to plot the EPS compound annual growth rate, the average return on assets, the 1982 price-to-earnings ratio, the market capitalization, and the percent difference between target price and current price for a number of stocks we are comparing, in this case ten. We would need to set up DIF files for the categories EPSGR, AVG ROA, P/E82E, MKT CAP, and PCTCHTGTP.

Before entering the DIF files, move the column containing the Standard and Poor's 400 values out of the way. They aren't part of the data you wish to plot for the firms. To move these values, type >B5Ⓡ/MA5Ⓡ.

Next type >B15Ⓡ to move to cell B15, which contains the EPSGR label. Type /S#SEPSGR.DIFⓇ L15ⓇⓇ. This will give all the data on line 15 from column B through column L the file name EPSGR.DIF and it will store the figures. Set up the next four files by typing the following commands:

```
>B20Ⓡ/S#SAVG ROA.DIFⓇL20ⓇⓇ
>B23Ⓡ/S#SP/E82E.DIFⓇL23ⓇⓇ
>B28Ⓡ/S#SMKT CAP.DIFⓇL28ⓇⓇ
>B29Ⓡ/S#SPCTCHTGTP.DIFⓇL29ⓇⓇ
```

To check the five new files you have created, type /SLⓇ. Then scroll through the file names by pressing the arrow keys.

Figure 3

SYMBOL	SPIN	AAPL	AVAK	CCBL	CUL	ESY	HBOC	INGR	MOLX	NEWP	VRB
FY	12	9	12	6	4	12	3	12	6	7	6
EPS79	16.21	0.12	0.28	0.20	0.44	1.47	0.39	0.29	2.28	0.33	0.30
EPS80	16.13	0.24	0.43	0.53	0.73	0.93	0.51	0.50	2.62	0.79	0.45
EPS81	16.70	0.70	0.55	1.12	1.10	1.67	0.74	0.75	3.15	1.24	1.80
EPS82E	14.50	1.00	0.65	1.65	1.40	2.25	1.00	1.15	3.75	1.60	2.30
EPS83E	17.25	1.50	0.85	2.15	1.80	2.80	1.30	1.65	4.00	2.20	2.75
TGTP	140.00	18.00	17.00	24.00	32.00	34.00	31.00	33.00	48.00	35.00	36.00
CURP	125.17	13.25	13.88	20.00	28.13	33.00	24.50	23.38	44.25	26.00	31.13
SHS80tMM	1.00	48.40	16.30	2.70	2.70	13.80	4.00	9.50	6.50	2.10	2.10
SHS81tMM	1.00	56.20	18.10	3.00	3.10	14.00	7.20	11.50	6.60	5.40	5.40
AST80tMM	108.10	65.40	43.70	3.80	13.70	236.00	25.00	42.80	94.50	36.10	36.10
AST81tMM	117.22	254.80	76.50	10.00	38.60	280.00	41.00	87.00	116.20	59.00	59.00
Y1EPS		0.12	0.28	0.20	0.44	1.47	0.39	0.29	2.28	0.33	0.30
EPSGR		86.03	32.00	81.07	42.22	17.48	35.12	54.44	15.09	60.69	74.00
RELEPSGR		56.19	20.42	51.75	26.95	11.16	22.42	34.75	9.63	38.73	47.23
ROAEPS	1.00	1.00	0.65	1.65	1.40	2.25	1.00	1.15	3.75	1.60	2.30
ROA:CUR	22.06	22.06	15.38	49.50	11.24	11.25	17.56	15.20	21.30	14.64	21.05

Figure 3, *continued*

SYMBOL	SPIN	AAPL	AVAK	CCBL	CUL	ESY	HBOC	INGR	MOLX	NEWP	VRB
ROA:PRE		51.80	20.51	79.58	21.68	9.77	11.84	16.65	21.67	7.21	10.47
AUG ROA		36.93	17.95	64.54	16.46	10.51	14.70	15.92	21.48	10.93	15.76
REL ROA		1.78	1.24	4.00	0.91	0.91	1.42	1.23	1.72	1.18	1.70
P/E81		18.93	25.24	17.86	25.57	19.76	33.11	31.17	14.05	20.97	17.29
P/E82E		13.25	21.35	12.12	20.09	14.67	24.50	20.33	11.80	16.25	13.53
P/E83E		8.83	16.33	9.30	15.63	11.79	18.85	14.17	11.06	11.82	11.32
RELP/E81		2.53	3.37	2.38	3.41	2.64	4.42	4.16	1.87	2.80	2.31
RELP/E82		1.53	2.47	1.40	2.33	1.70	2.84	2.36	1.37	1.88	1.57
RELP/E83		1.22	2.25	1.28	2.15	1.62	2.60	1.95	1.52	1.63	1.56
MKT CAP		744.65	251.23	60.00	87.20	462.00	176.40	268.87	292.05	140.40	168.10
PCTCHTGT	LIMIT	35.85	22.48	20.00	13.76	3.03	26.53	41.15	8.47	34.62	15.64
EPSGRLOL	30.00*	*		*			*			*	
ROALOLI	20.00*	*		*							
P/EHILI	15.00*	*			*			*	*	*	
PCTCHLOL	30.00*					*					
MKTKLOLI	60.00*	*		*	*	*	*	*	*	*	
MKTKHILI	300.00	*		*		*	*	*	*	*	
COMPANY	S&P 400	APPLE C	AVANTEK	C-CORE	CULLINA	E-SYSTE	HBO&CO	INTERGR	MOLEX	NEWPRT	VERBATI

At this point the Techinvestor data disk, which now also includes the DIF files you have chosen for plotting, should be removed. Put in the VisiPlot program disk and type **/SQ6Ⓡ**. The 6 stands for slot 6, to which your disk drive is connected. If your drive is connected to a different slot, say 3, you must type that number instead.

The command you have just given the computer instructs it to drop VisiCalc and load VisiPlot. VisiPlot, by the way, loads slowly. Like a television commercial break, it gives you time to get up, stretch, and raid the icebox.

When the VisiPlot menu finally makes its appearance on the screen, move the cursor to "Load" if it is not already there. Put your Techinvestor data disk back in the drive and press Ⓡ. The DIF files will now be displayed.

Check that the cursor is on EPSGR.DIF. Then press Ⓡ again. The computer will beep and display the word "Periodicity" on the prompt line. Press Ⓡ once more. Now the display should read "Major Start (Year)?" Again press Ⓡ. The message "Continue" will appear. Make sure that's the word highlighted by the cursor, not "Print," then press Ⓡ. That's it for loading the first DIF file.

The computer will bring the prompt line back to the menu with the cursor on "Load." Press Ⓡ and you will once more receive a display of the DIF directory. Follow the same sequence outlined above for ESPGR.DIF to load AVG ROA.DIF and the remaining three DIF files in the present example, checking each time that the cursor is on the appropriate file listing before proceeding.

When the last DIF file you plan to use has been loaded, press Ⓡ one more time to bring the VisiPlot menu up on the prompt lines. You're ready to plot. So move the cursor to "Plot" and press Ⓡ.

You will be requested to "Type y to confirm." Do so, and the prompt will read, "Put in program diskette, press any key." When you press a key, the disk will spin, the computer will beep, and the same message will be repeated—over and over again, as often as you press a key. You are in a loop. The operative phrase in such an event is "program diskette"—theirs, not yours. Take out the Techinvestor disk and replace it with VisiPlot if you haven't already done so. Then press any key and wait while the computer fetches the plot program.

Next you will be asked to choose the type of graph desired. Move the cursor to "Scatter." That's the type of graph we will be using in our example.

Like most graphs, the one displayed on the screen will have a y and an x axis. In response to "Select x-axis series," move the cursor to MKT CAP and press Ⓡ. For the y-axis, indicate that you wish to use P/E82E.

From the next menu selections, choose "Plot" and press Ⓡ. You will have to wait while the computer adjusts the scaling and lays out the graph. Beep, beep, and you will see a replication of Figure 4, although without the stock labels.

To obtain a printout, hit Ⓡ for yet another display of the menu. Move the cursor to "Print" and press Ⓡ. In answer to the query about the slot number that will appear next on the screen, enter 1Ⓡ. The printer will suddenly come to life. That's all there is to requesting a printout. But you've done more than obtain a pretty picture. You've produced a new analytical tool, a way of visualizing the data you have painstakingly acquired on the various companies you are studying so that potentially good buying opportunities jump out at you.

Look at the graph you've achieved with VisiPlot, and you will notice right away that without the labels appended in Figure 4 you can't tell which dot represents which company. Fill in the symbols on your printout by hand, determining the appropriate coordinates from your data. While your software could be modified to print these symbols in their proper places, wherever you had a concentration of companies in one area, they would overlap each other and become indistinguishable.

Figure 4

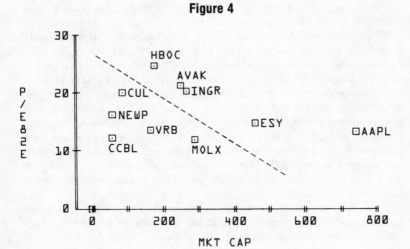

Once your graph is properly labeled, you are ready to analyze the data it portrays. In July 1982, when the plot shown in Figure 4 was made, the market was in a risk-averting mood. Investors simply didn't want to take any chances. Stocks overall dragged their feet. In a situation such as this, financially well-established companies, those with secure revenues and profits, tend to command the highest P/Es for their stock prices. As you can see from Figure 4, HBOC had the highest P/E of the stocks we were comparing, even though its market capitalization was a relatively low $200 million. The explanation for this phenomenon is to be found in the company's position in the medical industry, a comparatively safe investment area during economic storms. Furthermore, following the current financial news, you would have known that medical-technology stocks were in the forefront of investor interest at the time.

Nevertheless, HBOC's stock lies relatively close to the trend line, the dashed line you draw on such graphs as more or less an average between the extremes of the points plotted. The perpendicular distances of the entries lying above the line should total nearly the same as those below the line. The two companies farthest from the trend line in Figure 4 are CCBL and AAPL. Their position should catch the investor's keen eye. As time was to prove, both of these stocks did very well in the months that followed.

it's wise to plot several sets of variables. Comparing the different aspects of companies you are following gives you additional insights into their relative valuations. Figure 5 shows the same ten companies we have used previously as examples plotted by their return on assets relative to that of Standard and Poor's 400 and their target stock price relative to their current price.

What you would like to see here is companies in the upper right hand corner of the plot, with high numbers on both coordinates. The dashed trend line shows that higher ROA's have higher price potentials. Here again AAPL looks interesting (as do INGR and NEWP).

In Figure 6, the stocks are graphically compared on the basis of their relative estimated 1983 P/E and their relative estimated compound annual growth rate. In this plot the central tendency is to form a hump, with high relative P/E's in the center. Again, in the risk-averse July 1982 climate, investors did not believe that high growth rates would be realized. They would not pay for rates over 22 percent. If you felt that AAPL, CCBL and VRB could produce, opportunity was knocking.

These two graphs confirm the visual conclusions of the first graph and reinforce the suggested profitable outcome of the AAPL stock purchase tentatively indicated by Figure 4.

Figure 5

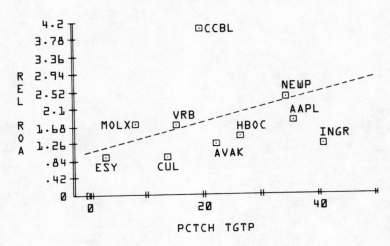

PCTCH TGTP

Figure 6

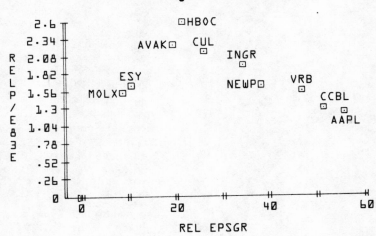

REL EPSGR

Plotting is by no means an absolute guarantee of wise stock choice. There is no system or method that will do all the decision-making work for you. However, graphic plotting used in conjunction with your other analyses can give you some awfully good leads for profitable high-tech investment.

Index

387